DATE DUE

~~MY 26 95~~			
DE 19 97			

Monetary Policy

for a VOLATILE

GLOBAL

ECONOMY

MONETARY POLICY

for a VOLATILE

GLOBAL

ECONOMY

Edited by
William S. Haraf and Thomas D. Willett

THE AEI PRESS

Publisher for the American Enterprise Institute
Washington, D.C.

Distributed by arrangement with

UPA, Inc.
4720 Boston Way   3 Henrietta Street
Lanham, Md. 20706   London WC2E 8LU England

Library of Congress Cataloging-in-Publication Data

Monetary policy for a volatile global economy / William S. Haraf and
  Thomas D. Willett, editors.
    p.   cm.
  Includes bibliographical references.
  ISBN 0-8447-3713-5 (alk. paper)

  1. Monetary policy—United States.   2. International finance.
I. Haraf, William S.   II. Willett, Thomas D.
HG540.M655   1990
332.4'973—dc20   89-18486
                                                           CIP

1 3 5 7 9 10 8 6 4 2

AEI Studies 503

THE AEI PRESS
Publisher for the American Enterprise Institute
1150 Seventeenth Street, N.W., Washington, D.C. 20036

Printed in the United States of America

Contents

Foreword

In recent years we have witnessed tremendous changes in financial markets and institutions as a result of new technology, market innovations, and greater international interdependence. Although these changes have largely been beneficial, they have also raised important new issues for monetary policy. These issues range from relatively narrow and technical questions about appropriate operating procedures, the role of intermediate targets, and the means of controlling risk in the payments system, to very broad questions about the ultimate objectives of monetary and exchange rate policy and the value of coordinating those objectives across nations.

To explore the implications of developments in domestic and international financial markets for the conduct of U.S. monetary policy, the American Enterprise Institute brought together leading experts from government, business, universities, and international institutions at a conference in Washington, D.C., November 16–17, 1988. The essays generated by this conference are being published in two volumes. This volume focuses on the international dimension. A companion volume, *Monetary Policy for a Changing Financial Environment*, edited by Phillip Cagan and William Haraf, concentrates on domestic issues. As repeatedly emphasized at the conference and clarified in essays in both volumes, increased international interdependence has blurred many of the traditional distinctions between domestic and international monetary analysis. Thus the domestic volume should provide considerable relevant analysis even for those whose interests are primarily international while this international volume deals with many issues important for domestic monetary analysis and policy.

Two predominant issues cut across most of the chapters in this volume: (1) the choice of an exchange rate regime and (2) the influence of international capital mobility on both the choice of the exchange rate system and domestic financial policy strategies. The debate over pegged versus flexible exchange rates is an old one, but it retains its relevance. For the United States, few argue today for a return to a full-fledged system of pegged rates, but since the dollar was floated in the

1970s, periods of relatively free floating have alternated with efforts at heavy official management. The debate over a fixed versus flexible rate has also been manifested in recent international discussions of a proposed system of target zones for the exchange rates of the major industrial countries. Indeed the press often reports beliefs that secret target zones have in fact been set for the dollar against the German mark and Japanese yen. Another issue concerns the efforts to create a zone of fixed exchange rates among the members of the European Monetary System.

Hali Edison and Michael Melvin survey the considerable body of empirical research relevant to such issues, while Gottfried Haberler focuses on prospects for the European Monetary System. He stresses how high international capital mobility complicates the operation of adjustably pegged exchange rates, a theme that Thomas Willett and Clas Wihlborg also emphasize. The weight of Haberler's analysis is not that international capital mobility is bad but rather that it increases the need for consistency between domestic monetary and exchange rate policies.

The rapid rise of the dollar in the 1980s and its subsequent fall have heightened the debate over managed versus free exchange rates. To a large extent, positions in this debate turn on whether one views the course of the dollar as broadly justified by underlying fundamentals. As discussed by Alan Stockman and by Willett and Wihlborg, the considerable effort devoted to exchange rate analysis over the past decade has not led to a consensus. In part because of expectations, no exchange rate models do well by traditional econometric standards. This leaves considerable room for disagreement among experts. In the academic literature, Keynesian models of exchange rate overshooting in response to monetary and fiscal shocks despite high international capital mobility have become quite popular. While such models can explain the substantial rise in the dollar in 1984, they cannot explain its continued rise to its peak in 1985.

The behavior of the dollar over this period has resurrected interest in speculative bubbles as a possible explanation. The analysis of Stockman and of Willett and Wihlborg offers reasons for caution in jumping onto this bandwagon. They suggest that there are strong empirical reasons for rejecting the perfect capital mobility–Keynesian overshooting models. Alternative models may offer a basis for explanations that do not require destabilizing speculative bubbles. As discussants William Branson and Jeffrey Frankel comment, however, we have no strong scientific basis for determining whether we have suffered from excessive volatility of exchange rates.

From the behavior of floating exchange rates we can conclude, however, that countries that are following sound financial policies are not typically subject to arbitrary speculative attacks. Invariably debate over the behavior of speculation has occurred only after underlying policy developments have already stimulated major movements in exchange rates. Thus emphasis on the need for sound domestic financial policies to bring about greater stability with exchange rates and the domestic economy does not require a belief that the foreign exchange markets work perfectly. Indeed the possible susceptibility of foreign exchange markets to speculative excesses during periods of stress increases the case for sound domestic financial policies.

Willett and Wihlborg also argue that to the extent we may have suffered from excessive volatility of exchange rates, the current state of research does not allow us to discriminate between explanations based on excessive destabilizing speculation and those based on insufficient stabilizing speculation. Until we can distinguish better between these alternatives, the cases for taxing or putting controls on international capital flows and for engaging in heavy official management of the exchange rate are substantially reduced.

Richard Cooper and Guido Tabellini deal with issues related to the emergence of the huge U.S. trade deficits in the 1980s. In considerably less than a decade the United States has gone from being the largest net international creditor in the world to the largest debtor. While official statistics tend to overstate U.S. indebtedness, the United States is unquestionably now a large net debtor. Much of the U.S. debt is held in the form of nominal dollar-denominated assets. While some argue that the accumulation of such international debt increases the need for financial prudence on the part of the United States, the existence of these foreign claims increases the base from which a surprise inflation can generate net revenues for the government. It would be supremely ironic if concerns about reducing the U.S. budget deficit gave rise to such a use of the inflation tax, but concerns about this possibility could quite rationally give rise to disincentives to the continued capital inflows needed to finance the U.S. trade deficits while they are gradually reduced. This gives rise to a new form of international monetary interdependence, analyzed by Tabellini. (Readers interested in the inflation tax should also consult the essays by Herschel Grossman and by Thomas Sargent in the companion volume.)

Cooper argues that while the U.S. trade deficit need not be reduced to zero soon, a substantial further reduction over the next five years is required to maintain the international credit worthiness of the United States. While he concludes that such an adjustment is technically feasible, Cooper analyzes political and economic difficulties that must be faced on both the domestic and international sides. He illustrates the need for global analysis of the consistency of the positions of domestic savings, investment, and the balance of payments. Management of the international debt situation of developing countries, for example, should not proceed independently of U.S. objectives to reduce the trade deficit.

Most participants in the conference were skeptical of proposals that would rigidly link U.S. financial policies to international developments such as movements in the exchange rate or balance of payments. There was general agreement, however, that important international interdependencies should be taken into account in analyzing U.S. economic and financial developments and in formulating U.S. monetary and fiscal policies. In general, international interdependencies increase the cost of U.S. macroeconomic policy instability both to the United States and to our trading partners. Thus the need for pursuing sound domestic financial policies is greater than ever.

WILLIAM S. HARAF
THOMAS D. WILLETT

About the Editors and Authors

WILLIAM H. BRANSON is the Jacob Viner Professor of International Economics at Princeton University. He was a visiting scholar with Banca d'Italia and the International Monetary Fund and visiting professor at Johns Hopkins University's Bologna Center and at the Athens School of Economics and Business Sciences. Mr. Branson is an associate member of the Institute of Fiscal and Monetary Policy, Japanese Ministry of Finance, and member of the advisory board for the Institute for International Studies, Stockholm University.

RICHARD N. COOPER is the Maurits C. Boas Professor of International Economics at Harvard University. He was under secretary of state for economic affairs, provost and professor of international economics at Yale University, deputy assistant secretary of state for international monetary affairs, and senior staff economist for the Council of Economic Advisers. Mr. Cooper is deputy chairman of the Federal Reserve Bank of Boston, chairman of the advisory committee and director of the Institute for International Economics, and chairman of the Advisory Committee for the Committee for Economic Development.

JACOB S. DREYER is vice president and chief economist of the Investment Company Institute and adjunct professor of economics at Virginia Polytechnic Institute. He was deputy assistant director and acting assistant director in the Fiscal Analysis Division of the Congressional Budget Office. Mr. Dreyer also worked for the U.S. Treasury Department.

HALI J. EDISON is vice president of Edison and Associates and an economist in the Division of International Finance of the Board of Governors of the Federal Reserve System. She has taught at the University of Maryland and the Institute of Economics, University of Bergen. Ms. Edison was a consultant for the Norwegian Central Bank.

JEFFREY A. FRANKEL is a professor of economics at the University of

California, Berkeley, and a research associate of the National Bureau of Economic Research. He was a visiting professor of public policy at the Kennedy School of Government, Harvard University. Mr. Frankel was with the International Monetary Fund, the Institute for International Economics, the Federal Reserve Board, the World Bank, and Yale University.

MORRIS GOLDSTEIN is deputy director of the research department of the International Monetary Fund. He was a research fellow at the Brookings Institution, senior technical adviser at the U.S. Treasury, and visiting research associate at the London School of Economics. Mr. Goldstein has written widely about international economics.

GOTTFRIED HABERLER is professor of economics emeritus at Harvard University and a resident scholar at the American Enterprise Institute. He was Galen L. Stone Professor of International Trade at Harvard University and president of the National Bureau of Economic Research, American Economic Association, and International Economic Association. Mr. Haberler was a consultant to the Treasury Department and economic specialist at the Federal Reserve Board. He is the author of numerous books, including *The Theory of International Trade with its Applications to Commercial Policy* and *Prosperity and Depression.*

WILLIAM S. HARAF is vice president of policy analysis at Citicorp. He was the J. Edward Lundy Visiting Scholar and director of the financial markets project at the American Enterprise Institute. Mr. Haraf was special assistant and senior staff economist to the Council of Economic Advisers and a consultant to the World Bank. He was a contributing editor of *Regulation* magazine. Mr. Haraf has taught at Brown University.

MICHAEL MELVIN is associate professor of economics at Arizona State University and coeditor of the *Journal of International Money and Finance.* He worked with the Federal Reserve Board, the National Bureau of Economic Research, and the University of California, Los Angeles.

ALAN C. STOCKMAN is economics professor and undergraduate program director at the University of Rochester. He is a research associate at the National Bureau of Economic Research, visiting scholar with the Federal Reserve Banks of Richmond and Cleveland, and member of the National Science Foundation Economics Advisory Panel. Mr.

Stockman taught at Vanderbilt University; Institute for International Economic Studies, University of Stockholm; and University of California, Los Angeles.

GUIDO TABELLINI holds the Political Economy Fellowship at Carnegie Mellon University. He taught at Universita' Bocconi, Milan; University of California, Los Angeles; and Stanford University. He was visiting scholar at the Board of Governors of the Federal Reserve System and visiting fellow with the Institute for International Economic Studies, Stockholm. Mr. Tabellini is affiliated with the National Bureau of Economic Research, Center for Economic Policy Research (London), and American Economic Association.

CLAS G. WIHLBORG is the Felix Neubergh Professor of Banking and Finance at Gothenburg University. He was visiting associate professor at the Claremont Graduate School and at the University of Southern California and assistant and associate professor at New York University.

THOMAS D. WILLETT is the director of the Claremont Center for Economic Policy Studies at the Claremont Colleges, where he is the chairman of the graduate faculty in economics. He is adjunct scholar with the American Enterprise Institute. Mr. Willett taught at Johns Hopkins University, Cornell University, Fletcher School of Law and Diplomacy, Harvard University, and University of Virginia. He also served as deputy assistant secretary of the Treasury for international research and planning.

1
The Determinants and Implications of the Choice of an Exchange Rate System

Hali J. Edison and Michael Melvin

Since 1973, the major industrial countries have generally allowed their currencies to float in value against each other. This choice of a floating nominal exchange rate system by large developed countries masks the fact that most of the world's currencies have limited foreign exchange rate flexibility because of conscious government policy. Today, ninety-four of the one hundred fifty-one International Monetary Fund (IMF) member countries reporting their status claim to follow some form of fixed nominal exchange rate system, as shown in table 1–1. Only eighteen countries claim to have freely floating exchange rates vis-à-vis the rest of the world. Given the great diversity of exchange rate systems in the world today and the frequent calls for reform, it is particularly appropriate to take inventory of what economists have learned regarding the determinants and effects of a country's choice of exchange rate system.

This overview focuses on the empirical evidence. Although the theoretical literature on the choice of an exchange rate system is large and growing, reformists typically appeal to perceived real-world problems, so the emphasis will be on reporting and interpreting the available evidence relating to the incentives for choosing a particular exchange rate policy. Even though the evidence is not always conclusive and controversies surely exist, it is time to define the areas of agreement, the sources of disagreement, and the potential for resolving the remaining controversies.

First, the choice of nominal exchange rate system does indeed matter for real economic behavior. Economic magnitudes are not neutral with regard to the choice of an exchange rate system. Countries with floating exchange rates face much more variability in real exchange rates than do countries with fixed exchange rates. Evidence

TABLE 1–1

EXCHANGE RATE ARRANGEMENTS OF MEMBER COUNTRIES OF THE INTERNATIONAL MONETARY FUND

Exchange Rate Arrangement	Number of Countries
Currency pegged to	
U.S. dollar	39
French franc	14
other currency	5
IMF Special Drawing Rights (SDR)	7
currency basket	29
Limited flexibility with respect to a	
single currency	4
Cooperative arrangement (EMS)	8
Adjusted according to a set of	
indicators	5
Managed floating	21
Independent floating	18

SOURCE: *International Financial Statistics*, August 1988.

to this effect is provided by Alan Stockman, who compared the real exchange rate experience of countries that float with that of countries that peg, including countries that had floating exchange rates prior to 1973.[1] By including the experience of early floaters, he provided evidence more on the effects of exchange rate system choice itself than on any effects that might be specific to the 1970s. Stockman concludes that floating exchange rates are associated with significantly greater variability of real exchange rates.

Michael Mussa also examined the data on real exchange rates and produced evidence similar to Stockman's. Mussa concludes that "the choice of nominal exchange rate regime has important economic consequences. Real exchange rates do exhibit substantially and systematically different behavior under different nominal exchange rate regimes. These differences may have had an important influence on choice of exchange rate regimes by particular countries."[2]

The last sentence of the Mussa quotation raises an issue that is a major focus of this chapter: What are the implications of the choice of nominal exchange rate system? The fact that real exchange rates have been more variable under a floating-rate system than under a fixed-rate system is interesting and raises the obvious question of why. The typical answer, as found in Mussa, is that nominal exchange rates are more variable under a floating-rate system than under fixed rates and that goods prices are sticky relative to exchange rates. Having slowly adjusting goods prices and rapidly adjusting nominal foreign exchange rates means that the real exchange rate will be variable, and all the more so under floating exchange rates than under fixed rates, since a float by definition has greater nominal exchange rate variability than does a peg. If a policy change occurs that would cause domestic prices to rise and the domestic currency to depreciate, for instance, the exchange rate change occurs immediately, but prices adjust slowly over time; this difference between the speed of adjustment of exchange rates and the speed of adjustment of prices results in greater real exchange rate variability the greater the nominal exchange rate variability. Stockman offers an alternative "equilibrium theory" of greater real exchange rate variability under floating exchange rates that does not require a slow adjustment of goods prices relative to the speed of adjustment of exchange rates.[3]

The current chapter does not focus directly on *why* real exchange rates are more volatile under a float, although the analysis does offer some insights. Instead, it focuses on the *effects* of choosing a float or a peg in the first place. If real exchange rates have been more variable under floating nominal exchange rates, for example, then what have been the effects of such variability and why might countries be expected to prefer one system to another?

The first major section of the chapter reviews the empirical papers that have directly addressed the question of what determines the choice of an exchange rate system. Researchers have generally approached this question in terms of the following two criteria: Which system will provide the most efficient allocation of resources and which system best protects the domestic economy from foreign or domestic shocks? The latter may involve an assessment of the desired effectiveness of domestic policy instruments; policy makers setting targets related to monetary and fiscal policy may place a very high value on choosing instruments that best allow the attainment of these targets, even if heavy costs may be realized in another dimension related to the choice of an exchange rate system.

The second major section responds to the often-asserted criticism that floating exchange rates have been "too volatile." Researchers have used different points of reference to address this issue. Since all must ask, "Too volatile with respect to what?" the choice of a base for comparison will vary and can have an important effect on the conclusions reached. Reviewing the variety of studies in this area allows a general answer to the question of excess volatility of floating exchange rates.

One of the two criteria used in assessing alternative exchange rate systems is, as mentioned, the relative allocative efficiency of different systems. If floating exchange rates involve large premiums in terms of foreign exchange risk, then international trade and investment may possibly be depressed relative to what they would be under a fixed exchange rate regime. Therefore, the third major section of this chapter reviews the evidence regarding whether floating exchange rates have in fact depressed the volume of trade and investment relative to what they would be under fixed rates. The choice of an exchange rate system is often accompanied by supporting or related changes in economic policy. In practice, rarely will a country alter its exchange rate policy while holding all other policies unchanged—particularly in the case of policy on capital controls. Countries that peg their exchange rates tend to have much stricter capital controls than do countries with floating exchange rates. Thus, a choice to switch to a floating exchange rate may be made as part of a broader policy change to increase trade volume if the policy uncertainty facing traders under fixed rates exceeded the foreign exchange risk faced under floating rates, in which the effects on resource allocation and trade volume work in opposite directions.[4] Despite the seemingly set nature of country response, there is a large and still-growing literature on exchange regime choice and trade volume that offers interesting new insights into this area.

The fourth major section reviews the evidence provided by simulation studies that consider the broader area of the effect of the exchange rate system on other macroeconomic variables such as money, prices, and income or gross national product (GNP). Considering the close link between the exchange rate system and other policy instruments, many researchers have emphasized exercises of macroeconomic model building using simulations to indicate how the choice of exchange rate system will affect key macroeconomic variables. These models cover a crucial area of interest to the policy maker charged with controlling inflation and combating unemployment.

The fifth and final major section offers an analysis of the findings with regard to the current state of knowledge on the determinants and implications of the choice of an exchange rate system and the lessons contained for economic policy makers. Here we tie together the various strands of the literature to identify areas of general agreement and areas where disagreements exist, as well as the potential for resolving the remaining controversies. The reader uninterested in a detailed review of the current state of knowledge may turn immediately to that final section for a summary and analysis of our findings.

The Choice of Exchange Rate System

This section surveys the empirical literature on the choice of exchange rate regime. Most of the empirical literature, unlike the theoretical literature, focuses on the characteristics of the economy as the crucial determinants of the exchange rate arrangement, along the same lines as the literature on optimal currency areas.[5] The more recent empirical literature, however, also considers the nature of disturbances that buffet the economy. The central question addressed in this section is the following: Is it possible to predict empirically what exchange rate regime a country will or should adopt? In particular, can this line of research help guide U.S. policy makers in making a choice among different exchange rate arrangements?

Evidence on the Determinants of Exchange Rate System Choice. The study by Robert Heller provides useful insights into the empirical literature.[6] Heller's study is one of the first in the area, and most subsequent studies follow his general approach, so we shall discuss it in some detail. The main difference between the Heller study and subsequent studies relates to the definition of the dependent variable and the method of estimation.

Heller bases his study of the choice of an exchange rate regime on the economic characteristics of a country. Thus, the theoretical literature he draws upon is more closely related to that on optimum currency areas than that on the effects of stochastic disturbances. Heller argues that as long as countries differ in their economic characteristics, no single exchange rate regime is likely to be appropriate for all of them. Table 1–2 presents the characteristics Heller and others have associated with different exchange rate regimes. In this study, Heller uses five of these attributes, as follows: the size of the country, its openness, the degree of international financial integration, the inflation differential, and the foreign trade patterns of the country.

Given this background, Heller uses the exchange rate arrangements of eighty-six IMF countries, as of July 1976, to identify those country characteristics that help predict whether a particular country will be a floater or a pegger.[7] He excludes from his sample all countries that do not either float or peg their exchange rates. The dependent variable in this study is discontinuous and is not amenable to standard regression analysis. Therefore, Heller applies the statistical technique of discriminant analysis.[8] A positive value of the discriminant score indicates that the country has the characteristics of a floater; a negative value indicates the characteristics of a pegger.

5

TABLE 1–2
CHARACTERISTICS ASSOCIATED WITH EXCHANGE RATE REGIMES

Peggers	Floaters
Small country	Large country
Open economy	Closed economy
Low capital mobility	High capital mobility
Low inflation differential	High inflation differential
Concentrated trade	Diversified trade
Product concentration	Product diversification
Large domestic monetary shocks	Small domestic monetary shocks
Small foreign price shocks	Large foreign price shocks

The function Heller derives indicates that a country with the following characteristics will tend to be a floater: a large GNP, a low degree of openness, a high degree of international financial integration, a high inflation differential, and a low trade concentration. Having established the discriminant function, Heller extends his analysis by trying to predict whether countries participating in the European snake resembled floaters or peggers.[9] The analysis showed that among the countries participating in the European snake, only Germany had the characteristics associated with floaters; the other countries were all identified as being peggers. Carrying this analysis further, Heller tries to use discriminant analysis to identify the appropriate currency to peg to, if a country pegs to a single currency. In general, Heller concludes that certain identifiable characteristics determine the choice of an exchange rate system. These results also may be useful in providing a guide today when considering alternative exchange rate systems. Heller's results predicted, for example, that the United States would (as it has done) select a floating exchange rate regime.

Jacob Dreyer econometrically analyzes the choice of exchange rate regimes of a large sample of developing countries by using essentially the same explanatory variables used in Heller's study.[10] The major difference between Dreyer's study and Heller's study is that Dreyer uses a probit-type estimation technique as opposed to Heller's discriminant analysis. Dreyer's results are similar to those of Heller in that he finds that countries with a high degree of openness tend to adopt fixed exchange rate systems. On the other hand, he reports that the size of the economy does not influence the choice of exchange rate regime and that the greater the diversification of foreign trade, the more likely a country is to peg its currency. These latter results differ from Heller's initial findings and indicate that the choice of exchange rate regime is not as clear-cut as Heller's results suggest.

Paul Holden, Merle Holden, and Esther Suss study the choice of exchange rate policy using a similar approach to that of Heller and Dreyer.[11] They circumvent the problem of using a qualitative, zero/one type of dependent variable by developing an index of exchange rate flexibility. This index is defined as the ratio of the sum of the absolute value of the monthly percentage changes in the trade-weighted exchange rate to the sum of the absolute changes in official holdings of foreign exchange expressed in U.S. dollars. Then this ratio is divided by the sum of imports plus exports to yield the index. They propose this index as a way to evaluate the extent to which exchange market intervention arrangements are being used to offset market forces. This set of explanatory variables is quite similar to those used by Heller and Dreyer. Holden, Holden, and Suss regress the exchange rate flexibility index on these variables using ordinary least squares (OLS) techniques on cross-sectional data for seventy-five countries; they find that 42 percent of the variance of the flexibility measure is explained by their set of variables and that the direction of influence of all the variables is as predicted by theory. These results support an approach similar to that found in the literature on optimum currency areas in providing insights into the formulation of exchange rate policy.

Departing from the literature on optimum currency areas, Michael Melvin argues that modern open-economy macroeconomic theories suggest consideration of the role played by the nature of disturbances to the economy in the choice of exchange rate system.[12] In particular, Melvin considers two testable hypotheses regarding the choice of floating or pegging: the greater the foreign price shocks, the more likely it is that a country will float; and the greater the domestic money shocks, the more likely it is that a country will peg.

Melvin defines the choice of exchange rate system by assigning countries to one of three different categories: A value of one is assigned to single-currency peggers, a value of two to basket peggers, and a value of three to those with crawling pegs and to floaters. Melvin uses an N-chotomous logit estimation routine and evaluates exchange rate policy for sixty-four countries. The evidence Melvin reports is consistent with theory, that is, the greater the foreign price shocks the more likely a float, and the greater the domestic money shocks the more likely a peg.

To provide a link to the earlier literature (by Heller, Dreyer, Holden, and others), Melvin includes the variables from the optimum currency area approach in his logit equations and tests whether they

7

are important determinants of exchange rate system choice. His empirical evidence shows that once the shock effects are accounted for, these other variables used in the earlier studies are generally insignificant.

Some conflict seems to exist in the literature as to whether or not real exchange rate variability should have any impact on the choice of nominal exchange rate regime. Stockman argues that theoretically the choice of nominal exchange rate system should be neutral with respect to real exchange rate variability, although his empirical results do not confirm the neutrality proposition. Andreas Savvides extends the Melvin study further by estimating a model that accounts for the simultaneity between real exchange rate variability and the choice of nominal exchange rate regime.[13] Savvides's results support the proposition, as demonstrated by Melvin, that countries experiencing greater real exchange rate variability will tend to opt for more flexible exchange rate arrangements. Unlike Melvin, however, Savvides finds that variables from both the optimum currency area and the modern open-economy approaches are significant determinants of the choice of exchange rate regime.

Jean-Claude Nascimento's is the only study in this genre to consider what kind of exchange rate regime a single country ought to follow.[14] Nascimento develops a system of three equations based on the literature on exchange rate market pressure (managed floating). Four exchange rate regimes are considered (fixed rate, fixed basket rate, crawling peg, and crawling basket rate) in order to assess which is preferable for the West African Monetary Union. Nascimento estimates the model using full information maximum likelihood (FIML) techniques and concludes that the trade-weighted basket peg is optimal for the West African Monetary Union. This single-country approach of Nascimento may be informative, but several complicated econometric issues still must be addressed before it can be widely applied.

The six studies reviewed thus far in this section represent empirical papers that relate directly to the choice of exchange rate regime. The general approach has been to identify characteristics that predict whether a country participates in one regime or another. As seen from the discussion, this area of applied work, though difficult, is still fairly underdeveloped, owing in part to the difficulty of developing empirically testable hypotheses. Nevertheless, the cross-section studies indicate that countries with the following attributes will tend to adopt a flexible exchange rate arrangement: large, closed economies that have diversified trade, divergent inflation rates, and are financially integrated with a high degree of capital mobility. These findings tend to suggest that one would expect to find that countries such as the United States, West Germany (FR), and Japan would have flexible exchange rate arrangements. As Savvides has pointed out, however, one must consider other factors simultaneously with the choice of exchange rate regime. If Germany pegged its exchange rate, for example, it would not be surprising that some sort of capital controls would emerge that do not currently exist today, making that country appear more like a candidate for fixed exchange rate arrangements.

Related Studies on Currency Substitution and Optimal Currency Baskets. Two other bodies of economic literature also contain implications for exchange rate system choice, namely, the literature on currency substitution and that on the choice of optimal currency basket. The theory in the area of currency substitution indicates that if currencies are highly substitutable, then countries are not able to follow independent monetary policies. In the extreme case of perfect substitutes, fixed exchange rates must exist or else the depreciating currency would not be held. Empirical studies of currency substitution have not generally addressed the implications of this for choice of exchange rate system. Melvin provides evidence that western European monetary unification may be driven by a high degree of substitutability among European currencies.[15] The currency substitution argument is important in that it indicates that the choice of an exchange rate system may not always be at the discretion of policy makers. A high degree of substitutability among moneys results in a market-imposed discipline on monetary policy.

The theory in the area of optimal currency baskets discusses the currencies to which a country should peg its exchange rate. Hali Edison and Erling Vardal show that in extreme cases in which purchasing power parity holds between the home country and all other countries, no unique optimal weighting scheme exists and the country should adopt a floating exchange rate system.[16] This literature, in general, tends to be useful in guiding policy makers once they have made the decision to peg the exchange rate and they are deciding on the currencies to which they should actually peg the rate.

Have Floating Exchange Rates Been Excessively Volatile?

The argument against the float is usually based on the assertion that floating exchange rates have displayed excessive volatility. Exchange rates clearly have been more variable during the period of floating than during the fixed-rate period. Table 1–3 lists the standard deviations of monthly real exchange rate changes over the 1957–1971 pe-

TABLE 1–3

STANDARD DEVIATIONS OF MONTHLY REAL EXCHANGE RATE CHANGES

Exchange Rate	Peg (January 1957 to March 1971)	Float (March 1973 to May 1988)
Dollars per yen	0.0031	0.0333
Dollars per franc	0.0189	0.0329
Dollars per mark	0.0060	0.0353
Dollars per pound	0.0106	0.0319
Yen per franc	0.0192	0.0290
Yen per mark	0.0065	0.0308
Yen per pound	0.0108	0.0324
Francs per mark	0.0230	0.0166
Francs per pound	0.0030	0.0040
Marks per pound	0.0121	0.0297

riod of fixed exchange rates compared with the 1973–1988 period of floating rates for the yen, franc, mark, and pound relative to the U.S. dollar. The standard deviations generally range from roughly two to ten times greater for the floating rates than for pegged rates.[17] The exception is the franc-mark exchange rate, because the European Monetary System (EMS) has reduced variability in the recent period.

The Meaning of Excess Volatility. The fact that exchange rates have been more variable under the recent float than in prior years does not address the question of whether they have been excessively volatile. The most straightforward definition of excess exchange rate volatility would be high variability with much or most of the movement being unpredictable so that an undesirable level of risk is added to international transactions. If exchange rates have been unpredictable, this means either that they are not well explained by economic fundamentals or that many surprising changes have occurred in these fundamentals. Yet even if exchange rate changes indeed have been largely unpredictable, it is still not clear that an undesirable level of risk has been added to international transactions so that traders would prefer fixed rates. The evidence available on these issues is considered in a moment, after we consider a second possible interpretation.

This alternative interpretation of excess volatility is that nominal exchange rates have moved out of line with changes in prices for international goods, with the resultant "misalignment" of exchange rates causing changes in the international competitive positions of nations. This is really not volatility per se but more a persistent tendency for exchange rates to move apart from purchasing power parity. Yet perhaps it is precisely these deviations of nominal exchange rates from purchasing power parity that underlie most criticisms of floating exchange rates by economic policy makers. Therefore, let us take a brief detour to give some attention to this so-called misalignment interpretation of excess volatility.

Exchange Rates and Goods Prices. Evidence regarding the volatility of exchange rates relative to goods prices is presented in table 1–4. The standard deviations of nominal exchange rates have exceeded the standard deviations of consumer or wholesale price ratios by a factor of 2.5 to 7.5. Exchange rates have moved much more than the ratios of the prices of foreign goods to the prices of domestic goods.[18] Exchange rate volatility in this sense means that exchange rates have changed for reasons other than simply to offset movements in the prices of international goods. Those who think of equilibrium exchange rates in a purchasing power parity sense will believe that exchange rate volatility has been associated with a misalignment of nominal exchange rates that in turn has caused changes in trade flows and in the international distribution of income. Policy activists would then argue that policy should be aimed at moving the exchange rate back to its true equilibrium position, thereby achieving an improvement in the international allocation of resources. The underlying basis

---

TABLE 1–4

STANDARD DEVIATIONS OF MONTHLY PERCENTAGE CHANGES IN
EXCHANGE RATES AND OTHER PRICES, JULY 1973–DECEMBER 1985

Prices	Japan	France	West Germany	U.K.
Exchange rates (domestic currency per dollar)	0.0274	0.0279	0.0288	0.0255
Ratio of domestic consumer price index to U.S. consumer price index	0.0094	0.0037	0.0039	0.0081
Ratio of domestic wholesale price index to U.S. wholesale price index	0.0106	0.0123	0.0078	0.0090

SOURCE: Richard C. Marston, "Exchange Rate Policy Reconsidered," in Martin Feldstein, ed., *International Economic Cooperation* (Chicago: University of Chicago Press, 1988).

11

for such an activist policy is the assertion that misalignment can cause temporary resource allocations that will be reversed later when the exchange rate returns to its equilibrium value. In order to avoid such costly temporary resource movements, the authorities could push the exchange rate to the equilibrium level. Marie Thursby demonstrates, however, that the alleged resource reallocation costs associated with flexible exchange rates are likely to be much lower than is commonly believed.[19] Even so, some observers still focus on resource movements as a major problem that comes with flexible exchange rates, as emphasized in several of the studies found in the volume edited by Sven Arndt, Richard Sweeney, and Thomas Willett.[20]

One problem with this activist policy prescription is that if everyone knows that the exchange rate has strayed only temporarily from its equilibrium level, then why would resources move in a less than optimal manner? An additional problem with this misalignment view of excess volatility comes in identifying the source of exchange rate variability: If purchasing power parity gives the long-run equilibrium, then what is responsible for movements away from this equilibrium? The answer could conceivably lie in exchange rate overshooting caused by the fast adjustment of exchange rates coupled with the slow adjustment of goods prices in the face of new information. In this case, the problem would be but a temporary one, since the exchange rate would move toward the long-run equilibrium as goods prices adjust. This kind of exchange rate pattern would suggest recurrent temporary deviations from some mean value, with the real exchange rate expected to return to the mean after a shock occurs. Nevertheless, since much empirical evidence indicates nonstationary movements and a lack of reversion to the mean in real exchange rates, these temporary overshooting deviations from equilibrium may not reasonably be perceived as being the source of misalignment. Instead, the sources of the alleged misalignment would by default be the same sources that would contribute to the first interpretation of excess volatility, that of high exchange rate variability with much or most of the movement being unpredictable so that an undesirable level of risk is added to international transactions. A popular argument used for activist exchange rate management in the context of misalignment or excessive risk is that exchange rate changes have not followed economic fundamentals. This line of reasoning has been subjected to empirical scrutiny as discussed in the following section.

Variance Bounds and Speculative Bubbles. Exchange rate volatility is often termed excessive if it exceeds the volatility implied by the factors believed to determine the exchange rate. The empirical studies that address this issue include variance bounds studies and speculative bubbles studies. Variance bounds tests determine whether the variance of the exchange rate is less than the variance of a linear combination of fundamentals hypothesized to be the primary determinants of exchange rates. Studies on variance bounds have been performed by Roger Huang, R. H. Vander Kraats, L. D. Booth, Kenneth West, and Sushil Wadhwani.[21] This literature has been reviewed by Jeffrey Frankel and Richard Meese.[22]

Huang specifies a simple monetary model of the exchange rate in which the spot rate is a function of domestic and foreign money and interest rates; he finds that the variances of the dollar-mark, dollar-pound, and pound-mark exchange rates all exceed the model-implied variances. Vander Kraats and Booth test three monetary models of the exchange rate and find evidence of excess volatility of exchange rates. Behzad Diba criticizes Huang and Vander Kraats and Booth on the basis of their model specification; using what he claims is a more plausible value for the interest elasticity of money demand, he shows that Huang's and Vander Kraats and Booth's volatility tests do not indicate excess volatility.[23] West uses a model of the mark-dollar exchange rate with money and industrial production identified as the fundamental determinants, in which the variance of the exchange rate exceeds the variance implied by the fundamentals alone; however, when regression disturbances are added to the structural equations and allowed to enter the variance, the exchange rate variance becomes consistent with the model, leading West to conclude that shocks to money demand and purchasing power parity (through real relative price changes, for instance) play a major role in making the model consistent with the data. Wadhwani specifies an overshooting exchange rate model for the effective foreign exchange value of the pound (weighted average value against major currencies), with fundamentals including money, gross national product, interest rates, and prices; he finds that the exchange rate variance exceeds the variance implied by the fundamentals.

Overall, the few variance bounds tests conducted for exchange rates provide some evidence that exchange rates have been excessively volatile. Before evaluating this evidence, let us consider the evidence on a potential source of such excess volatility, namely, speculative bubbles. Speculative bubbles refer to patterns of exchange rate movements that cannot be explained by economic fundamentals. Such speculative runs are thought to reflect self-fulfilling expectations of market participants rather than actual fundamentals. An influential early discussion of the dollar behaving as though following a bubble is that of Paul Krugman; in an informal policy discussion Krugman

13

argued that the dollar had moved away from its long-run equilibrium value in the early to mid-1980s and was due to depreciate in the future (a prediction that proved quite accurate).[24] More formal empirical studies of speculative bubbles include those by George Evans, Richard Meese, and Wing Thye Woo.[25] Evans calculates what is essentially a runs test for the pound-dollar exchange rate and finds that too many periods of negative excess returns to the holding of pounds exist over the 1981–1984 period to be attributed reasonably to chance; this evidence is consistent with the presence of a speculative run. Meese examines the dollar-mark and dollar-pound exchange rates over the 1973–1982 period for evidence of a speculative bubble, finding mixed evidence because his monetary model of the exchange rate seems to perform differently as the U.S. monetary policy regime changes from interest rate targeting to money aggregate targets; still Meese does provide some evidence consistent with the presence of speculative bubbles. Woo investigates the dollar exchange rate versus the mark, French franc, and yen for evidence of bubbles in the context of a portfolio balance model over the 1973–1982 period, arguing that the usual failure of such models to explain exchange rates is because of a failure to model the presence of such bubbles; he identifies two periods of bubbles, namely, a 1978 bubble and 1979–1980 bubble.

Woo's results are instructive not only for the statistical evidence presented but also for his linking of empirical results with a policy discussion. He presents quotations from official sources that are probably representative of what many observers believe during periods asserted to contain bubblelike behavior. Bubbles are often thought to result from individual agents' self-fulfilling forecasts in which each speculator expects to exit the market before the bubble bursts. In the 1979 *Economic Report of the President*, for instance, it is stated:

> Market participants continued to shift out of dollars, despite an apparent consensus that the dollar was undervalued from a long-run point of view. Almost all market participants commenting in the press or in discussions during the fall of 1978 expected an eventual turnaround of the dollar. Only the timing and duration of the expected recovery were uncertain . . . the continued decline of the dollar had become disorderly and was not justified by fundamental economic conditions.[26]

Such a belief that extraneous information (extraneous in terms of econometric models) drives exchange rates is likely to reflect the beliefs of many who argue that exchange rates are too volatile.

What should we make of the evidence on variance bounds tests and bubbles? Unfortunately, such tests cannot distinguish between bubbles and incorrect model specification. Clearly, the fundamental determinants of the exchange rate must be correctly modeled. The researcher must know the correct variables to include, as well as their model coefficients. Diba has illustrated just how sensitive conclusions are with respect to selection of coefficient values. Considering the poor performance of exchange rate models, this assumption of knowing the correct model is quite unrealistic today. Kenneth Singleton forcefully argues the case against the presence of speculative bubbles in the foreign exchange market:

> Most of the exchange rate models that have been examined to date imply that bubblelike behavior of exchange rates must be reflected in the behavior of goods prices or equilibrium consumptions and other asset prices. In fact, these comovements are not observed in the data. This observation casts considerable doubt on the bubble explanation of exchange rate behavior. It also suggests that the empirical exchange rate models within which the presence of bubbles has been studied are seriously misspecified, *with or without the bubble terms.*[27]

Singleton is not alone in his skepticism regarding the presence of speculative bubbles in the foreign exchange market. Yet even those who are doubtful of the relevance of bubbles have difficulty explaining the path of the dollar in the 1980s. The relevant fundamentals that could be responsible for the appreciation and depreciation of the dollar are hard to identify.

Exchange Rates as Asset Prices. Aside from the limited usefulness of empirical exchange rate models, the question still remains whether exchange rates have in fact been excessively volatile. Table 1–4 showed that exchange rates were much more variable than goods price indexes over the 1973–1985 period. Table 1–5, however, shows that exchange rates have not changed "excessively" relative to prices of other financial assets.

As asset prices, exchange rates should behave like stock prices. As new information is revealed, asset prices react immediately. If for some reason investors expect future fundamentals to change in value and to affect the future spot exchange rate, this expectation is reflected in the current spot exchange rate, even though current fundamentals may not be changing. A major challenge for empirical researchers is to incorporate such expected changes in future fundamentals into exchange rate models. Today's exchange rate reflects traders' opinions of the future in the same way as do stock prices and interest rates.

TABLE 1–5

TWO MEASURES OF EXCHANGE RATE CHANGES VERSUS STOCK PRICE
CHANGES FOR FOUR EUROPEAN COUNTRIES, 1973–1975 AND 1973–1983

	Japan	France	West Germany	U.K.
Standard deviations of monthly percentage changes, July 1973 to December 1985				
Exchange rates (domestic currency per dollar)	0.0274	0.0279	0.0288	0.0255
Stock indexes	0.0294	0.0580	0.0315	0.0597
Average absolute monthly percentage changes, April 1973 to February 1983				
Exchange rates (domestic currency per dollar)	2.04	1.99	2.19	1.85
Stock indexes	2.36	4.92	2.61	4.60

SOURCES: See source for table 1–4 and Jeffrey H. Bergstrand, "Is Exchange
Rate Volatility Excessive?" *New England Economic Review,* Federal Reserve Bank
of Boston (September-October 1983), pp. 5–14.

Since currencies are financial assets, evaluations of whether exchange
rate changes have been too volatile are better made by using com-
parisons to other financial assets, as in table 1–5, than by using goods
price indexes, as in table 1–4.

The major question raised at the beginning of this section still
awaits an answer: Have floating exchange rates added an undesirable
level of risk to international transactions? The third major section of
the chapter will review the evidence on this question from the perspective of whether trade in real goods and services has been ad-
versely affected. First, however, let us consider the issue from the
investor's point of view.

Investor Preferences for Fixed or Floating Exchange Rates. A major
part of the controversy surrounding the debate over the adoption of
floating exchange rates was whether floating rates would add an
undesirable element of risk to international financial transactions relative to fixed exchange rates (see Milton Friedman or George Halm).[28]
This argument has recently received new attention. Ronald McKinnon argues as follows:

> I hypothesize that a floating foreign exchange market is so-
> cially inefficient because private foreign exchange traders
> face a huge gap in relevant information: the relative future
> purchasing powers of national fiat moneys, none of which
> has any intrinsic value, are highly uncertain. Thus the as-
> sessments of international investors of whether dollar, or
> yen, or mark assets provide the best combination of yield
> and safety are unnecessarily volatile.[29]

We might suppose, then, that this excess volatility of a float will
reduce international investment activity relative to what a fixed-rate
regime would encourage. Such informational problems could apply
also to an adjustable peg.

Another example is provided by Jacques Artus, who states the
following:

> If investors are risk averse, an increase in exchange rate
> uncertainty should, in itself, generate a decrease in the
> amount of savings transferred among countries (as economic
> agents refrain from accumulating financial assets denomi-
> nated in foreign currencies in their portfolio). Apart from the
> question of transfers of savings, there could also be fragmen-
> tation of the international capital markets so that the com-
> parative advantages of each market over different types of
> transactions and maturities could not be fully exploited.[30]

Michael Darby and James Lothian, however, give evidence that
capital markets have become more, rather than less, integrated. They
argue as follows:

> The continued substantial or rising correlations between
> bond yields in the United States and abroad and the appar-
> ent continued relationship between the scaled balance of
> payments and monetary growth in most major countries
> suggest that interdependence of capital markets, in par-
> ticular, increased and that central bankers often hesitated to
> go it completely alone.[31]

Aside from the issue of capital market integration, one should
consider the evidence regarding individual investor preferences.
Many studies have shown evidence of the greater variability of exchange rates under floating rates. Andre Farber, Richard Roll, and
Bruno Solnik point out the following:

> The fixed rate period is characterized by much smaller indi-
> vidual variances. Thus, if the covariances have not changed
> drastically between the two periods, we should also find a
> smaller variance for a portfolio of currencies during the fixed

period. As a consequence, the use of Markowitz-style mean variance analysis is biased a priori against the flexible rate system, since it is likely to have missed other important changes in the multivariate probability distribution.[32]

If the relevant decision for individual investors deals with only the second moments of exchange rates, then we might be able to conclude that greater risk is associated with a float. But such a traditional mean variance analysis will not provide a useful comparison of fixed versus floating exchange rates. Floating exchange rates could, for instance, involve a high probability of a small change in the value of the exchange rate, while fixed exchange rates could be associated with a small probability of a very large change in the exchange rate. The greater variance of the float will not reflect this effect of higher-order characteristics of the distributions of fixed and floating exchange rates. Yet such higher-order statistics (like skewness and kurtosis) could be relevant to the problem of investor's choice.

Two papers have applied stochastic dominance analysis to the problem of choice of exchange rate system. Second-degree stochastic dominance is a technique for exploring whether all risk-averse investors prefer one distribution of returns to another. Farber, Roll, and Solnik apply stochastic dominance techniques to portfolio returns over the fixed-rate period of 1964–1971 and over the 1971–1975 period taken as representative of the early float. Their results suggest that investors could not unanimously rank the distribution of returns from one regime over the other. Based on this ambiguity, they conclude that "there can be no inference that a flexible-rate system created more uncertainty, diminished foreign trade, or caused destabilizing speculation."[33]

Michael Melvin and Michael Ormiston also study the investor's problem of ranking the distributions of returns from the fixed-rate period and the floating-rate period.[34] First, they estimate stochastic dominance rankings for pure foreign exchange returns, as done by Farber, Roll, and Solnik. Melvin and Ormiston, however, use monthly data from January 1957 to March 1971 for calculating the fixed-rate distribution and from March 1973 to July 1987 for the float. The 1971–1973 period is viewed as a transition period and excluded. Melvin and Ormiston find greater evidence of unambiguous rankings than did Farber, Roll, and Solnik, with fixed exchange rates generally preferred by risk-averse U.S. investors holding individual foreign currencies or a portfolio of foreign currencies.

Melvin and Ormiston argue further, however, that since investors are unlikely to hold portfolios of non-interest-bearing foreign currency, a more realistic sample consists of foreign currency positions in foreign shares of stock. The monthly dollar returns to holding foreign stocks offer much different rankings from the pure foreign exchange returns. First, the second-degree stochastic dominance results are ambiguous; it is not possible to state that all risk-averse investors prefer fixed or floating exchange rates. Estimating stochastic dominance over different ranges of risk-averse investors, however, shows that only at relatively high levels of risk aversion does a general preference exist for fixed exchange rates.

In short, the Melvin and Ormiston study indicates that investors will generally prefer fixed exchange rates if they hold portfolios of non-interest-bearing foreign currency. The investor's problem is interpreted as more likely to be associated with portfolios of foreign earning assets such as stocks and bonds, in which case only very risk-averse investors prefer the distribution of returns under fixed exchange rates. These results indicate that floating exchange rates have not created a level of risk that investors consider "excessive." The movements in currency values have partially offset changes in the yield differentials between domestic and foreign earning assets so that the distribution of returns under floating exchange rates are often preferred to those available under fixed exchange rates. Thus, no obvious basis exists for arguing that, because of the exchange rate volatility facing investors under floating exchange rates, fixed exchange rates are preferred to floating. The studies claiming evidence of excessive volatility of exchange rates are subject to substantial criticism. Overall, then, one must be very careful when drawing conclusions regarding the effects of exchange rate volatility. The next section provides evidence regarding the effect of exchange rate variability on the volume of international trade.

Exchange Regime Choice and International Trade

As pointed out in the preceding section, exchange rates do not appear to have been excessively volatile relative to other asset prices, nor does much evidence exist that floating exchange rates have added an undesirable level of risk to international transactions from the point of view of investors. In this section, we consider the issue of the effects of exchange rate volatility on the volume of international trade. Many economists and policy makers argue that variable exchange rates lead to a reduction in international trade. Such arguments are typically offered as part of a plan to impose greater exchange rate management. Let us first analyze how exchange rate volatility could be linked to the volume of international trade and then let us review the empirical literature that examines the evidence related to this issue.

19

How Exchange Rate Volatility Could Affect Trade Volume. Studies of the time series behavior of exchange rates have convinced economists that exchange rate changes are largely unpredictable. The greater the volatility of exchange rates, the greater are the unanticipated shifts in foreign currency values facing traders. This increase in uncertainty is what is supposed to produce lower trade volumes. If greater risk is associated with international trade, then the price of internationally traded goods is expected to rise and the quantity of goods traded is expected to fall.

The early proponents of floating argued that forward exchange markets would handle this problem by providing hedging opportunities for traders. The presence of forward markets, however, does not entirely eliminate this effect of greater risk associated with greater volatility of exchange rates. In the first place, forward markets exist for only a few currencies and short maturities. The lack of the needed broad coverage and large scale has led to the development of supplemental hedging facilities offered by futures and options markets and swap or barter contracts. All of these hedges are costly, however, and the cost is likely to increase in proportion to the uncertainty regarding future exchange rates. Furthermore, such hedging possibilities cannot eliminate all exchange rate uncertainty if traders do not know with certainty the magnitude and timing of all foreign exchange net payables or receivables.

If highly variable exchange rates increase the risk of trading internationally, then one might expect greater exchange rate volatility to depress trade volume directly. In addition, there could be indirect effects on trade volume if exchange rate volatility also influences international investment or the policies adopted by national and international authorities. The standard arguments, however, emphasize the direct effects of exchange rate volatility in increasing traders' risk and depressing trade volume. This could be a serious error, as the indirect effects may have an even larger role to play in understanding trade volumes.

Variable exchange rates could reduce the capital controls and other kinds of uncertainty facing traders. Exchange rates should change in response to economic events that shift relative prices of goods and absolute prices across countries. Traditionally, the nominal exchange rate is believed to shift to permit the balance of payments to attain the magnitudes consistent with current supply and demand conditions in markets for goods and financial assets. In this sense, the freely floating exchange rate is where it should be, based on market pressures. If the government authorities intervene to peg exchange rates at other levels consistent with some policy objective, they can do so only with the imposition of additional restrictions. An activist exchange rate policy may replace uncertainty regarding the exchange rate with uncertainty regarding capital controls and other restrictive measures. If the policy uncertainty affecting international traders is more repressive than the simple foreign exchange risk under a float, then it could be the case that trade volume will increase with a move from fixed to floating exchange rates.

As the discussion so far indicates, there are arguments to indict exchange rate variability as a reducer of trade, as well as arguments that associate exchange rate variability with greater trade volume. The actual effect that exchange rate variability has on international trade is an empirical question. Therefore, an examination of the pertinent evidence is in order.

Empirical Evidence on Exchange Rate Variability and Trade Volume. Many others have already examined the evidence related to exchange rate fluctuations and international trade. In 1984, for example, the International Monetary Fund published a study reviewing the evidence. The IMF study was conducted in response to a request from the director-general of the General Agreement on Tariffs and Trade. The officials of the GATT were concerned with the effects of the exchange rate volatility observed in the early 1980s, and so the IMF Research Department reviewed the existing evidence and conducted its own statistical tests. The report stated the following:

> The large majority of empirical studies on the impact of exchange rate variability on the volume of international trade are unable to establish a systematically significant link between measured exchange rate variability and the volume of international trade, whether on an aggregated or on a bilateral basis.[35]

An examination of the literature reviewed by the IMF study leads to concurrence with the conclusion stated in the preceding quotation. In addition, Willett offers a survey with a similar conclusion.[36] Many new studies, however, have been conducted since the IMF survey of the literature was made in the early 1980s. Let us examine some of these new studies to see if a new consensus emerges regarding the effects of exchange rate variability on international trade.

The studies reviewed are listed in table 1–6. The first study, that of M. A. Akhtar and R. Spence Hilton, was published shortly after the IMF study.[37] The authors note the lack of significant evidence prior to this time and agree with the conclusion of the IMF analysis as far as it went. They argue, however, that the use of more recent data allows

21

TABLE 1-6
RECENT STUDIES OF EXCHANGE RATE VARIABILITY AND TRADE VOLUME

Authors	Sample Period	Trade Flows	Measure of Variability	Conclusion
Akhtar and Hilton (1984)	1974–1981	Aggregate trade of United States and Germany	Standard deviation of nominal exchange rates	Negative effect[a]
Gotur (1985)	1975–1983	Aggregate trade of United States, Germany, France, Japan, and United Kingdom	Standard deviation of nominal effective exchange rate index	Little or no effect
Kenen and Rodrik (1986)	1975–1984	Aggregate manufactured imports of the eleven largest industrial countries	Standard deviation of real effective exchange rate and standard error of AR1 real exchange rate equation	Negative effect[a]
Bailey, Tavlas, and Ulan (1986)	1973–1984	Aggregate real exports of the seven largest OECD countries	Absolute value of quarterly change in nominal effective exchange rate	No effect
Bailey, Tavlas, and Ulan (1987)	1962–1985	Aggregate real exports of eleven OECD countries	Absolute value of quarterly change in real and nominal effective exchange rate, standard deviation of real and nominal effective exchange rate	Little or no effect
Thursby and Thursby (1985)	1973–1977	Real bilateral exports for twenty countries	Standard deviation of nominal and real trade-weighted exchange rates and absolute values of percentage changes in nominal and real exchange rates	Mixed effects

Study	Period	Trade flow	Measure of variability	Conclusion
Cushman (1986)	1965–1977 1973–1983	Real bilateral exports of United States to six major trading partners	Standard deviation of the change in the bilateral real exchange rate along with standard deviations and covariances with other major currencies	Negative effect[a]
Cushman (1988a)	1974–1983	Real bilateral exports of United States to six major trading partners	Five alternative measures of standard deviations on real exchange rates or forward rate forecast errors	Negative effect on imports, inconclusive on exports
Maskus (1986)	1974–1984	Real bilateral exports and imports by industry of United States with four major trading partners	Unexpected change in real exchange rate based on forward rate and inflation forecasts	Negative effect in some industries
DeGrauwe and De Bellefroid (1987)	1960–1969 1973–1984	Real bilateral export growth among the ten largest industrial countries	Standard deviation of exchange rate change and mean absolute change	Negative effect on growth rate not level
Perl (1988)	1975–1986	Real bilateral trade of United States with four major trading partners	That part of exchange rate variability not explained by relative money supply variability	Ambiguous effects
Brada and Mendez (1988)	1972–1977	Real bilateral exports of thirty countries	Dummy variable for exchange rate system	Positive effect

a. Authors' conclusions appear to be either too strong or incorrect based on either the results reported in the study or later research.

them to turn up significant evidence of a negative effect of variability on trade volume. They find that the aggregate exports and imports of the United States and Germany are lowered by greater exchange rate variability. Variability is measured by the standard deviation of nominal exchange rates.

The second study, by Padma Gotur, is an extension and reestimation of the work of Akhtar and Hilton.[38] Gotur criticizes the latter's use of only two countries, as well as their econometric technique. When the model of Akhtar and Hilton is extended to other countries and more recent dates, the strong negative effects of exchange rate variability on trade disappear.

Peter Kenen and Dani Rodrik analyze the response of aggregate manufactured imports of the eleven largest industrial countries to several alternative measures of exchange rate variability.[39] They conclude that greater variability of real exchange rates depresses import volumes. Yet a cursory glance at their estimation results indicates that this is not a universal result. Of the eleven countries in their sample, only the United States, Canada, Germany, and the United Kingdom had negative exchange rate variability effects that were statistically significant. The other seven countries had either positive or negative coefficients that were statistically insignificant. It would seem reasonable to consider their conclusion that "the volatility of real exchange rates appears to depress the volume of international trade" as rather strong given the fact that seven of eleven equations do not display this result.

Other studies of the effect of exchange rate variability on aggregate trade flows include the two studies by M. J. Bailey, G. S. Tavlas, and M. Ulan.[40] The first study examines the volume of real exports as a function of the absolute value of the quarterly change in nominal effective exchange rates (along with other variables in the export equation) for the seven largest countries of the Organization for Economic Cooperation and Development (OECD). In no case was the exchange rate variability term statistically significant, even after experimenting with lag structures. In a follow-up study, they added several countries and experimented with alternative measures of exchange rate uncertainty. They estimated their equations separately for the fixed-rate period and the floating-rate period. Of the forty equations estimated, only eight displayed a statistically significant effect of exchange rate variability. Of these eight coefficients, five were positive and three were negative. Overall, the work of Bailey, Tavlas, and Ulan suggests that exchange rate variability has no significant effect on trade volume.

The studies cited thus far have all used aggregate trade data.

Other studies have explored bilateral trade data for evidence of a negative impact of exchange rate variability. J. G. Thursby and Marie Thursby, for example, estimated real bilateral export equations for twenty countries as a function of several alternative measures of exchange rate variability. The evidence is mixed. In forty-one cases, exports are significantly increased by variability. In eighty-five cases, exports are significantly decreased by exchange rate variability. Thursby and Thursby do not claim any net effect of exchange rate variability but instead simply state that "our bilateral trade results provide support for the hypothesis that exchange rate variability affects the pattern of trade."[41]

David Cushman has been an active contributor to the literature on exchange rate variability and trade volume. He brings the issue of third-country risk into the empirical literature.[42] Cushman argues that researchers are mixing effects when they ignore third-country risk in studies on bilateral trade flow. An increase in the uncertainty associated with the pound-dollar exchange rate, for instance, could depress the level of trade between the United States and the United Kingdom. But an increase in the uncertainty associated with the dollar-mark exchange rate could increase trade between the United States and United Kingdom. Ideally, the researcher would like to hold constant such third-country effects. Cushman estimates real exports from the United States to its major trading partners as a function of proxy variables for the risk attached to each bilateral currency and proxy variables for the risk attached to third-party currencies (along with other determinants of exports). Cushman claims that his results suggest that exchange risk has "played a significant role in depressing international trade during floating."[43] But a look at his tables indicates that his results yield mixed evidence. For each sample period and each specification, he provides six equations, one for each trading partner. When the third-country risk terms are omitted, the bilateral risk coefficients yield one positive value, three negative values, and two insignificant values for the 1965–1977 period. For the 1973–1983 period, only one significant negative is found, with one significant positive and otherwise insignificant results. When the third-party risk terms are included, the results are similar. In no case do more than half the coefficients have statistically significant negative signs. The other coefficients are either significantly positive or else insignificant. The author's conclusion would seem to be rather strong given the reported findings.[44]

In a recently published paper, Cushman ignores the third-country risk terms altogether.[45] He studies the same real export flows for the 1974–1983 period as were studied in his previous paper but also

25

includes U.S. imports. The novelty of the newer paper is that he experiments with five alternative definitions of exchange rate variability. In his best bilateral export equations, the exchange risk coefficient is significantly negative twice, significantly positive once, and otherwise insignificant. His best bilateral import equations yield five significantly negative coefficients with one positive and insignificant coefficient. Cushman concludes that the evidence on U.S. exports is inconclusive but that U.S. imports have been reduced by exchange rate variability.

Keith Maskus examines the effect of unexpected real exchange rate changes on U.S. bilateral trade with Japan, the United Kingdom, West Germany, and Canada. The Maskus paper differs from other studies in that he explores bilateral trade by industry. Of his sixty-four equations, twenty-six had significantly negative coefficients on unexpected real exchange rate changes. Agriculture was the industry most susceptible to the negative effects of exchange risk, which Maskus attributes to the openness and lack of concentration of that industry. Even though Maskus finds some evidence of statistically significant negative effects of unexpected real exchange rate changes on trade, he concludes that "trade gains associated with lower exchange risk are likely to be modest, at least for the United States."[46]

Paul De Grauwe and Bernard de Bellefroid analyze the effect of exchange rate variability on the growth rate of bilateral trade. They compute the standard deviation and mean absolute change in annual exchange rates over the 1960–1969 and 1973–1984 periods for ten large industrial countries. They regress the growth rate of trade on income growth, a dummy variable for customs unions, and exchange rate variability. They have a cross-section regression using the rate of trade growth over the periods studied as their dependent variable. Their finding of a significant negative effect of exchange rate variability on real trade growth across countries must be interpreted carefully. The countries with lower growth rates of trade, for example, could also have the highest levels of trade; in such a case, we may not want to claim that exchange rate variability has depressed the volume of trade. Furthermore, a dummy variable for Japan is included in their equations for no better reason than to capture the rapid growth of Japanese trade "which we cannot explain by income growth or by exchange rate variability."[47] It would be enlightening to see what would happen to the overall results in the absence of this ad hoc dummy variable for Japan.

Tijana Perl uses a novel measure of exchange rate variability. She defines "pure" foreign exchange risk as that part of exchange rate variability that cannot be explained by the unanticipated volatility of

U.S. and foreign money. By decomposing exchange rate variability into sources (like monetary policy) and a residual, she finds that the residual effect of foreign exchange risk has mixed effects on trade volume. Perl concludes that "a major portion of the overall uncertainty effects of exchange rate volatility on trade should be ascribed to uncertainty in the underlying environment (like money supplies) rather than to floating exchange rates per se."[48]

The last study to be reviewed is quite different from the previous studies in that it is the only one that actually addresses directly the issue of exchange rate regime choice and trade volume. Earlier we noted that trade volume could increase with the move from fixed to floating exchange rates if the policy uncertainty facing traders under fixed exchange rates exceeded the foreign exchange risk faced under floating rates. Josef Brada and Jose Mendez attempt to estimate this effect in the context of a "gravity" equation for real bilateral trade flows between countries. A gravity equation is an equation specifying trade flows as a function of incomes, populations, and distance between countries. Brada and Mendez add dummy variables for the exchange rate system to this model. The equation is estimated for bilateral trade flows between thirty countries for each year from 1973 to 1977. They find that, other things being equal, bilateral trade flows are higher between countries that maintain floating exchange rates than between countries with fixed exchange rates. Their conclusion is that although exchange rate risk may lower the volume of trade, such effects are less "than the trade-reducing effects of restrictive commercial policies imposed by fixed-exchange rate countries."[49]

Lessons of the Empirical Studies. Taking the newer studies cited here together with the earlier studies reviewed by the IMF, we can fairly say that the research has not produced one-sided evidence that exchange rate variability has any particular effect on the volume of international trade. The papers dealing with aggregate trade flows claimed to have found either a negative effect or no effect. The Kenen and Rodrik evidence, however, appears to be much more consistent with inconclusive evidence rather than a negative effect, and the Akhtar and Hilton results were overturned by Gotur. Therefore, the first five studies in table 1–6 do not as a whole reveal a systematic relationship between exchange rate variability and trade volume.

The remaining studies listed in table 1–6 are on bilateral trade. Since the first Cushman study reports evidence that is quite mixed, we should discount his evaluation that exchange rate variability depresses the volume of trade. Then the last seven studies in table 1–6, taken as a whole, suggest that the evidence regarding the effect of exchange rate variability on trade volume is inconclusive. One certainly cannot examine the empirical evidence reviewed in this section, or the earlier papers not examined here, and claim that greater exchange rate variability reduces the volume of international trade.

Simulation Studies of the Choice of Exchange Rate Regime

Despite the importance of the question of fixed versus flexible exchange rates, until recently very few empirical studies have attempted to evaluate international monetary systems quantitatively.[50] We have already considered empirical studies that examined what determines the choice of exchange rate regime. In this section we focus on literature that evaluates the effect of the choice of exchange rate regimes on key macroeconomic variables and that examines the effectiveness of policy instruments over alternative exchange rate regimes. The literature surveyed uses multicountry model simulations to evaluate and compare alternative exchange rate systems when policy variables are perturbed or when the economy undergoes an exogenous shock.

The early theoretical literature on the choice of exchange rate regime focused on comparing the capabilities of fiscal and monetary policies in stabilizing output (GNP) under different exchange rate regimes, as did the early model simulation literature; the first part of this section therefore examines the effectiveness of monetary and fiscal policy under alternative exchange rate arrangements, as addressed by the early model simulation literature. Over the years, with the large movements in the foreign currency market there has been a surge of interest in considering alternative exchange rate arrangements; the second part of this section therefore considers model studies that not only examine a larger range of alternative exchange rate scenarios but that also assess how economies react to different stochastic shocks under these different exchange rate arrangements. Finally, in the last part "target zones" for exchange rates are analyzed in detail, because they have received so much attention in policy-making circles.

The papers discussed use various multicountry models to evaluate the differences in exchange rate regimes. In conducting the simulation experiments, base line paths are typically generated using actual values for all the exogenous variables. The residuals of the behavioral equations are added back to make the endogenous variables follow their actual historical paths in the base line. The model is then run to consider each policy action compared with the base line. The general simulation properties of the model are conditional not only on the parameters of the model but also on the cyclical state of the economy.

This simulation approach does raise problems of implementation, in that parameters in the model may change when there is a change in policy regime—or, as in our example, a change in exchange rate regime. In general, one would want to be able to model how parameters change under different policy regimes, but, as Robert Lucas has noted, econometric models typically assume fixed parameters, making such models less well suited for analyzing how economies might respond under alternative policy scenarios.[51] Most of the papers discussed do not deal directly with the Lucas critique. Implicitly most simulations studies assume that parameter shifts resulting from changes in policy regimes are small relative to the perturbation and that therefore the model simulations can offer some useful information. One must keep this qualification in mind when considering the simulation results in this section. The papers examined here are compiled and listed in table 1–7 in the order in which they are discussed.

Early Model Simulations. The early simulations surveyed here typically evaluate the effectiveness of fiscal and monetary policy under different exchange rate regimes. This literature tends to be linked to the early Mundell-Fleming theoretical literature on choice of exchange rate regimes. As is well known, these results are quite strong and are dependent on the assumptions embodied in the model. The principal results of the Mundell-Fleming model, which tend to be evident in the macroeconometric models, is that monetary policy is effective in influencing output under flexible rates and fiscal policy has no effect; similarly, fiscal policy is effective in influencing output under fixed exchange rates and monetary policy has no effect.

Ernesto Hernandez-Cata and others produced one of the first model simulation studies to consider the impact of monetary policy under alternative exchange rate assumptions.[52] The paper uses an early version of the Federal Reserve Board staff's multicountry model (MCM) as described by Stevens and others.[53] The model simulates a contractionary monetary policy in the United States (produced by an open-market operation) under (1) flexible exchange rates and under (2) conditions in which the monetary authorities do intervene in the foreign exchange market (managed float). The simulations are evaluated for the United States, West Germany, and Japan, focusing primarily on gross national product, prices, and the trade balance.

The simulation results show that the contractionary monetary policy has a negative impact on U.S., German, and Japanese GNP

29

TABLE 1–7

SIMULATION STUDIES ON ALTERNATIVE EXCHANGE RATE REGIMES

Authors	Model	Conclusions
Hernandez-Cata et al. (1979)	FRB MCM	Managed rates greater impact.
Amano (1983)	EPA	Mixed depending on country evaluated.
OECD (1984)	OECD mini-interlink	Flexible rates tend to insulate more.
Helliwell and Padmore (1985)	Survey	
Darby (1983)	Mark III	Inconclusive.
Boughton et al. (1986)	IMF minimod	Fiscal effects independent of flexibility.
Taylor (1986)	Taylor	Flexible rates insulate; flexible less fluctuation.
McKibbin and Sachs (1985)	MSG	Country-specific—flexible better; global—fixed better.
McKibbin and Sachs (forthcoming)	MSG	Depends on disturbance.
Edison et al. (1987)	FRBMCM	Target zones perform well.
Currie and Wren-Lewis (1987)	NIESR (Global Econometric Model) GEM	Target zones perform well.
Frenkel et al. (1988)	Multimod	Target zones perform well.
Hughes Hallett et al. (1988)	MCM multipliers	Target zone gains are small.
Levine et al. (1988)	Minilink	Gains from using simple rules.
Minford (1988)	Liverpool	Fixed rates are somewhat better.
Blake et al. (1988)	Glasgow	Target zone gain depends on wage indexation.

under both exchange rate scenarios. Interestingly, the effect on U.S. GNP tends to be stronger and to start earlier in the managed-float case than under flexible rates, because under the managed float the weighted average dollar initially tends to appreciate, leading to a reduction in the U.S. trade surplus. Similarly, the price effect tends to be stronger in Germany and Japan under managed rates than under flexible rates, because here, too, the effect of GNP is stronger in the managed case. The overall results reported in this paper suggest that monetary policy can be effective in influencing output under both free and managed-floating exchange rate arrangements.

Two other well-known multicountry models have also studied the different effects of policy changes under different exchange rate arrangements. Akihiro Amano discusses the differences in macroeconomic behavior under alternative exchange rate arrangements (fixed versus floating) using the Japanese Economic Planning Agency (EPA) model.[54] An OECD paper examines the impact of exchange system choice on macroeconomic policy and exchange rates (floating versus managed) using a scaled-down seven-country version of the OECD "interlink" model.[55] The general methodology that these papers apply is much the same as that used by Hernandez-Cata and others. The results of both studies indicate that fiscal policy tends to influence output under different exchange rate regimes. In all cases a cut in government purchases leads to a fall in gross national product; the effect tends to be stronger, however, under fixed exchange rates. The rise in interest rates in both studies tends to lower GNP and tends to be transmitted abroad. The EPA model simulation exercise shows different results for different country models, which suggests that the different country models have different transmission mechanisms incorporated into their structure. John Helliwell and Tim Padmore survey multicountry macroeconometric models with two or more countries.[56] Included in this survey is a comparison of transmission of fiscal and monetary shocks under fixed and floating exchange rates for the EPA model and for a linked Canadian RDX2 and U.S. MPS model. The results of the EPA model as reported earlier are replicated with the same findings.

Michael Darby also considers the different transmission mechanisms under fixed and flexible exchange rates.[57] The model that he uses is at a more experimental stage than the other linkage models, and the results are preliminary. The model offers useful inference in other areas, but the results are inconclusive regarding the differences between fixed and floating rates.

In general, the results of most of these early simulation studies are consistent with the theoretical findings, although they do blur the stark results of the theoretical models somewhat. The results also appear to be dependent on the model to some degree. In a recent paper, for example, Boughton and others show, using the IMF's "minimod," that the effect of fiscal policy on home country output is not dependent on the degree of exchange rate flexibility, yet they also show that monetary policy is most effective when the exchange rate is flexible.[58] The overall conclusion that one can draw from this literature is that the choice of exchange rate regime depends somewhat on the choice of the instrument (fiscal or monetary) that the policy maker wishes to use.

More Recent Simulations. This subsection considers the more recent simulation studies on the choice of exchange rate regime. The focus in these studies vis-à-vis the earlier studies has been more on evaluating several alternative exchange rate regimes using newer empirical techniques such as stochastic simulations. These newer studies address the question of which exchange rate regime is better able to stabilize output and inflation when the economy is buffeted by disturbances. Another difference is that these models tend to introduce forward-looking expectations.

John Taylor evaluates and compares systems of flexible versus fixed exchange rates by using a small rational-expectations model.[59] In the first part of the paper he reports on the effects on endogenous variables of unanticipated changes in monetary and fiscal policy under both fixed and flexible exchange rates. This is similar so far to the studies reported in the preceding subsection. All the experiments also involve changes in the U.S. money supply or U.S. government spending. Taylor's results are somewhat different from those discussed earlier; he finds that there is no marked difference for the United States between exchange rate regimes but that the effects on Japan and Germany vary between exchange rate regimes, because of how the shocks are transmitted abroad. Under flexible rates, for example, the empirical model predicts, in response to a monetary shock, an initial increase in U.S. GNP that slowly dissipates monotonically over time, as well as a gradually rising U.S. price level, with almost no change in the other countries' GNP. Under fixed rates, compared with the United States, in response to a U.S. monetary shock Japan's GNP expands by almost the same amount and Germany's GNP expands by almost three times as much; prices in the other countries also are affected under fixed exchange rates.

In the second part of the paper, Taylor reports on the evaluation of alternative monetary systems using stochastic simulations. This method differs somewhat from the standard deterministic simulations. In this paper, Taylor considers shocks that affect only the "contract" wage equations. The stochastic simulations are performed both for fixed exchange rates and for flexible exchange rates. The main results are that the fluctuations in real GNP in the United States are about the same under both exchange rate regimes. On the other hand, the fluctuations in real GNP in the other countries are much larger under fixed exchange rates than under flexible exchange rates. The fluctuations in the price level are higher under fixed exchange rates for all the countries of the Group of Seven except for the United States and Germany. Taylor also finds that the fluctuations in imports and exports are greater under fixed exchange rates.

Warnick McKibbin and Jeffrey Sachs study the operating characteristics of a number of alternative monetary arrangements using a large-scale simulation model (MSG) of the world economy.[60] They examine the asymptotic variances of key macroeconomic target variables for a range of stochastic disturbances under a variety of exchange rate regimes. They consider the outcomes when policy makers do or do not observe the shock and when policy makers infer the shocks using an optimal filtering rule. McKibbin and Sachs's methodology is somewhat similar to the second approach used by Taylor, augmented to include a summary measure of performance of each regime using a welfare function. They consider seven alternative monetary regimes under various assumptions about the observability of the shocks and the regimes, as follows: a pure float, noncooperation, cooperation, nominal GDP targeting, McKinnon rule, global nominal GDP targeting, and leaning with or against the wind. They find that the performance of each regime depends crucially on the nature of the shocks impinging on the economy. For the country-specific shocks, the fixed exchange rate regimes perform poorly in the sense of leading to a large variance of a set of macroeconomic target variables. When a shock requires adjustment of the real exchange rate, a regime of fixed exchange rates in a sticky-price world does not produce adjustment of the real exchange rate in the short run and thus results in increased variance of target variables. For global shocks, such as a change in world oil prices, fixed exchange rates perform tolerably well. For other shocks, such as negatively correlated monetary shocks, the fixed-rate regime proposed by McKinnon performs quite well.

In an earlier paper, McKibbin and Sachs, using the same McKibbin and Sachs global (MSG) model, analyzed the implications of alternative monetary regimes in the OECD for the transmission of fiscal policy and for the efficiency of strategic interactions across the major OECD economies.[61] In this paper they found that the nature of fiscal interactions will vary greatly depending on the nature of the monetary regime. Under floating exchange rates, transmission of fiscal policy tends to be positive, while under fixed rates, fiscal policy can actually be negatively transmitted. The question of which regime is better is shown to depend on which stochastic disturbances are dominant. On the whole, the results are not very favorable to fixed exchange rates.

These papers have presented an alternative method for examining the operating characteristics of different exchange rate systems that is linked to the theoretical literature that emphasizes the nature of the shocks to the economy. As shown in table 1–2, an economy faced with foreign price shocks tends to be better insulated by flexible exchange rates. In general, it is hard to draw any specific conclusions from these papers because the results tend to be not only model specific but also dependent on the nature of the shocks considered.

Evaluation of Target Zone Proposal. Recent years have brought a renewed interest in issues of international macroeconomic policy co-ordination and in forms of exchange rate targets or zones. In the Bretton Woods system of fixed exchange rates, policy makers were committed to limiting a country's exchange rate movements to one percent of the currency's exchange rate par value vis-à-vis the dollar. The target zone system, which has been advocated by John Williamson, also has bands for exchange rates, but these bands are much wider apart, more on the order of 10 percent; this target zone system allows considerable fluctuation in the exchange rate but attempts to eliminate the large gyrations, or so-called misalignments.

The first empirical paper in this genre is that by Hali Edison, Marcus Miller, and John Williamson.[62] It examines the target zone proposal for exchange rate management by presenting the results of simulations performed on both a large macroeconometric model (the Federal Reserve Board staff's multicountry model, or MCM) and a small analytical model. In the first part of the paper, the question posed to the large macroeconometric model (the MCM) is how economic outcomes with respect to output, inflation, interest rates, and exchange rates would have differed in the five MCM countries had the assignment of monetary policy in these countries been changed to limit deviations of the real effective exchange rates from a target value.[63] To evaluate this counterfactual situation, the historical values are taken as the base line, and then the model is rerun under the assumption that the monetary authorities had started adjusting interest rates from their historical levels according to a simple hypothesized reaction function starting in the first quarter of 1976.

The essence of the policy reaction function used in the MCM simulations is that monetary authorities are assumed to have adjusted interest rates whenever the real exchange rate deviated from the center of the target zone. The interest rate adjustment is rather small when the exchange rate still lies within the target zone, but the adjustment increases rapidly once the exchange rate leaves the zone. Although a country does not have an absolute obligation to keep the exchange rate within the target zone ("soft buffers"), as the currency leaves the target zone, the monetary authorities do increasingly act to bring the exchange rate back toward its target, but their action is not abrupt.

The MCM simulation results presented in the paper suggest that countries' coordination of monetary policy following a target zone rule can diminish the misalignments of exchange rates somewhat but cannot completely remove the historical misalignments. The "success" of the use of monetary policy for each of the five countries depends on each one's historical situation.

To push the analysis of policy design further, Edison, Miller, and Williamson considered a second set of MCM simulations in which they supplemented the monetary rule with compensatory changes in fiscal policy directed at holding real GNP at its base line level. The results suggest that the change in the policy blend in each country tends to eliminate some of the exchange rate and current account misalignments without sending countries into an inflationary spiral. These results, as noted earlier, do depend heavily on the MCM structure, which has been documented elsewhere.[64]

In the second part of the paper the analysis shifts from the complexities of a large macroeconometric model to a simple linear description of the determination of output (GNP) prices, and exchange rates. The analytical model follows the MCM in assuming that output is determined by demand and that inflation depends upon demand pressure and past inflation. In the small model, however, exchange rates are assumed to reflect the rational expectations of agents who are fully informed both as to these characteristics of the model and of policies designed to control it. As a result, one should get some idea of how a policy regime might operate as and when rules of the game become well understood.

In general, the main conclusions derived from the analysis with the MCM are (1) that a monetary policy oriented toward exchange rates could have curbed some possible misalignments without completely undermining counterinflation policies and (2) that flexibility in fiscal policy also is needed, to eliminate some of the imbalances that arose historically in current account positions. The results of the analytical model suggest that real interest rate differentials can be used for exchange rate management and that fiscal policy can be aimed at achieving national nominal income targets.

David Currie and Simon Wren-Lewis provide an assessment of the proposal on the extended target zone using the NIESR global economic model (GEM) of the world economy.[65] The essence of the extended, or "blueprint," proposal as laid out by Miller and Williamson can be summarized as follows:[66]

35

- Countries should determine a set of real exchange rate targets chosen so as to be consistent with simultaneous internal and external balance in the medium term.
- Countries should choose targets for the rate of growth of domestic demand according to a formula designed to promote the fastest growth of output consistent with a gradual reduction of inflation.
- Differences in interest rates among countries should be varied to limit the deviation of currencies from their target levels.
- Average world interest rates should be varied to stabilize the aggregate growth of nominal demand.
- National fiscal policy should be used to achieve national target rates of growth of domestic demand.

As in the Edison, Miller, and Williamson study, the two Currie and Wren-Lewis studies evaluate the extended target zone proposal using simulations over the historic period of 1975 to 1986. To evaluate the target zone proposal, they use optimal-control simulation methods. The parameters on the proposed feedback rules are determined using optimal control. The results of both of the Currie and Wren-Lewis papers suggest that policy cooperation using the optimal feedback rules leads to substantial Pareto improvement when compared with history.[67] Real exchange rate variability tends to be reduced. Their simulation results also show that under the counterfactual simulation, the large interest rate hike around 1980 would have been avoided. In general, the Currie and Wren-Lewis simulations give support to the target zone blueprint scheme of Williamson and Miller. They do stress that the support tends to come from changes in fiscal policy relative to the historical policy rather than from the use of monetary policy to stabilize the real exchange rate.

Jacob Frenkel, Morris Goldstein, and Paul Masson also report simulations from the global "multimod" macroeconomic model developed at the IMF Research Department. In this paper they evaluate the target zone scheme.[68] Multimod differs from the MCM and the NIESR GEM that have investigated target zones in the sense that expectations are forward looking and reflect the stance of policy. In many ways this model is similar to the small rational-expectations model used by Taylor, as described earlier in this section.

Frenkel, Goldstein, and Masson consider two simulations to evaluate the target zone proposal. The first simulation relates to the original target zone proposal, which considers only a monetary reaction function to movements in the exchange rate. The second simulation relates to the so-called blueprint target zone proposal, which augments the simple target zone proposal with a fiscal policy reaction function.

The monetary reaction function used by Frenkel, Goldstein, and Masson is like those in the MCM study by Edison, Miller, and Williamson, augmented by a target monetary base term. The fiscal policy reaction function is more attuned to the latter blueprint proposal than to the study by Edison, Miller, and Williamson in their simulation with the MCM. Fiscal policy is assumed, as in the blueprint proposal, to be targeted on domestic demand growth. In general, Frenkel, Goldstein, and Masson find that the simple target zone simulations had little success in limiting real exchange rate movements and that they led to more variable inflation rates, in part because of their wider bands and in part because of the forward-looking expectations assumption.[69] Nevertheless, as did Edison, Miller, and Williamson, they found that the current account imbalances are reduced for the major countries when fiscal policy is used.

In a recent Center for Economic Policy Research (CEPR) conference, several empirical papers on analyzing international exchange rates were given. Andrew Hughes Hallett and colleagues, for example, use MCM multipliers in a dynamic game to consider exchange rate targeting as a surrogate for international policy coordination.[70] Paul Levine and colleagues assess simple rules for policy coordination using the OECD "minilink" model.[71] Patrick Minford reevaluates the blueprint proposal using his multicountry model, while Andrew Blake and others emphasize the importance of the structure of the labor market for the operation of exchange rate targeting.[72] The conclusions of these studies for the target zone proposal were mixed. Levine and colleagues find that there are gains for coordination using simple rules, while Hughes Hallett and others find small gains. The conclusion that emerges from the conference was that the results are highly sensitive to the assumptions embedded in the models. Blake and colleagues, for example, show that with a moderate degree of wage indexation, it would be difficult to implement target zones. This diversity in findings is similar to the conclusions that emerge from empirical models that measure the gains from coordination: Different models reveal different results.

Summary of Simulation Findings. What should we make of the evidence on simulations of exchange rate regime choice? First, little consensus exists among the models about the exact response to changes in policy variables and to changes in exogenous disturbances; however, the general response to changes is fairly consistent. This finding has also been documented in the work by Bryant and others for the case of twelve multicountry models under the floating exchange rate regime. Second, the general conclusion that emerges from the earlier simulation studies is that monetary policy tends to be more effective in influencing output under flexible rates and that fiscal policy tends to be more effective under fixed rates, the standard Mundell-Fleming result. Third, the more recent simulation studies tend to find flexible rates performing better in the sense of leading to smaller variances of the key macroeconomic variables, at least when the shock is global. Fourth, the conclusion that emerges from the target zone studies is that the policies described in the blueprint and in the empirical evidence tend to lead to a welfare improvement when compared with history. Of course, such studies do not ensure that future welfare would be improved by such policies nor that the required cooperation among countries can even be achieved.

Analysis and Implications for Policy

The empirical studies reviewed offer selective ammunition to the reform-minded economist and policy maker. Rather than selectively appealing to one or another study that best supports a particular viewpoint, the approach taken here is one of evaluating the whole body of literature addressing each area of concern. After summarizing the current state of the evidence in each area, we discuss the key policy issues.

The Issues. The issues considered in this chapter have included the determinants of exchange rate system choice; the hypothesized excess volatility of floating exchange rates, or exchange rate "misalignment"; the effects of volatility on international trade; and the implications of the choice of exchange rate system for the effectiveness of monetary and fiscal policy and for the behavior of macroeconomic variables. These are important issues in current policy discussions that warrant further investigation.

Determinants of exchange system choice. Empirical studies of the determinants of the choice of exchange rate system have identified certain characteristics that systematically differ across countries depending on whether the countries float or peg their exchange rates. Floaters tend to be large, relatively closed countries following an inflation rate that differs from that of trading partners. Floaters also tend to be well developed financially and to have diversified trade with the rest of the world. They are more likely to face greater foreign price shocks and smaller domestic money shocks than peggers. These results are quite sensible in light of the received theory on choice of the exchange rate system.

The literature in this area is sparse, and the studies that do exist have not given proper consideration to the simultaneity that exists between the determinants of the choice of exchange regime and the causal effects of such a choice on economic variables related to the determinants. Countries that choose floating exchange rates, for instance, have more variable real exchange rates than countries that peg; if real exchange rate variability has an impact on government policy goals, then this variability may affect the choice of regime. Such two-way causal links have not been given adequate consideration in this literature. Nevertheless, the characteristics shared by countries that choose flexible versus fixed exchange rates are important to recognize as we seek to understand the incentives and effects regarding the choice of an exchange rate system.

Excess volatility. One criticism of floating exchange rates is that they have been too volatile, adding an undesirable level of risk to international transactions. Some studies show exchange rates moving more than is implied by the fundamentals associated with a particular model. This line of research, however, has generally been considered unconvincing because of the poor explanatory power of the models and because of the fact that exchange rates are actually asset prices, which should be expected as a matter of course to be more variable than the prices and incomes that enter as fundamentals in many models. Jacob Frenkel and Morris Goldstein have argued as follows:

> There is an intrinsic difference between asset prices on the one hand and wages and prices on the other hand. The former are auction prices that depend heavily on expectations about the future, whereas the latter are more sticky in the short run, reflecting in large part contractual arrangements made in the past. Thus, wages and prices of national output may not serve as a proper yardstick for assessing exchange rate volatility. Indeed, some would say that it is precisely because wages and prices are so slow to adjust to current and expected economic conditions that it is desirable to allow for "excessive" adjustment in exchange rates.[73]

Even though no strong evidence seems to exist that flexible exchange rates have been too volatile relative to fundamentals, it is still true that nominal and real exchange rates have been much more variable under floating than under pegged exchange rates. An important question, then, is whether this variability has added an excessive level of risk that has retarded international capital flows and financial integration. The evidence on this question is overwhelmingly in favor of a negative response. International capital mobility appears to have increased rather than decreased over the period of floating rates. Capital markets are more closely linked than ever, and studies show that investors do not have a clear preference for fixed exchange rates. Fixed exchange rates typically induce capital controls as part of the policy required to maintain the fixed parity; such controls can be quite damaging to capital flows, more so possibly than volatile exchange rates.

When critics of floating exchange rates argue about the volatility of exchange rates under a float, in many cases they are referring to a perceived misalignment of exchange rates. The issue of exchange rate misalignment is problematic because no accepted methodology exists for determining a "correct" exchange rate. John Williamson defines a misalignment as "a persistent deviation of the real effective exchange rate from the 'fundamental equilibrium exchange rate,' the level that can be expected in the medium term to reconcile internal and external balance."[74] The problem comes in identifying a "fundamental equilibrium exchange rate." Williamson asserts that the dollar (the real effective exchange rate) was overvalued by 39 percent by the end of 1984.[75] Other economists disagree with such interpretations of the recent experience. One person's misalignment is another's equilibrium adjustment (see Stockman for an equilibrium theory explaining why real exchange rates are more variable under a float than a peg).[76]

It seems fair to conclude that, at this point, the issue is still unresolved as to whether or not floating exchange rates have been associated with a misalignment of exchange rates. Furthermore, proponents of misalignment-related policy prescriptions have yet to convince all observers how such misalignments could occur; proponents argue that there are three potential sources of misalignment, namely, misguided intervention, market inefficiency, and the stance of macroeconomic policy. They cannot point to speculative bubbles as a source, because the evidence on speculative bubbles in exchange rates is questionable.

Effects on trade. A common argument against floating is that greater exchange rate variability will depress the volume of international trade because of the increased risk associated with international transactions. If fixed exchange rates are associated with restrictions on trade and capital flows, however, then a move from floating to fixed exchange rates replaces foreign exchange risk with uncertainty regarding government-imposed regulations. Conceivably, then, the volume of trade could be larger under floating exchange rates than under a pegged-rate system.

As discussed in detail by Thomas Willett, the effect of exchange rate shifts on trade cannot be analyzed in isolation, since this effect will often depend on the cause of the shift.[77] Furthermore, if exchange rate misalignment is present, a problem may exist in separating volatility effects from misalignment effects. Richard Marston gives an example of how misalignment can shift production and consumption and change the volume of trade.[78] An overvaluation of the mark relative to the dollar, for instance, could induce the relocation of producing units from Germany to the United States and consequently lower the trade volume between the two countries. The reduction in trade is not a result of exchange rate variability, but if exchange rate misalignment is highly correlated with exchange rate volatility, then empirical studies of volatility effects may find spurious significant negative effects.

The evidence regarding the effects of exchange rate volatility on trade volume was summarized in the third major section of the chapter. Studies have found negative effects, positive effects, and no effects. The lack of a consensus one way or the other suggests that the threat of spurious results from misalignment effects is probably unimportant. The body of knowledge now existing on the issue of volatility and trade volume indicates that it is clearly inappropriate to claim that floating exchange rates have depressed the volume of international trade substantially below what would have existed in the presence of fixed exchange rates.

This issue became important for policy discussions in the early 1980s as trade volumes fell. Yet, as many observers have reminded us, the *effects* of floating exchange rates must be separated from the *period* of the float. The recession years of the early 1980s might have been expected to yield a falling level of international trade regardless of the exchange rate system. In fact, under fixed exchange rates, more restrictive trade measures might have been imposed than actually occurred under floating rates. In any event, world trade has risen rapidly in recent years, increasing by about 10 percent in 1986 and by about 18 percent in 1987. The rapid growth of world trade over the past few years suggests that the presence of floating exchange rates has not had the depressing effect feared in the early 1980s.

Other issues. One of the important issues in early discussions of the choice of an exchange rate system was how floating or fixed rates would alter the effectiveness of monetary and fiscal policy. A number of simulation studies have addressed this issue and found support for the standard theoretical result: Monetary policy tends to be more effective in changing output under floating exchange rates, while fiscal policy has a greater effect on output under fixed rates.

41

Recent simulation studies yield a great variety of evidence, depending upon the nature of the shocks allowed to enter the analysis. Generally, these studies have found that key macroeconomic variables such as prices and incomes have less variability under floating exchange rates than under fixed rates. Such a finding indicates how important it is to isolate the effect of the exchange rate system from other sources of change. The actual variability of incomes and prices has been greater during the period of generalized floating rates since 1973 than during the period of fixed exchange rates prior to 1971; the recent research, however, suggests that this variability is more the result of the macroeconomic shocks arising from oil price changes and other government-induced and exogenous real disturbances than it is the result of shocks from the move to floating exchange rates.

Simulations of "target zone" proposals indicate that such international policies of cooperatively maintaining a target value of the real or nominal exchange rate can reduce real exchange rate variability as well as inflation and interest rate differences among countries. If the major shocks buffeting the world since the advent of floating exchange rates have been induced by governments, then it is reasonable to expect more stable government policies to have a beneficial effect on most macroeconomic variables. A question often raised in the context of cooperative arrangements is whether governments will subordinate national policy goals to international policy goals related to fixing exchange rates at some equilibrium level. The record of history is not favorable in this regard. The Bretton Woods era of fixed exchange rates eventually broke down because national authorities would not support the system at the expense of domestic priorities. An additional practical problem associated with a cooperative arrangement is the identification of the equilibrium exchange rate. As was discussed earlier in the context of misalignment, no agreed-upon method exists for determining such an exchange rate.

Conclusions. Reform-minded economists and policy makers often appeal to empirical studies to support a particular policy prescription. The goal of this chapter has been to examine the empirical literature on the determinants and implications of the choice of an exchange rate system to see what consensus emerges. The result has been more to define what cannot be said than to define what can be said with certainty.

The literature on the determinants of choice of an exchange rate system is unclear as to whether system choice depends primarily on traditional characteristics related to optimum currency area, such as the country's economic size and its level of financial development and trade diversification, or on the nature of the shocks that buffet the country's economy. Furthermore, it is unclear whether causality runs from such variables to the choice of fixed or flexible exchange rates, or whether the exchange rate system determines the values of the variables often referred to as "determinants" of system choice; two-way causality is probably important.

It does seem clear that the choice of nominal exchange rate system has implications for the real exchange rate. Across countries and across time, real exchange rates are more variable when nominal exchange rates are flexible than when they are fixed. Whether the exchange rate system itself can take credit or blame for the statistical properties of any other macroeconomic variable is not established. It is true that key macroeconomic variables have been more variable since the early 1970s, but several studies indicate that this is not because of the presence of floating exchange rates. One recent study by Marianne Baxter and Alan Stockman examines the evidence from countries that changed their exchange rate regime at a time other than the 1971–1973 period of widespread change of exchange rate regimes. Baxter and Stockman conclude that aside from the real exchange rate, there is "little evidence of quantities for which the exchange rate system is an important determinant."[79]

Since clear agreement exists that real exchange rate variability increases with nominal exchange rate flexibility, the issue of the effects that such real exchange rate volatility may have becomes important; if such volatility of real exchange rates has clearly harmful effects, then fixed exchange rates become more attractive. It cannot be said, however, that any widely acknowledged effects of greater real exchange rate volatility have been found. With regard to the contention that greater exchange risk harms international investors and depresses the volume of international trade, the evidence does not support any conclusions against flexible exchange rates. The evidence suggests in fact that international investors may actually prefer the distribution of returns under floating exchange rates to that realized under fixed rates. The evidence on the effects of greater exchange risk on trade is mixed and at best leans slightly in the direction of suggesting that exchange rate volatility reduces the level of trade. In any case, the evidence on exchange rate volatility cannot be used to argue the case for fixed exchange rates.

The evidence on exchange rate misalignments is highly controversial in the absence of agreement on how to identify a fundamental equilibrium exchange rate. The causality of such misalignments is also uncertain even if cause could be identified. Furthermore, the evidence on variance bounds tests and speculative bubbles is dependent on exchange rate models with extremely poor explanatory power; as a result, such tests are rendered highly suspect. Therefore, any appeals to exchange rate misalignment as a motivation for policy reform must be cautiously considered, since such arguments are still quite speculative at this point.

The pessimistic conclusion from our consideration of the current state of knowledge on the determinants and implications of the choice of an exchange rate system is that any discussion of the proper role for policy must be based on conviction rather than on fact. If we are unsure of the implications of the choice of an exchange rate regime, then we cannot be sure of the results that any proposed reform will have on the achievement of the policy maker's goal. Reformers should therefore proceed with a degree of humility and realism consistent with the limited knowledge possessed.

Effects of an
Exchange Rate System

A Commentary by Morris Goldstein

Hali Edison and Michael Melvin are to be commended for writing a most comprehensive and useful survey of the empirical literature on the determinants and implications of the choice of an exchange rate system. They have asked most of the right questions and have come to most of the right conclusions.

Four issues, however, may deserve more emphasis and attention than they perhaps receive in the Edison-Melvin discussion. These four issues are as follows: (1) Can the choice of the exchange regime have much effect on the authorities' ability to discipline fiscal policy? (2) How would the inflexibility of fiscal policy limit the lessons we can draw from simulation studies of alternative exchange rate and macroeconomic policy reform proposals? (3) What kinds of lessons and unanswered questions about the choice of exchange regime are suggested by the experience of the European Monetary System (EMS)? and (4) What are the implications of exchange rate uncertainty when it is combined with substantial sunk costs associated with entering a foreign market?

Disciplinary Effects of the Exchange Rate Regime on Fiscal Policy

One of the oldest arguments for greater fixity in exchange rates is that the commitment to defend the parity provides economic agents with increased discipline to avoid inflationary policies. The traditional province of the discipline hypothesis is monetary policy. Under the well-known Mundell-Fleming model, monetary policy is completely ineffective for a small country with fixed exchange rates in a world of high capital mobility. This is merely one application of the dictum that

The views expressed in this commentary are the author's alone and do not necessarily represent the views of the International Monetary Fund.

policy makers who seek to achieve simultaneously fixed rates, open capital markets, and an independent monetary policy will be frustrated. The best they can do is to achieve any two of the three objectives. Thus, once the choice is made for fixed rates and open capital markets, monetary policy is effectively disciplined.

Surprisingly enough, disciplinary effects of the exchange rate on fiscal policy have only recently begun to be subjected to close scrutiny—and this despite the role often attributed to lax fiscal policy in both the breakdown of Bretton Woods and in the large real appreciation of the dollar during the first half of this decade. Let us consider four alternative exchange regimes and how each would influence fiscal policy.[1]

Fixed rates. With high capital mobility, a fiscal expansion under fixed exchange rates will yield an incipient positive interest rate differential, a capital inflow, and a balance of payments surplus, as opposed to a deficit. Hence, exchange rate fixity helps to finance—and by no means disciplines—irresponsible fiscal policy. As suggested in the recent literature on "speculative attacks," only if and when the markets expect fiscal deficits to be monetized will they force the authorities to choose between fiscal policy adjustment and devaluation. The better the reputation of the monetary authorities, the longer in coming will be the discipline of markets. In this connection, it is worth observing that whereas the EMS has produced significant convergence of monetary policy, convergence of fiscal policies has not taken place.

Target zones. Suppose there are target zones that are to be defended by monetary policy. In that case, a fiscal expansion that puts appreciating pressure on the exchange rate will produce a loosening of monetary policy to keep the rate from leaving the zone. Again, the exchange rate regime will have exacerbated—not disciplined—the basic cause of the problem. Target zones will discipline fiscal policy only if the threatened departure of the exchange rate from the zone initiates a multilateral review of the whole range of policies that succeeds in tilting the balance of power in the domestic debate toward fiscal responsibility. This missing link between exchange rate movements and fiscal policy under target zones is being increasingly recognized. Note that whereas first-generation target zone proposals spoke mainly of monetary policy, second-generation proposals have added a specific rule to rein in fiscal policy—a topic to which I shall return in a moment.[2]

Floating rates. With high capital mobility, one would expect fiscal expansion under floating rates also to prompt appreciation of the real exchange rate. Pressures for reversal are then likely to come from the beleaguered traded-goods sector, as it looks for ways to turn around its decline in competitiveness. The trouble here is that there is also the protectionist alternative to fiscal discipline, which, if adopted, would again mean that one inappropriate policy is being followed with another.

Managed floating with international economic policy coordination. One immediate advantage under a managed float with international economic policy coordination is that the potential for a perverse monetary policy response is reduced, since specific fiscal policy commitments can be specified directly as part of a negotiated policy package—that is, one avoids the intermediate link between the exchange rate signal and the policy response. But this regime, too, fails to overcome all the problems. For one thing, the responsibility for implementation of fiscal policy lies with different branches of government in different countries. For another, no automatic mechanism exists for sharing the fiscal adjustment across participants.

The main point of all this is that if modification or reform of the exchange rate system is really to lead to more disciplined macroeconomic policies, more thought must be directed to determining if and how the exchange rate regime can discipline fiscal policy. Some observers respond by maintaining that fiscal reform must precede reform of the system. Others argue that the better route to disciplining fiscal policy is via mechanisms outside the exchange rate system; examples of such mechanisms include Gramm-Rudman legislation in the United States and the recent move from secret to public voting in the legislature in Italy. And for still others, the present writer included, the peer pressure incorporated in the ongoing process of policy coordination may be a helpful tool in achieving greater fiscal responsibility. In any case, it is a key issue. Let us now turn to the second point.

Simulation Studies and the Inflexibility of Fiscal Policy

As Edison and Melvin document, the last few years have witnessed a burgeoning of empirical studies that attempt to simulate the hypothetical properties of alternative reform proposals using global macroeconomic models. Two types of simulation are often done, namely, historical and single shock.

Historical simulations are typically directed at the following question: How would the historical record have looked if macroeconomic and exchange rate policies had behaved differently from what was actually observed? In operational terms, the general procedure for answering this question is the following: First, the model is constrained to replicate history exactly by adding the appropriate residuals to each equation of the model, thereby providing a base line scenario. Next a number of counterfactual scenarios are performed using the same residuals as in the base line scenario, but in each scenario a different policy rule is postulated, be it simple target zones, target zones with a fiscal policy rule, nominal income targeting, money targeting, or the like. Finally, the differences between the base line scenario and the counterfactual scenarios, are noted and recorded.

With the second type of simulation, or single-shock simulation, one disregards the historical record and focuses instead on hypothetical shocks to different individual behavioral equations in the model, be it to the demand for money, to aggregate supply, to asset preferences, or the like. One then examines these shocks under alternative policy rules and again records the differences.

We have done some of these simulation exercises in the IMF Research Department and have obtained many interesting results, a few of which are described in the Edison-Melvin chapter.[3] Here, let us briefly consider two of them.

One finding is that placing too much of a burden on monetary policy and allowing fiscal policy to roam free can get one into trouble. Let us suppose, for example, that a simple target zone involving only monetary policy existed during the time of large U.S. fiscal deficits (1981–1985); the associated loosening of monetary policy implied to keep the dollar within a target zone could well have produced considerably higher U.S. inflation than actually occurred. In contrast, if fiscal policy is better tied down, then the results are more favorable.

A second simulation finding is that, under flexible exchange rates, fiscal policy actions have more potent effects on current account imbalances than do monetary policy actions. This is because the expenditure-switching and expenditure-reducing effects of fiscal policy actions reinforce each other, whereas they offset each other under monetary policy. But there is an important catch to the implication that policy rules and scenarios that rely heavily on fiscal actions do better than those that use monetary policy. The catch is that the simulation studies do not take account of the relative inflexibility of fiscal policy in most industrial countries; they assume that it has the same flexibility as monetary policy. Yet the facts are that fiscal policy is not oriented to short-run stabilization goals in most industrial countries; it is rather guided by other considerations (for example, reducing the share of government in gross national product or reducing the burden of taxation). Until simulation studies take this practical feature into account, the lessons we can draw are more limited.

The European Monetary System

The European Monetary System (EMS) has recently celebrated its tenth anniversary. For anyone interested in studying the implications of the choice of exchange rate regime, the EMS is a most interesting laboratory. I should like to offer just a few observations in that regard.

One is that the experience of the EMS seems to support the importance that Edison and Melvin attribute to openness and trade interdependence in the choice for greater fixity of exchange rates. With an approximately 12 percent share of imports in gross domestic product, the European Economic Community (EEC) as a whole is only marginally more open than either the United States or Japan (which have import ratios of about 10 to 11 percent, respectively). But the striking thing is that individual countries in the EEC have separate currencies and have openness ratios (extending up to the 60 percent to 70 percent range for the smaller countries and the 25 percent to 30 percent range for the larger ones) that are much higher than that of the region as a whole. A more powerful incentive to limit exchange rate fluctuations exists within the EEC itself than between the EEC and other regions.[4]

A second observation is that the EMS experience illustrates the limits of trying to explain the choice of an exchange rate regime without reference to wider integration goals and related institutional mechanisms. In this connection, Francesco Giavazzi and Alberto Giovannini have shown how the stability of intra-European exchange rates aids the survival of the common agricultural market, in the sense that exchange rate realignments could produce large shifts in the profitability of the farming sector across Europe.[5] Factors like this will not be picked up in the studies surveyed by Edison and Melvin.

Finally, the EMS also raises the question of how the choice between monetary independence and greater fixity of exchange rates will be resolved when (in 1990) member countries can no longer resort to capital controls. What variables and mechanisms will then take care of adjustments among members? Will labor mobility and wage flexibility increase, will transfer payments have to carry a much bigger load, will interest rate variability increase, or will new institutions be created to improve harmonization and coordination of macroeconomic policies? There is food for thought.

Exchange Rate Uncertainty, Sunk Costs, and the Delinking Hypothesis

Now we come to the issue of exchange rate uncertainty and international trade. Here, Edison and Melvin have done an admirable job of surveying the traditional econometric evidence. But this controversy has a new twist that they do not address.

Recently, Paul Krugman has argued that exchange rate fluctuations are excessive not because they matter so much but rather because they now matter so little. Krugman argues that the substantial sunk costs associated with entering a foreign market and the greater volatility of exchange rates have combined to render trade prices and volumes unresponsive to exchange rate fluctuations, much in the same manner that certain viruses become resistant to antibiotics when the latter are used too much. Krugman concludes, in other words, that exchange rate uncertainty has increasingly "delinked" the real sector from floating rates.

Four of the seeming implications of the delinking hypothesis are the following:

- Price elasticities of import and export demand should not be as great as they once were during periods of lower exchange rate variability.
- These same price elasticities should be relatively greater for "large" price changes that overcome sunk costs than for small ones.
- Lags in traditional trade volume equations should have become longer in the floating-rate period.
- There should be lower pass-through of exchange rate changes into import prices (that is, more reliance on pricing-to-market strategies by exporters) than there once was during periods of lower exchange rate variability.

Suffice it to say that the empirical evidence to evaluate the delinking hypothesis is not yet in hand.

2

International Capital Flows, the Dollar, and U.S. Financial Policies

Thomas D. Willett and Clas G. Wihlborg

The environment facing U.S. monetary and fiscal policy makers has changed drastically in recent years. The growth of international capital mobility has been an important contributor to these changes. Perhaps the most dramatic effect of the growth of capital mobility has been its contribution to the collapse of the Bretton Woods system of pegged exchange rates.[1] Under the current system of flexible exchange rates, domestic and internal financial innovations have stimulated the continued growth of international capital mobility, thereby contributing to the increase sensitivity of national economies to external developments and also greatly influencing the impact of given domestic economic and financial developments and policy changes on domestic and international economies.

International capital flows and exchange rate movements are frequently viewed as primarily disruptive elements. This interpretation has led to numerous proposals for direct governmental actions to restrict capital flows and limit exchange rate variations through official intervention in the foreign exchange markets. The present chapter focuses on the implications of international capital mobility for U.S. financial policies (including monetary, fiscal, and exchange rate policy strategies), for international policy coordination, and for both sides of the argument concerning restrictions on capital flows.

The chapter begins with an overview of some of the major financial policy issues related to international capital mobility. In the first

We are indebted to Massoud Darbandi, Pamela Martin, and David Taylor for research assistance and to William Branson, Phillip Cagan, Hansen Cheng, Milton Friedman, Reuven Glick, Christine Hekman, Randall Henning, and Alan Stockman for helpful comments and suggestions on earlier drafts.

51

major section we review the major strands of international finance and open-economy macroeconomic theory that are relevant for analyzing these financial policy issues. A major conclusion is that simple generalizations cannot be drawn about the effects of the growth in international capital mobility on exchange rate variability and on national economic stability. In each case, more detailed analysis of the causes of capital flows is required. Depending on these causes, as well as on the kind of exchange rate regime in operation and the nature of the financial policies being considered, international capital flows can either increase *or* reduce the size of exchange rate variations, can help move the domestic economy toward *or* away from internal equilibrium, and can enhance *or* retard the effectiveness of national monetary and fiscal policies. Thus, sensible discussion of the implications of international capital mobility for national financial policy strategies (including their international coordination) requires a careful analysis of the likely patterns of disturbances that countries will face.

In the second major section of the chapter, we review the arguments about the contribution of speculative capital flow activity to exchange rate volatility. It often is difficult to determine empirically which exchange rate shifts have been caused by changes in fundamentals and which exchange rate shifts have been caused by the existence of destabilizing speculation. This difficulty raises the issue of who should be assigned the burden of proof for government intervention, to stabilize the exchange rates, or against government intervention, to allow fundamentals to be reflected in the rates.

The existence of destabilizing speculation in an economic sense can be determined only in relation to an equilibrium path. Most economists identify such paths by models in which market participants are assumed to have rational expectations based on substantial knowledge about the economy. In the third major section of the chapter we argue that neither the popular rational-expectations model based on perfect capital mobility nor the destabilizing-speculation model seems to fit the evidence. In our view, much more care must be taken in modeling exchange rates to determine market participants' information sets and their ability to gather and cope with relevant information. One possible approach, based on the concept of reasonable behavior or bounded rationality, is presented in the third section. Thereafter, the fourth section, our view and other contending views of the behavior of the dollar are evaluated in light of events during the 1980s.

We conclude in the fifth section with a discussion of some of the major implications of the analysis for U.S. financial policies. One of these implications is that speculative capital mobility could be considered too low as often as it is considered too high, thus calling into question the basis of proposals to tax capital flows in the hope of reducing exchange rate volatility. Another is that, although in principle and in an ideal policy environment, high international capital mobility does strengthen the case for internationally coordinated discretionary macroeconomic policies, under present real-world conditions of uncertainty and in view of the limited credibility of government policies, the first practical priority should be the establishment of more stable domestic macroeconomic policies in the major industrial countries. Consideration of strategies for establishing limits on the instability of national monetary and fiscal policies should be an important element in discussions of international policy coordination.

Overview of Financial Policy Issues Related to International Capital Mobility and the Open-Economy Model

Popular discussions of international capital flows tend to focus almost exclusively on these flows' perceived roles in creating exchange rate and macroeconomic instability and in undercutting national economic policies' ability to influence the performance of the domestic economy.[2] Capital flows can indeed have such destabilizing effects in some cases, but capital flows can also help to reduce fluctuations in exchange rates and the domestic economy. Furthermore, depending upon the exchange rate regime in operation and the policy blend in use, international capital flows can enhance rather than undercut a national government's ability to achieve domestic macroeconomic objectives. For many decades, for example, it has been known that under fixed exchange rates, high international capital mobility will reduce the effectiveness of domestic monetary policy.[3] Under floating rates, however, higher international capital mobility will actually increase the speed with which tight monetary policies can slow inflation, since the current exchange rate appreciates in response to higher real interest rates. The unusual speed of the U.S. disinflation in the early 1980s is an important case in point.[4]

What the growth of international capital mobility and of economic interdependence in general clearly does do is increase the level of sophistication needed for intelligent discussion of economic policy strategies. Although much remains to be discovered, a very substantial body of theory already exists in which to draw in framing policy discussions.[5] The literature clearly shows that few simple generalizations can be made about the effects of international capital mobility. More than one answer exists, for example, to the question of whether an increase in international capital mobility will increase or reduce exchange rate fluctuations, or domestic macroeconomic stability, or the strength of the transmission of the effects of economic developments in one country to its trading partners.

Although the popular view does still seem to be that increases in international capital mobility will aggravate exchange rate fluctuations, domestic macroeconomic instability, and the international transmission of disturbances, counterexamples to each of these conclusions can easily be produced. Consider, for example, the widely used Mundell-Fleming model, which shows that under a domestic fiscal expansion, as capital mobility increases from very low to very high levels, the magnitude of the resulting exchange rate fluctuations will first fall and then rise, with the direction of movement reversing as capital mobility reaches a middle range.[6] Likewise, although high international capital mobility in some cases can indeed increase the disruptive effects of foreign disturbances on the domestic economy, it can also help stabilize the domestic economy by reducing the extent to which the effects of domestic shocks are bottled up at home, by helping to spread these shocks across the world economy. Furthermore, although the growth of international capital mobility is often viewed as increasing the riskiness of the international environment, such mobility also increases the scope for risk reduction through international financial diversification.

In short, sensible discussion of the economic effects of increased international capital mobility requires detailed analysis focusing on particular situations. In general, the effects of higher capital mobility will vary greatly depending upon the types of disturbances that are generating the capital flows, as well as the type of model used for the analysis. In Keynesian open-economy models, for example, the optimal response to international currency switching would be unsterilized official intervention to keep exchange rates constant. Belief in the prevalence of this type of currency substitution disturbance underlies Ronald McKinnon's proposals for a return to fixed exchange rates, with domestic monetary policy determined by developments in the balance of payments; such a change in exchange rate regime would indeed neutralize the tendency of currency switching to create domestic financial instability.[7] Nevertheless, most of the latest empirical research suggests that, at least for countries like the United States, international currency substitution has not been a dominant type of disturbance. Thus, the empirical basis for McKinnon's proposals is weak.[8]

Furthermore, if we take the point of view that currency switching is not in itself an exogenous disturbance but that it depends, for example, on changes in risk perceptions, then exchange rate changes may simply move relative rates of return in different currencies toward equilibrium. If the exchange rate is not allowed to change, then relative rates may adjust in other ways, with different welfare effects from each alternative adjustment path, according to the particular model adopted. In Keynesian fixed-price models with their emphasis on output and employment effects, the optimal response to currency switching is to peg the exchange rate, while in flexible-price models with utility-maximizing individuals, no such conclusion can be drawn.

Another illustration of the importance of distinguishing between the symptoms and the underlying causes of disturbances as well as among model frameworks is the analysis of the huge capital flows into the United States and the associated trade deficits in the 1980s. These flows have frequently been viewed as examples of the imposition of disruptions on the U.S. domestic economy by the international economy. Keynesian models suggest, however, that a major cause of these capital inflows was the large U.S. budget deficits. If so, what were viewed by many as an international disturbance were, in fact, largely the consequences of U.S. domestic policies in an interdependent world. As will be discussed in the fourth section of this chapter, academic economists disagree about the correctness of this particular analysis, because the models of the new classical economists lead to substantially different conclusions. Recent contributions to the literature on open-economy macroeconomics have demonstrated that the choice of desirable policy strategies depends not only on beliefs about the sources of disturbances but also on beliefs about the structure and operation of the economy in question. A disturbance that would suggest a particular policy response in a Keynesian fixed-price model, for instance, might call for a substantially different response in models assuming different types of short-run inflation-unemployment trade-offs, and it might call for no response at all in many new classical models.[9]

Besides illustrating how the choice of optimal monetary and exchange rate regimes can depend crucially on both the type of disturbances and the degree of international capital mobility, the Keynesian macroeconomic literature demonstrates that ignoring international considerations can easily lead to serious policy mistakes. Although our reading of the empirical evidence suggests to us that international financial integration is still far from perfect and need not overwhelm domestic monetary policy in the major industrial countries under flexible exchange rates, the failure to take open-economy considerations into account could substantially reduce the ability of national monetary policies to promote domestic economic stability.

55

An effort to catalog the various ways in which the source of disturbance, degree of international capital mobility, and different models of the economy can interact would go well beyond the scope of this chapter. In the overwhelming majority of approaches, however, there is a strong presumption that the existence of destabilizing speculation will reduce net economic efficiency and welfare. In the Keynesian literature, for instance, although the optimal response to induced capital flows varies in accordance with their causes, autonomous shifts in asset preferences generally call for compensating policy adjustments in asset supplies rather than adjustments in interest and exchange rates. In such models, destabilizing speculation can be thought of as an autonomous international shock. Alternatively, within a standard microeconomic framework, destabilizing speculation can be seen as generating incorrect prices, reducing the information content of the price system, and leading to distortions similar to those resulting from government price fixing in an efficient market or the arbitrary introduction of excise taxes and subsidies.[10]

Exceptions may exist, but in general it seems a safe bet that if destabilizing speculation could be clearly identified and effectively offset at reasonable costs, it would be desirable to do so.[11] Nevertheless, besides the normal problems of identifying shocks and actually implementing optimal policy responses—considerations that lead some economists to question the desirability of having governments even attempt to practice discretionary policy strategies—particularly difficult problems exist in attempting to decide whether a given shift in international capital flows is truly the result of an autonomous shift in preferences or rather is an induced response to perceived changes in risk and return. Similar difficulty exists in attempting to distinguish between stabilizing and destabilizing speculation. We turn to this issue in the following section.

Destabilizing or Stabilizing Speculation, and When Should Government Intervene?

No necessary connection exists between whether capital flows are disruptive in the everyday sense of the term and whether they are destabilizing or stabilizing in the sense implied by economic theory. As Milton Friedman pointed out in his classic reevaluation of flexible exchange rates, one of the major reasons that most analysts of the disastrous 1930s had concluded that speculation was commonly destabilizing was that they were using a faulty concept.[12]

The Concept of Destabilizing Speculation. At that time, capital flows were classified as "destabilizing" if they tended to increase payments imbalances. Thus, capital outflows from a deficit country and inflows to surplus countries were labeled as destabilizing. Clearly, to refer to such flows as being "disruptive" to efforts to restore payments equilibrium at the current exchange rate is certainly consistent with common usage; besides making life more difficult for officials, such flows could be disruptive in the sense of increasing volatility or instability in domestic financial markets. As Freidman emphasized, however, the normal criterion used in economic theory to classify whether speculation is actually destabilizing or not is whether the speculation tends to move prices toward or away from their equilibrium levels.

The faulty classification of capital flows as stabilizing or destabilizing according to whether they reduce or increase payments imbalances under pegged rates has an exact analogue under floating rates in the classification of capital flows as stabilizing or destabilizing according to whether they reduce or increase exchange rate movements. Although these faulty classifications continue to prevail in popular discussions, they correspond to the economic concept of stabilizing or destabilizing speculation only under the assumption that the initial exchange rate level was at equilibrium and that no changes have occurred to redefine this equilibrium level. This more appropriate definition of speculation as destabilizing if it moves currency prices away from rather than toward equilibrium underlies the concept of excess volatility that refers to volatility greater than is justified by changes in the fundamentals, that is, actual volatility greater than the volatility of equilibrium prices.

The need to consider currencies' price movements in relation to equilibrium values rather than to initial values does not simplify the task of identifying destabilizing speculaton. But the importance of using this economic concept can be easily illustrated. Consider the case of an exchange rate pegged at a fixed nominal level and diverging farther and farther over time from an equilibrium because of, say, rapid inflation in the domestic country. In these circumstances, speculative capital outflows would reflect prudent financial behavior and would be stabilizing in the economic sense in that they would increase pressure for the exchange rate to move toward equilibrium. Such speculative capital outflows could be disruptive to domestic financial markets, but the blame for these disruptions should be placed on the developments and policies that created and maintained the exchange rate disequilibrium. Of course, the tendency to blame the symptoms or the messenger of bad tidings is quite human, but it is a poor guide to policy analysis.

The major difficulty with moving from a statistical to an economic definition of stabilizing and destabilizing is that use of the economic definition undermines the observer's ability to classify capital flows unambiguously. Analysis becomes based on movements relative to equilibrium, but in real-world situations, reasonable people may differ substantially in their estimates of equilibrium. As Fritz Machlup stressed long ago, equilibrium conditions can be specified only within the context of specific models, but considerable disagreement often exists about the best models to use.[13]

Considerable disagreement certainly exists among leading international monetary economists about the best model of the foreign exchange market. And even with agreement on a specific model, considerable disagreement can exist on the empirical values of the key parameters in the model. The available empirical research would not allow one to argue confidently that the sum of demand elasticities for U.S. exports and imports is definitely well above two or definitely well below four. Thus, depending on whether one were inclined toward elasticity optimism or pessimism, considerable disagreement could exist about how far the dollar would need to fall to bring about a given improvement in the trade balance.

The difficulty of empirically estimating the equilibrium level of exchange rates is also increased by the difficulty of quantifying expectations. In speculatively efficient markets, expectations about future developments in fundamentals should influence current prices. Thus, for example, the fact of whether one took or did not take as credible the announcement of a new anti-inflation policy could have a substantial influence on one's estimate of equilibrium interest and exchange rates. Under such circumstances, policy officials would quite understandably describe as destabilizing those capital flows not based on full belief in official forecasts and announced policy intentions; yet the historical record clearly shows that believing such official pronouncements could often provide a quick path to financial ruin.

We must accept that we possess only limited scope to make operational statements about equilibrium values. Nevertheless, it is still much better to use correct, albeit somewhat fuzzy, concepts than to use wrong, albeit precise, concepts.

The inherent difficulties in developing precise estimates of equilibrium values make it inevitable that frequent cases will occur in which reasonable people differ in their estimates or judgments. This area calls for a good bit of humility; yet one often encounters forcefully made statements that some particular currency is clearly overvalued or that some particular development has clearly been caused by destabilizing speculation. Frequently one does not have to look far to find equally confidently made statements of contradictory conclusions. This can occur when individuals develop a great deal of confidence in the correctness of a particular model or way of looking at the world that many other experts do not share.

The Burden of Proof. We also find that some strong differences in statements are caused by different assumptions about where the burden of proof should lie. Given the inherent uncertainties in judging equilibrium prices, it makes a tremendous difference whether capital flows and exchange rate movements are assumed to be stabilizing or destabilizing when the opposite is not clearly shown. Almost all economists, for example, would agree that a considerable portion of the exchange rate volatility observed under floating rates has been the result of instabilities in underlying economic policies and conditions. But what about the possibility that the remaining autonomous exchange rate instability is the result of destabilizing speculative capital flows? Advocates of floating rates tend to assume that speculation moves exchange rates to equilibrium unless strong evidence exists to the contrary, while critics of floating tend to assume just the opposite.

What is the right way to assign the burden of proof? Unfortunately, little effort is currently being made to answer this question, despite its tremendous importance for the evaluation of exchange rate policy and most other types of economic policy as well. Just as with the debates over the allocation of balance-of-payments adjustment responsibilities between surplus or deficit countries, we are not sure of the best answer. We should reveal to the reader that our own set of assumptions includes considerable skepticism about the prevalence of destabilizing speculation and about the type of ideal farsighted speculators facing little uncertainty as assumed in many (but not all) rational-expectations models. We have attempted to be objective in our presentation, but undoubtedly our biases have crept in here and there—probably most notably in our tendency to refer to capital flows and exchange rate movements as being economically justified, not destabilizing, as long as we can find plausible stories consistent with this interpretation. When expectations are important and disagreement exists about the appropriate economic model, we cannot expect believers in market efficiency to be able to explain precisely every dip and surge in prices. On the other hand, if plausible stories cannot be offered to explain major exchange rate swings, then we believe points must be awarded to those who believe in speculative inefficiencies.

Insufficient Stabilizing Speculation. The debate about the degree to which speculation is destabilizing is usually based on the presumption that capital mobility is high. Nevertheless, high exchange rate volatility can also be caused by a low degree of capital mobility causing what may be called an insufficiency of stabilizing speculation.[14] Elasticities in goods markets, for example, are often much lower in the short run than in the long run, such that in the absence of speculation, the price changes needed to clear the market after a real shock could be much greater in the short run than in the long run. Under many circumstances, the existence of stabilizing speculation would reduce the magnitude of this short-run price overshooting. If high exchange rate volatility were due primarily to an insufficiency of such stabilizing speculation, then public policy should focus on measures to increase rather than reduce capital mobility, and official intervention should be geared to reinforcing rather than offsetting the effects of speculative flows.

Although the empirical literature has found greater profits from simple trading rules than can be easily explained by normal risk aversion in efficient markets, it typically has not attempted to discriminate among different possible causes of seeming speculative inefficiencies.[15] We return to this issue in the next section; we simply note here that the results are consistent with bubbles and destabilizing speculative-bandwagon effects, but they are equally consistent with a relatively low degree of capital mobility combined with heavy leaning-against-the-wind official intervention policies. Either scenario would create runs in the exchange rate data; yet in one case greater official intervention would be called for, while in the other official intervention should be reduced. This is clearly an important topic for further research.

Toward a Theory of Reasonable Exchange Rate Behavior

In the previous section we contrasted two views of foreign exchange market behavior. In the first view, most exchange rate changes are equilibrium responses to news about fundamental determinants of the exchange rate in a world of high international capital mobility and stabilizing speculation. In the second view, many exchange rate changes are caused by the existence of destabilizing speculation on the part of market participants who are irrational or less informed about the equilibrium value of the exchange rate than are central bankers and governments. We argued that destabilizing speculation under high capital mobility is not easily distinguished from insufficient stabilizing speculation under low capital mobility in response to real changes in the demand and supply for foreign exchange.

In the present section we present a view of foreign exchange

markets in which periods of what appears to be destabilizing speculation may exist, as well as periods with insufficient stabilizing speculation. This view is based on the near-tautological assumption that
market participants are indeed rational but that because the information required to obtain equilibrium (as commonly defined in terms of
a stable relationship between exchange rates and fundamentals) is
overwhelming, market participants are characterized by merely reasonable behavior, or bounded rationality, to borrow a term from the
industrial organization literature.

Models with Perfect Capital Mobility Do Not Fit the Data. The
current popularity in the academic literature of the assumption of
very high international capital mobility leads us to discuss briefly the
empirical evidence on exchange rate models that are based on the
assumption of perfect capital mobility—in particular those based on
the real interest rate parity (RIRP) theory—before giving our alternative view.

The building blocks of real interest rate parity are perfect capital
mobility or uncovered interest rate parity (UIRP), a long-term trend
toward purchasing power parity (PPP), and rational expectations in
the sense that agents form exchange rate expectations based on
knowledge about the long-term purchasing power parity trend. Uncovered interest rate parity implies perfect capital mibility in the sense
that risk-neutral speculators force equality between the interest rate
differential and the expected rate of change of the exchange rate.

The attraction of these assumptions for model building is easy to
understand. In the early postwar period, many open-economy models assumed away international capital mobility. Deep research is not
required to see that such an assumption is untenable in today's world;
international capital mobility is clearly important. Model construction
generally is greatly simplified by making extreme assumptions, and it
probably strikes most economists today that among the industrial
countries, capital movements' elasticity of response to changes in
interest rates is more closely approximated by infinity than by zero.
As an initial modeling strategy and for ease of exposition in classroom
presentations, we believe the current popularity of the uncovered
interest rate parity assumption combined with rational expectations is
quite understandable and is well justified. As we argue later, however, this view is not always suitable for analyzing real-world developments and policy issues.

The uncovered interest rate parity theory allows for differences in
real rates of return between countries if there are expected *real* exchange rate changes, but equilibrium requires that nominal interest

61

differentials just be offset by expected changes in nominal exchange rates. Thus, uncovered interest rate parity is based on the existence of risk-neutral speculators with an unlimited supply of funds facing zero transactions costs. If purchasing power parity holds, then differences in expected inflation rates would be the sole cause of differences in nominal interest rates and expected exchange rate changes. Real interest rates would be equalized internationally. Considerable evidence exists of variability in real interest rates across countries and over time, however, and exchange rates often deviate from purchasing power parity. In the long run, purchasing power parity should be approximated unless substantial relative price shifts occur. Under uncovered interest rate parity, a real interest rate differential signifies expected real exchange rate changes, generally toward the long-run purchasing power parity level if expectations are rational. Under real interest rate parity, an increase in real interest rates should be associated with a stronger, not a weaker, currency but one that is expected to depreciate in real terms.

Parity conditions require that the currency with a high real interest rate be expected to depreciate in real terms at a rate equal to the real interest differential. This comes about by the currency's appreciating so much with the rise in the real interest rate that it is expected to depreciate toward long-run equilibrium. Thus, the short-term equilibrium exchange rate changes by more than does the long-term equilibrium rate. Exchange rate overshooting occurs in response to disturbances that influence real interest rates. The amount of the overshooting and the size of the interest differential depend on how long it is expected to take to restore purchasing power parity. Thus, for example, a 2 percent higher real interest rate on one-year treasury notes as a result of temporary tight money would require an initial exchange rate overshooting of 2 percent, while a 2 percent real differential on ten-year bonds caused by expectations of a continued budget deficit would cause an exchange rate overshooting of 20 percent.

Models based on this type of reasoning have frequently been used to show why the U.S. budget deficits could explain a large rapid appreciation of the dollar in the early 1980s and why the strong dollar would be only temporary, the sudden appreciation being followed by a gradual depreciation.[16] A simple glance at a chart of the dollar (see figure 2–1) indicates, however, that the expected accompanying pattern of a quick jump followed immediately by the beginning of depreciation did not hold. Nevertheless, many monetary and fiscal disturbances may occur over a time period, and it can be argued that gradual learning about monetary policy and the outlook for the deficit caused further appreciation rather than depreciation to follow the initial overshooting. The timing of a disturbance and the expectations about future policies, in combination with a multitude of other smaller unanticipated shocks, may hold off the depreciation phase for some time after a shift to a tight monetary policy and an associated higher real interest rate. The consistent large forward discounts on the dollar over the period of continued appreciation in the early 1980s and the expectations of even more rapid depreciation revealed in the surveys analyzed by Jeffrey Frankel and Kenneth Froot are in keeping with this view.[17]

In its 1984 annual report, the Council of Economic Advisers was able to present evidence broadly consistent with this real interest rate parity overshooting view. Frankel, who was on the senior staff of the CEA at that time, repeats this evidence in his recent papers on international capital flows.[18] Calculations showed a real interest rate differential of approximately 3 percent on ten-year bonds, suggesting

FIGURE 2–1
REAL EFFECTIVE EXCHANGE RATE OF U.S. DOLLAR,
JANUARY 1978 TO APRIL 1988
(1980 = 100)

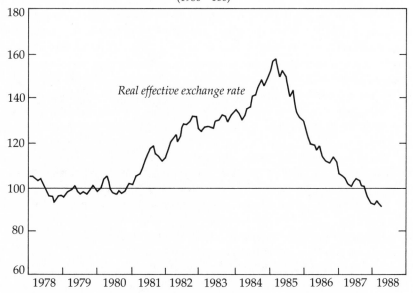

NOTE: Real effective exchange rates are calculated on the basis of normalized unit labor costs. Monthly average exchange rates are shown.
SOURCE: International Monetary Fund, *Annual Report* (Washington, D.C.: IMF, 1988).

63

temporary real appreciation (overshooting) of the dollar of about 30 percent. This figure was roughly in line with many of the calculations of the misalignment of the dollar being made at that time.

This story did not hold up through the year, however, as the dollar continued to climb in real terms while both the nominal and real interest differentials in favor of the United States began to fall. This lack of correspondence between the predictions of the real interest rate parity theory and the facts was one of the causes of increased interest by economic researchers in the possibility of speculative bubbles.[19]

More careful analysis would have already suggested before these developments in 1984 that it was hard to make the real interest rate parity theory fit the facts.[20] One simple check would have been to look at still-longer maturity interest differentials. It turns out that the twenty-year nominal differentials were of approximately the same size as the ten-year differentials, suggesting that unless reasons existed for expecting a particular change in inflation differentials, a real depreciation of at least 60 percent, not just 30 percent, was expected.[21]

At a more technical level, the perfect capital mobility/real interest rate parity story implies the prevalence of patterns in spot and forward exchange rates that generally are not found to hold. Contrary to the initial expectations of many economists, deviations from purchasing power parity were not found to be strongly self reversing, and forward rates were found to be biased predictors of future spot rates.[22] Thus, both building blocks of real interest rate parity theory were shaken. The bias of forward rates as predictors of future spot rates violates uncovered interest rate parity and suggests that the foreign exchange markets operate with risk aversion.[23] Many of the movements in exchange rates are caused by expectations about real effects that are not expected to be reversed over the time horizon relevant for private market participants. When risk aversion is important, sterilized official intervention in the foreign exchange market can have a short-run market impact, for better or for worse. Of course, not every empirical study has reached these conclusions, and indeed many of the earliest studies during the floating-rate period found opposite results. The trend of most recent empirical research findings, however, is in this direction.[24]

The real interest rate parity theory is most easily tested after isolated shifts in fundamentals and real interest rates, but during the 1980s disturbances were large and frequent, and it is difficult in hindsight to identify market participants' expectations at different times. Nevertheless, the foregoing discussion still casts serious doubt on the real interest rate parity theory. Conceivably, the lack of fit between the predictions of real interest rate parity and reality may be the result not only of misspecified expectations about future disturbances but also of violations of one or all of the assumptions of perfect capital mobility (uncovered interest rate parity), long-run purchasing power parity, and rational expectations. But less-than-perfect capital mobility is not going to have a strong impact on the predictions of the theory, and the long-run purchasing power parity assumption has been questioned but is still the subject of serious debate, so it remains to ask whether foreign exchange market participants do not take this long-run tendency into account because they are irrational.

A good deal of criticism in recent years has been based on the contention that U.S. financial markets have too short a time horizon. Even though one can present counterexamples to many of the most extreme versions of alleged myopia, relatively little formal research has been undertaken on the effective time horizons of different markets. This will not be an easy topic to investigate, but it nevertheless is one that is quite important.[25]

The Speculative-Bandwagon View. Some critics of floating rates have stressed such arguments about the extremely short time horizons of foreign exchange dealers (often measured in minutes and hours, not months and years) and the propensity for bandwagon effects to dominate foreign exchange markets. As descriptions of very short-term behavior, such views may hold some truth. But frequently the bandwagon effects so vividly described by exchange dealers are fleeting phenomena lasting minutes or hours at most.[26] Even Shafigul Islam, a steady believer in the importance of bandwagon effects, identifies them primarily with exchange dealers and short-term speculators and notes that "portfolio managers and long-term investors usually play the role of stabilizing speculators" and that "no bandwagon started by the market makers can survive for long if challenged by the longer-term investors."[27] Furthermore, Islam notes that the dealers themselves will limit the size of such speculative runs. He argues, "Of course, if rates move 'too fast' in one direction, traders engage in short-term 'profit taking' by closing their positions and slowing down the bandwagon."[28] We doubt that the blips in exchange rates caused by such short-term bandwagon effects can even be noticed in the charts and tables typically used to analyze the fluctuations of the dollar.

Islam argues that bandwagon effects also influence longer-term investors and that, in the absence of official intervention, they lead to larger movements of the dollar. We are much more skeptical about the importance of such longer-term bandwagons. We do agree with Islam's view that there is no agreed-upon exchange rate model of the fundamentals on which exchange market participants can rely and that as a consequence many market participants may from time to time switch the weight that they give to various factors in forming their longer-term views on the outlook for currencies. The average level of sophistication in the exchange markets could certainly be increased by better utilization of professional economists' input and the findings of economic research. The lack of use of sophisticated economic analysis is understandable, however, given the wide range of conflicting perspectives among economic experts and the near-total lack of agreement on the correct specification of a comprehensive exchange rate model as opposed to a mere checklist of factors that should influence the market. Evidence about the relative forecast accuracy of advisory services using more or less sophisticated forecasting models indicates that sophisticated econometric techniques do not generally beat judgmental forecasting.[29]

In situations of considerable uncertainty and ambiguity, compounded by the lack of credibility of policy announcements, it is not appropriate to label all shifts in the mood of the market as irrational. Mood and confidence arguments can often be translated into more formal arguments to the effect that risk-averse investors are responding to uncertainty about rates of return. Indeed, just such risk considerations as these may provide much of the basis for the arguments that "safe-haven" considerations and bolstered confidence in the U.S. economy relative to that of Europe may at times have significantly influenced capital flows into the United States.

Though changes in confidence have undoubtedly influenced capital flows at times, we remain unconvinced by the argument that bandwagons explain major ups and downs of the dollar. The surveys of expectations of exchange market participants analyzed by Frankel and Froot show quite clearly that, with the possible exception of the very last portion of the rise of the dollar in the mid-1980s (this period will be discussed later), speculative expectations were stabilizing, not destabilizing—that is, the market participants seem to have expected exchange rates to return toward earlier levels and not to continue to move in the current direction. Thus, unless these surveys were completely wide of the mark (which seems highly unlikely, especially since forward rates tended to give qualitatively the same signals), most of the time we cannot look to destabilizing speculation as the origin of the major, nor indeed of many of the minor, swings in the dollar.

Viewing Decision Makers as Reasonable but Not Perfect. If destabilizing expectations and bandwagons do not explain the major ups and downs of the dollar and if the real interest rate parity theory does not fit the facts well either, then we must begin to ask what kind of theory of foreign exchange markets could explain consistently the events of the last decade. It is not terribly satisfying to argue that some periods are explained by a monetarist view, others by Dornbusch-type overshooting, and yet others by the existence of destabilizing speculation. We need to attempt to develop a framework within which we can explain why the appropriate model of the economy would change frequently. We turn now to our own view of foreign exchange markets, which should help explain events more consistently.

Our starting point is that the foreign exchange market consists of heterogeneous participants who act according to the best of their knowledge and information under institutional constraints in an uncertain world.[30] Often their knowledge is of limited value, and decisions must be made on intuitive grounds. "Rationality" in the formal economic sense implies the satisfaction of extremely rigorous information requirements. Therefore, we characterize foreign exchange markets as being governed instead by "reasonable behavior" or "bounded rationality." Increasingly, economists are recognizing that the concept of bounded rationality may be useful for studying macroeconomic and finance issues.[31]

In foreign exchange markets the limits to rationality can be found in the lack of knowledge not only about fundamentals but also about the response of the exchange rate to a change in fundamentals. The effect of uncertainty about the response of the economy to policy changes has been analyzed in some detail by economists.[32] This uncertainty about response coefficients is in turn the result of uncertainty about structural parameters and policy rules, and associated with it is the additional uncertainty about others' expectations.

In a model of financial asset pricing, Clas Wihlborg shows how uncertainty about model parameters and policy rules influences price adjustment.[33] First and most obviously, learning about parameters and policy rules influences adjustments to shocks and can lead to changes in market prices even in the absence of shocks. In the theoretical literature on learning, the general conclusion seems to be that convergence to rational-expectations equilibrium in which structural parameters are known may occur if there is a "consensus forecast rule" that everybody applies. If such a rule is known, however, it is not optimal for individuals to use it.[34] Thus, convergence is not instantaneous but time consuming and possibly erratic.

Even if all individuals have the same perceptions, increasing the uncertainty about model parameters and policy rules causes an increase in the absolute value of response coefficients. The reason is that the response coefficients in a particular period depend multiplicatively on model parameters over all future periods. If imperfect knowledge about model parameters is recognized, then it follows that each individual is uncertain about the average expectation of others. Under such circumstances, "bubbles" as usually defined may arise when all market participants believe that they individually have some information that others have not incorporated into their expectations. The exchange rate will then depend on the average perception of others' expectations of future exchange rate changes, and these expectations differ from the average expectations of the equilibrium path based on fundamentals. On purely theoretical grounds, it is hard to believe that such a situation could be long lived.

Allowing for risk aversion, we would expect uncertainty about model parameters, policy rules, and others' expectations to reduce the elasticity of supply of speculative funds in response to a certain expected return differential between currencies. Therefore, in times of uncertainty we expect capital mobility to be reduced to a greater extent than is predicted by most models. The degree of capital mobility would vary over time with policy and model uncertainty. Periods of extremely high uncertainty may at times be associated with the development of disorderly markets because of a lack of speculative funds.

These aspects of exchange rate adjustment can be incorporated into modeling under the assumption that agents use "all available information" about parameters, policy rules, and others' expectations. The information gathering and analyses required to incorporate all these factors into expectations formation, however, is clearly time consuming and costly. The concept of using "all available information" does not have precise content. The crucial issue for market efficiency, in this view, is not whether all available information is used, which can be viewed as a tautology, but whether the information set in the hands (or the heads and computers) of agents is reasonable. In other words, out of the potentially available information, is the amount in use reasonable, given the costs and time required to gather and process information? As will be discussed later in this chapter, foreign exchange market behavior that is reasonable in the sense used here would still allow a case for ideal government intervention based on government's better information. In practice, however, government intervention is also often undertaken in a manner that is far from ideal. Realistic analysis must compare less than ideally efficient private behavior with less than ideally efficient public behavior.

Market participants must act on imperfect information about model structure and the behavior of others. Bounded rationality implies that at times market participants may rationally prefer to use checklists, rules of thumb, and technical rules for forecasting—or simply to abstain from trading—as substitutes for gathering information in order to derive exact predictions. Institutional constraints imposed on the sizes of the open positions traders can take may be rational responses under limited information and costly control mechanisms rather than arbitarily imposed sources of inefficiencies.

Our view of foreign exchange markets is consistent with the existence at times of what we have called insufficiently stabilizing speculation.[35] It is also consistent with temporary bandwagons and bubbles during periods of great uncertainty, while exchange rate changes driven primarily by changes in fundamentals would occur in periods of a stable relationship between these variables and expectations.

For empirical work that is relevant to policy, one must try to distinguish between variability caused by speculative bubbles and variability caused by perception errors about changing policies and structural parameters. James Hamilton and Charles Whiteman argue that current empirical methods cannot distinguish between these two sources of excess (or insufficient) variability relative to the variability that would occur under strongly rational expectations.[36]

As was discussed earlier, the empirical problem is also compounded by the need, from a policy point of view, to distinguish between excess variability caused by speculative flows under high capital mobility and excess variability caused by a low elasticity of supply of speculative funds. The latter phenomenon is particularly likely to occur if policy uncertainty is high. Econometric methods for identifying bubbles—such as, for example, the cointegration tests used by Meese—must be complemented with more detailed studies of actual capital flows and policy behavior in specific periods in order to make the distinctions necessary for drawing policy conclusions regarding capital mobility.[37]

The previous section raised the issue of the burden of proof for government intervention aimed at reducing destabilizing speculation. Our view of the foreign exchange market is consistent with the possibility of benefits of official intervention at times, but this does not resolve the issue of burden of proof and the role of government intervention. We must ask whether central banks have access to, or ability to use, an information set superior to that available to private market participants. If the presumption is that they do not, then one could argue that the burden of proof lies on those arguing that exchange rate changes warrant intervention.

One type of information to which governments do have potentially better access is information about their own future policy rules. Thus, government intervention would be warranted when exchange rate changes are clearly inconsistent with these planned future policies *and* if government plans are firm. This kind of intervention could lend credibility to government policy if market participants have learned that governments tend to follow up on policies signaled by intervention. In fact, little intervention would be needed under these circumstances.

A serious moral-hazard problem is involved in official intervention based on insider knowledge of policy intentions. The possibility of better information must be balanced against officials' natural propensities for wishful thinking. Given the frequency with which government exchange market intervention has not been followed in the past by complementary macroeconomic policies, at present the burden of proof that intervention has the purpose of correcting agents' information clearly should lie with the government or the central bank. If the government or the central bank does not act in a credible manner and does not follow up its signaled intentions with policy, then government intervention can only cause further uncertainty in the market and thereby contribute to exchange rate behavior that is less efficient, in terms of its informational foundation.

Much more analysis of these issues is needed, but given our current knowledge, we see no basis for a general presumption that government will act on the basis of better information than that available to private market participants. Official intervention may be able to play a positive role as a component of credible policy strategies, but governments must understand the need to establish their credibility. An important advantage of credible government behavior and signaling of intentions is that the likelihood of insufficiently stabilizing speculation is reduced, since the amount of uncertainty about policy parameters would be reduced.

International Capital Flows and the Behavior of the Dollar

In the preceding section we discussed some of the general empirical evidence relevant to assessing the major contrasting views of international capital flows and speculative behavior. In the present section we shall review the major movements of the dollar during the 1980s in terms of these movements' consistency with the same three con-trasting views. The association of international capital flows with the large fluctuations in the dollar over the past decade makes it easy to understand the widespread view that destabilizing capital flows have had a major disruptive effect on the U.S. economy.[38] The fall of the dollar in the late 1970s, followed by its dramatic rise through the mid-1980s and then its new plunge, makes it easy to understand why many observers believe that markets, if left to themselves, will always tend to overreact, creating a pattern of excessive volatility and dy-namic instability.

Recent empirical research finds that modern exchange rate mod-els have little predictive power and that theories of simple speculative efficiency do not fit the data. This is not surprising, in light of our view of foreign exchange markets, but it does not follow that one can describe speculative behavior as being dominated by herd instincts and bandwagon psychology. Such interpretations are often based on a failure to distinguish between the very short-term volatility of ex-change rates, which may be uncomfortable for many market partici-pants but is not tremendously costly, and large swings in the dollar, which may have very substantial economic effects.

Formal tests of the predictive power of exchange rate models have focused on short-term changes in exchange rates.[39] Given the impor-tant role of unquantifiable expectations in the determination of price in financial markets and given the lack of agreement among experts about the precise specification and parameter values of exchange rate models, it should not be surprising that we can neither predict nor explain very well the short-term dynamics of exchange rate be-havior.[40] Indeed, from this perspective the surprising fact is not that flexible exchange rates have displayed considerable short-term vol-atility but that by many measures they have displayed considerably less short-term volatility than have bond and stock prices over the same period.[41]

An Overview of the Fall and Rise of the Dollar. A substantial fall of the dollar such as occurred in the late 1970s can easily be explained by the highly expansionary macroeconomic policies adopted by the Car-ter administration. The failure to adopt coherent energy policies in the United States also contributed to lowering the equilibrium value of the dollar. Initially, capital flows helped to stabilize the dollar as market participants expected the worsening of the U.S. current ac-count to be only temporary. But as the rest of the countries of the Organization for Economic Cooperation and Development (OECD) continued to experience growth rates lower than had initially been projected and as accelerating inflationary pressures in the United States were fed by a growing loss of confidence in President Carter's economic policies, net capital flows quite understandably turned against the United States. Still, with the announcement of new measures to reduce inflation and stabilize the dollar in November 1978, the dollar immediately appreciated. These announcements were not backed by sustained policy changes, however, and the dollar soon resumed its downward course.

This last portion of the dollar's fall possibly went too far, in the sense that most market participants believed that the dollar should rise but were not willing to back up their best guesses with sufficient funds to halt the dollar's slide. Given the considerable uncertainty present at that time and the previous failure of U.S. policy makers to carry through on their promises, the development of an insufficiency of stabilizing private speculation could be explained by a combination of (1) the high risk of investing in dollar assets, which resulted in a low demand elasticity for dollars, and (2) rational expectations that the administration's promises to strengthen the dollar were not credible.[42]

For our later discussion of the proposals to tax international capital flows, it will be important to keep in mind that to the extent that speculative deficiencies were associated with an excessive fall of the dollar in the late 1970s, these deficiencies were more likely to be the result of an insufficiency of stabilizing capital flows because of high risk and a lack of policy credibility than a result of the pressure of actively destabilizing flows.

After a brief period of relative stability, the dollar began to climb sharply in 1981. Again, U.S. policy developments were crucial, first for ending the fall and then for initiating the climb. Although good reasons exist for believing that the combination of policies adopted by the United States is quite consistent with the rise of the dollar, much less basis currently exists for judging the comparative importance of these different policy changes. Many commentaries have presented an exaggerated view of current understanding of the causes of the strong dollar. A number of economists have stressed the U.S. budget deficit's role to the virtual exclusion of other considerations. In a recent analysis, for example, Branson argues that "the evidence . . . is clear" that expectations of the emerging structural budget deficit in the United States caused interest rates and the dollar to rise and that the expected reductions of the deficit associated with Gramm-Rudman caused the dollar to begin to decline in 1985.[43] Nevertheless, as a number of economists have argued—including Branson himself in another analysis—the full story is not that simple.[44]

The empirical study by Martin Feldstein,[45] on which Branson put considerable weight, was described by a recent critic as being "based on eleven annual observations with six or seven degrees of freedom. An economics undergraduate would be unlikely to receive a good grade on an econometrics term paper if he dared to use such a small sample to test the null hypothesis."[46] Some of the Reagan administration's challenges to the idea of the twin deficits—which holds that the budget deficit caused the trade deficit through the former's effects on capital flows and exchange rates—have been based on even less sophisticated analysis. Allegations that the budget deficit did not increase interest rates were sometimes based on simple correlations of the budget deficit and interest rates, with the data being dominated by the tendency for the budget deficit to increase and interest rates to fall during recessions. Likewise, whether a fiscal deficit would cause currency appreciation or depreciation in a standard open-economy Keynesian model depends crucially on the degree of capital mobility. The relationship will also be influenced by other important considerations such as the interest elasticity of the demand for money and the extent to which deficits are expected to be monetized. Thus, the failure to find strong, consistent cross-country and cross-time correlations between budget deficits and exchange rate changes tells one little about the role that the U.S. structural budget deficit may have played in causing the strong dollar.

The savings rate in the United States did not rise in the way expected by the new classical theories, which predict no effects on interest rates and capital flows from changes in the budget deficit unaccompanied by changes in government expenditures. It may be possible to argue that other factors were causing savings rates to fall so that the *ceteris paribus* effects of the budget deficit were consistent with the new classical deficit neutrality theory, but the burden of proof would certainly seem to fall on those wishing to make such arguments.

In accordance with the currently available research, the U.S. budget deficit probably did contribute significantly to the rise of the dollar.[47] The deficit, however, was only part of a much larger picture. The initial rise of the dollar was influenced by the tightening of monetary policy in the United States.[48] Furthermore, the Volcker factor was important not just in causing the initial tightening of monetary policy but also in establishing market expectations that the budget deficit would not be heavily monetized—a necessary condition for the budget deficit to cause currency appreciation, even assuming very high international capital mobility. There is also undoubtedly some truth to the argument that the investment incentives included in the Economic Recovery Tax Act of 1981 improved the investment climate in the United States and helped attract capital inflows.[49]

Much more research is needed in order to make possible a good understanding of the relative importance of the various underlying causes of the appreciation of the dollar. Fortunately, a full understanding of these causes is not needed in order to draw some important conclusions from this experience. Although it cannot be proved that this combination of policy developments was the dominant cause of the dollar appreciation, there exists at least a reasonable basis for concluding that the magnitude and timing of the appreciation were not inconsistent with reasonable responses by international investors and speculators to the growth of U.S. aggregate expenditures relative to output, whether this relative growth of expenditures to output was caused by fiscal policy, an increase in investments, or a decline in savings.

For our particular purpose it is not terribly important to distinguish among these particular causes. Admittedly, each could certainly have different implications for the long-run sustainability of capital flows, but, from the standpoint of the theory of economic policy discussed earlier in the chapter overview, all three of these causes are consistent with large capital inflows and currency appreciation. The alternative policy responses of maintaining constant exchange rates or controlling capital flows without reducing the fiscal deficit (or both) would have required either a monetary expansion, which could have been highly inflationary, or, if capital controls had been imposed, a rise in interest rates, which would have crowded out domestic investment. Although it may have been desirable to reduce the fiscal deficit to avoid substantial pressures for the reallocation of resources among sectors, it seems doubtful that desires to maintain exchange rate targets would have produced substantially stronger political pressure for changes in fiscal policy than did the appreciation of the dollar.[50] The same holds with respect to the adoption of direct measures to limit inflows.

The analysis of appropriate macroeconomic policies becomes more complicated if the safe-haven argument is accepted as the explanation of capital inflows.[51] To some extent this argument approximates the pure shift in financial asset preferences in which an adjustment in asset supplies at constant exchange rates is the optimal response. But taking into consideration that the safe-haven argument refers to the broader desire to have more real productive assets in the United States, a financial transfer and a consequent temporary appreciation of the dollar are required—thereby calling for a U.S. trade deficit. Nevertheless, if the safe-haven argument really provided the major explanation for the dollar appreciation and the trade deficit, one should have been able to observe a decline in the U.S. real rate of interest. It could also be argued that the world debt crisis in the 1980s, after heavy U.S. lending to the less developed countries in the 1970s, contributed to financial instability and that substantial cutbacks occurred in the flow of net lending to the developing countries—thereby calling for exchange rate and trade flow adjustments.

Speculative Bubble as Cause of Overpriced 1984–1985 Dollar? Did bandwagon effects or a speculative bubble cause an excessive run-up of the dollar toward the end of its appreciation? The evidence may be consistent with either a bubble or a combination of changes in fundamentals and structural changes in the international financial system. As mentioned earlier, the interest rate differential in favor of the United States had peaked by mid-1984 and subsequently began to decline; yet the dollar continued to rise rapidly into the first part of 1985. This behavior has suggested to some economists that a speculative bubble may have been in operation during this last portion of the dollar's climb.[52] The aforementioned surveys analyzed by Frankel and Froot indicate that during most of the dollar's appreciation, subsequent depreciation was expected, but that over this latter period, expectations of a continued climb predominated for time horizons of a week to a month.[53] Such evidence is consistent with the possibility of a short-term speculative bandwagon.

Nevertheless, a number of developments in the underlying fundamentals can also help explain this rise. One such development was the substantial tightening of monetary policy that occurred in the United States in 1984 after a period of relative monetary ease.[54] Furthermore, two actions directly affecting capital flows may have contributed to the continued rise of the dollar, namely, the liberalization of Japanese capital markets and the U.S. removal of withholding taxes on foreign investments in the United States.

The liberalization of Japanese capital markets, which started in 1980 but received a final push in May 1984, allowed substantial net capital flows from Japan to the United States, which contributed to further appreciation of the dollar against the yen. Coming as it did at a time when many thought, from a broad public policy perspective, that the dollar was already too high, this liberalization could easily be interpreted as a case of the imposition of instability costs on the United States by policy actions of other countries. Once again, however, in reality it was really just another case in which the United States has only itself to blame. The Japanese liberalization was at least in part the result of strong pressure from the United States, especially from Treasury Secretary Regan, who was apparently operating on the basis of the seriously flawed view that Japanese liberalization would generate greater capital inflows into Japan than outflows and would hence force up the yen.[55]

The second policy change that contributed to the continued rise of the dollar was the U.S. removal of withholding taxes on foreign investments in the United States in July 1984. Again, this created additional incentives for capital inflows and dollar appreciation. Though the interest rate differential in favor of the United States had decreased in 1984, it was still positive and capital flows still gravitated toward dollars, thus helping to account for the continuing appreciation during 1984. We know relatively little at present about this question of adjustment speeds. Foreign exchange markets do react quite rapidly to news, but this speed of response is not inconsistent with much lower adjustment speeds on the part of many long-term investors. Studies in the 1960s did find evidence of significant lags in the adjustment of the international allocation of long-term and even short-term financial investments.[56] This issue of response speed is one that needs revisiting.[57]

What kept the dollar appreciating during 1984 and early 1985, we suspect, was not primarily the behavior of speculators. It was rather the net excess demand for dollars that was resulting from non-speculative transactions, combined with only a modest influence from speculation. The continued large incipient longer-term capital inflows in excess of the deficit on the current account had greater effects than the speculative expectations by active market participants of a future fall in the dollar. The latter were not strongly enough held or not backed by sufficient access to funds (or both) to offset the net imbalance of other transactions in favor of a strengthening dollar.

Why did the dollar finally begin its downturn in early 1985? A number of explanations have been put forward. The bursting of a speculative bubble is one. Another, a policy rule shift that was gradually learned, is suggested by Shafigul Islam, who argues that the gradual shift of the U.S. government away from a laissez-faire attitude toward the dollar, manifested in part by an increase in official intervention in the United States and other major countries, gave important signals to the market that the central banks were committed to inducing the dollar to depreciate; these changes preceded the widely publicized Plaza Agreement by many months.[58] A third explanation is based on fundamentals in combination with a limited supply of speculative funds.

We are inclined to give some weight to Islam's argument about gradual recognition of a shift in policy. Changes in official attitudes and behavior can be important signals to market participants and can at times significantly shift market expectations. We further note that it is much easier for officials to talk down their currencies than to talk them up. Thus, we believe that these policy shifts involving government attitudes toward official intervention and the desirable course of the dollar had a nontrivial impact on market expectations about future policy even though they did not involve simultaneous changes in underlying fundamentals. The conditions for such a direct impact on the foreign exchange market were unusually favorable, however, for they did roughly coincide with the mentioned changes in the underlying U.S. policy fundamentals—all of which pointed in the direction of a lower dollar.

Another factor that may have contributed to the fall of the dollar is that foreigners, who had accumulated a large amount of dollar assets, may have been reluctant to invest in more dollar assets without increased compensation for risk. We would expect the elasticity of supply of additional funds to the United States to decrease with the size of the dollar asset holdings. Some evidence in support of this view can be gathered from the response of the dollar to news about the outlook for U.S. budget deficits. In the Mundell-Fleming theoretical framework, an increase in the exogenous portion of a budget deficit may lead to either appreciation or depreciation, depending in part on whether international capital mobility is high or low. The higher is capital mobility, the more likely is appreciation. If the continued attraction of funds after some point entails an increasingly less elastic supply of funds, then we might expect an appreciation in response to expectations of an increased budget deficit while a country is in a large net international asset position, but depreciation to such news if prolonged capital inflows are creating prospects of the emergence of a large net debtor position.

We have some weak evidence that this process may in fact have been at work in the case of the U.S. budget deficits. Using a data set developed by Thorbecke of government announcements that were likely to change market expectations about future U.S. budget deficits, we find that the average value of the dollar against the major industrial currencies fell after four of the five announcements of budget reduction measures during 1982.[59] This is what we would expect with high international capital mobility. In early 1984, responses to reduction announcements were mixed, but from June 1984 through 1985, reduction announcements were followed by appreciation in all six cases. This is consistent with a substantial reduction over time in the elasticity of supply of additional funds to the United States.

Although this view may have some merit, we do not wish to make too much of it. The evidence from announcements that should have led to larger expected deficits does not fit the hypothesis. The one such announcement in 1982 was accompanied by a fall of the dollar, and four of the five in 1985 were followed by appreciations.

Furthermore, this hypothesis of an increasingly less elastic supply of additional funds as a contributor to the decline of the dollar is not consistent with Frankel's argument that according to mean variance portfolio choice models, risk premiums in international financial markets are small.[60] Our view of behavior in foreign exchange markets contradicts Frankel's calculations, however, and one can get quite different results from other types of models.[61] In 1985 the dollar had appreciated to unprecedented heights, foreigners had accumulated more dollar assets than ever, and uncertainty about future policy was very high. Thus, it is not at all unreasonable to think that continued investment in the United States may have required a substantial increase in differential interest returns. A complementary explanation of the turning point is the working out of J-curve effects under low capital mobility conditions. The working out of these effects in 1984 and 1985 would imply that for a given change in capital inflows per time period, net nonspeculative demands for the dollar would initially be in an incipient surplus, causing a tendency toward appreciation in the absence of offsetting speculation. In such a nonspeculative world, the combination of continued appreciation and the working out of J-curve effects would cause an eventual switch to an excess supply of dollars as the growing current account deficit began to exceed the incipient autonomous capital inflow. The dollar would then begin to depreciate.

We cannot clearly discriminate among the budget deficit, investment incentives, monetary policy, risk premium, and J-curve arguments about the causes of the dollar's behavior. As advocates of the budget deficit view emphasize, the passage of the Gramm-Rudman-Hollings legislation (in late 1985) would be expected to cause a drop in the dollar; the credibility of this legislation can be questioned, however.[62] Advocates of the investment incentives view can point, however, to the surfacing of the Treasury Tax Reform proposals, which implied a substantial increase in the taxation of capital.[63] Monetary policy turned toward ease, and the growth rates of the monetary aggregates sped up substantially. Finally, substantial uncertainty existed about the future course of both fiscal and monetary policy and therefore about the dollar. In summary, although the precise timing is open to debate, there are a number of good economic reasons that the dollar should have begun to fall in 1985.

The fall of the dollar was a fairly gradual process rather than a precipitous plunge like the stock market crash of October 1987. No clear evidence exists of the bursting of a speculative bubble. The dollar's fall was nevertheless a good bit more rapid than one might be led to expect by popular theories based on perfect capital mobility in which international interest rate differentials are exactly offset by the expected rate of exchange rate changes. And the decline was slowed at times by massive official intervention, which for 1987 may have totaled more than $100 billion.

The Rebound of the Dollar in 1988. During 1987 and 1988, a number of official pronouncements were made by the United States and other summit countries during 1987 and 1988 that the dollar had fallen sufficiently. Such statements were and are not consistent with the estimates of most academic researchers who have studied this issue nor indeed with some high-quality analysis by economists with the U.S. government and major international organizations.[64] Initially the official pronouncements had relatively little credibility, and heavy interventions had to be made by both foreign and the U.S. governments to slow the fall of the dollar.

During 1988, favorable short-run developments—such as the unexpectedly rapid reduction in the U.S. trade deficits and the perceived tightening of monetary policy—began to buoy the dollar, and the official "targets" for the dollar began to gain credibility. In fact, the dollar strengthened to the point that official intervention was used to hold it down. Does this show that the governments were right and that they were the best judges of fundamentals in their initial announcements that the dollar had fallen enough? Not necessarily. This strengthening of the dollar was probably the result of the interaction of inappropriate policy actions and pronouncements by governments, on the one hand, and the limited effective time horizon of the private markets, on the other.

We have argued that international financial integration is sufficiently imperfect so that governments can typically have a substantial impact on exchange rates in the short run through official intervention policies. What are the odds that, if an administration could, it would not allow the market to generate a fall in the country's currency shortly before a presidential election? If a number of exchange market participants believe, as we do, that such odds are high and then act on that belief, then the probability at that time of a substantial drop in the dollar in the short term would be low. If considerable weight is given to a relatively short time horizon in the majority of forward-looking exchange market transactions, then the market could actually turn quite bullish on the dollar in the short term even though considerable depreciation was still expected over the next several years.

Note that the setting of an effective short-term floor on a currency can cause its value to rise well above the floor. This will occur if considerable diversity exists among the exchange rate forecasts of the different exchange market participants or even if forecasts are homogeneous but have a sizable probability distribution around the best estimate. In either case, there would be dispersion in the distribution of the aggregate market's judgment of the probability distribution of possible outcomes. In a risk-neutral and efficient market, the market price of the currency would be set near the mean of this distribution. By truncating the lower part of the distribution range, the setting of a price floor would raise the mean of the remainder of the distribution and hence lead to a rise in price. Thus, paradoxically, the government's own emphasis on a floor on the dollar may have given rise to its perceived need to intervene in the opposite direction.

Another complementary explanation for the dollar's rise is that the market began to believe at least partially the government's optimistic views that the dollar has fallen low enough. The recent unexpectedly large reductions in the U.S. monthly trade deficit understandably gave a short-term boost to the dollar. Such short-term trade developments, however, may give little cause for adjusting estimates of the amount of dollar depreciation needed to restore long-term balance of payments equilibrium. They could, for example, be merely a reflection of a faster-than-expected speed of trade adjustment rather than a greater long-run trade flow adjustment. Thus, this could be a case in which government pursuit of short-term political ends takes advantage of, rather than attempts to correct for, market imperfections.

Policy Implications

This concluding section addresses major specific policy implications of the analysis contained in the present chapter. The section begins with a discussion of proposals to limit capital flows through taxes or controls and then goes on to discuss strategies for U.S. macroeconomic and exchange rate policies and international policy coordination.

Administrative Measures to Reduce Capital Flows. Views that capital flows have been a major cause of exchange rate volatility and misalignments have given rise to a recent increase in interest in the possible desirability of the adoption of measures by the United States to restrict capital flows. Most economists have a healthy skepticism toward the effectiveness of many types of government controls and regulations, capital controls being a case in point. Many would join Frankel in concluding that "the controls on capital inflow into Germany and Switzerland, like the controls on capital outflows from the United States, were never very effective."[65] We believe that this view is too strong, however, if *effectiveness* is meant in its conversational sense of having a substantial influence on net capital flows. We agree with Dornbusch that "the record on capital controls is hard to interpret. The common argument is that they are circumvented the moment they are imposed. . . . Some evasion is inevitable. The question is whether the controls substantially work."[66] The episodes cited by Frankel, as well as numerous other episodes—including the recent experiences of France and Italy within the European Monetary System—demonstrate that capital controls can have a substantial impact, even though some evasion and slippage are inevitable.

The lesson to be drawn from these experiences is that in today's world of sophisticated financial markets, capital control measures that are selective and limited will have little effectiveness. Considerable fungibility exists among the various channels for moving funds, as was dramatically illustrated by the history of U.S. capital control measures during the 1960s.[67] The first measure adopted, the Interest Equalization Tax, was virtually 100 percent effective in terminating the issuance of foreign securities in the United States by making them subject to the tax. Little change occurred in net capital flows, however, as foreign lending by U.S. banks rose by an almost equal amount. After successive expansions of the domain of controls, controls finally became comprehensive enough to have a substantial effect. Ultimately, a considerable portion of the financing of U.S. corporate operations abroad was shifted to Europe. (This shift had a substantial beneficial effect on the development of European capital markets, but the overall benefits for the United States were not so clear.)

The fungibility among different channels for capital flows likewise forced Germany toward the adoption of more comprehensive measures; evidence that the German controls eventually developed considerable bite can be found in the substantial interest differentials that developed. Similar evidence is available on the effectiveness of Japanese, French, and Italian controls.[68] The lesson is that one cannot go only a little of the way toward capital control. Mild selective measures will not work. Comprehensive controls, with all their disadvantages, are required in order to produce a major short-term net impact.

Recently, an alternative approach to mild capital restrictions has been recommended by James Tobin and others in the form of a tax of, say, 1 percent on all foreign exchange transactions.[69] The Tobin proposal explicitly recognizes the need for comprehensive application but seeks to keep the effects mild by using the price system rather than direct administrative measures. The idea is that a uniform transactions tax would particularly discriminate against short-term speculative and interest-sensitive investors. A 1 percent tax would not seriously discourage trade flows, it is argued. Likewise, for a ten-year investment, a 1 percent transactions tax would have to be compensated by an interest rate differential of only $^2/_{10}$ of 1 percent to pay for the purchase and sale of foreign currency, but the interest rate differential would have to be 2 percent to cover taxes on a one-year investment and 8 percent for a three-month investment.

When destabilizing short-term speculative capital flows are a persistent major cause of exchange rate fluctuations, then Tobin's proposal might have much to commend it. As we have argued, however, to the extent that U.S. exchange rates have suffered from speculative flaws, these have probably resulted more from a lack of sufficient stabilizing speculation than from the presence of actively destabilizing capital flows. If this is true, taxing capital flows could lead to an increase in exchange rate volatility.[70] Thus, Tobin's tax could have an effect that is opposite to what is intended.

Substantial problems of enforcement could also arise. Furthermore, the approach would need to be adopted cooperatively by all of the major financial centers; otherwise, U.S. institutions would be put at a severe competitive disadvantage.[71] We also suspect that proponents of a tax on foreign exchange transactions have substantially underestimated the adverse effect on real trade and investment flows. As discussed earlier, when arrangements for financing trade and reducing exchange risk are taken into account, a single export sale can generate a number of financial transactions. Thus, the discouragement to trade flows could be considerable. With such a tax, efforts would undoubtedly be made to reduce the number of financial transactions associated with each real transaction. Nevertheless, it is difficult to see how the increased cost could be kept from being anything less than a multiple of the direct amount of the tax or how to avoid at least some degree of deterioration in the effective provision of cover against exchange risk. Thus, after careful consideration, the Tobin transactions tax proposal may be much less attractive than it may have appeared at first glance.[72]

Macroeconomic and Exchange Rate Policy. The major shifts in international capital flows and the consequent large swings in the dollar have resulted largely from reasonable market responses to major often unanticipated shifts in U.S. economic policies, as was discussed in the fourth major section of this chapter. Thus, the principal prerequisite for creating more stable conditions lies in the United States improvement of its own economic policies.

We have found that—contrary to the views of some—in a stable underlying environment, international capital flows and currency switching are not likely to be sources of instability. Even if the environment is unstable and even if the information available to market participants is highly imperfect, a government's ability to improve the information is limited to announcing credible policies and to signaling its plans by committing itself to intervening only when markets do not seem to act on these credible policies.

Another conclusion is that increased international capital mobility would not seriously undercut the ability of the United States to implement sound monetary and fiscal policies. Policy makers, however, must take into account a given policy's likely effects on capital flows and exchange rates. And conversely, as was discussed in the first major section of the chapter, the actual degree of international capital mobility and the choice of exchange rate regime can strongly affect the impact of given changes in fiscal or montary policy. In an open economy with significant international capital mobility, for example, formulating policies on the basis of closed-economy analysis can create serious problems. Considerable need still exists, in fact, for increased recognition of the importance of open-economy thinking on the part of top policy makers in Congress and the executive branch. (At the staff level in the executive branch and at the Federal Reserve, such thinking is already the general rule.) The adoption of such a perspective would substantially reduce the apparent attractiveness of using restrictions on trade and capital flows.

High international capital mobility does raise the costs of domestic policy instability and of lack of credibility in announcements and in market intervention. These consequences of capital mobility in the face of policy instability and uncertainty need not be a bad thing, however, in that they strengthen an already strong case for greater policy stability under flexible rates as well as for policy coordination under fixed rates.[73] To the extent that speculation may have failed to behave in a stabilizing manner, these failures have typically occurred when major policy swings have already created large swings in exchange rates and when analysis of future policy developments and of long-run equilibrium exchange rates has been particularly difficult to perform. This is consistent with our theory of exchange market behavior presented in the third major section.

In conventional economic theory, market "failures" present cases for ideal government intervention via capital controls, exchange market intervention, and the like to establish more appropriate levels of exchange rates. There is a major irony here, however, in that bad government policies can create conditions of market failure that, circularly, may be used to justify government intervention. One must adopt a political-economy perspective and ask how likely it is that in such conditions the government itself will adopt correct interventions.[74] We certainly do not subscribe to the extreme view that governments can do no right, but the analysis of recent U.S. and international actions to prop up the dollar, as presented in the second major section, suggests that such concerns are not purely imaginary.

Such considerations are in fact quite relevant to the debate over strategies for achieving greater exchange rate and macroeconomic stability. One school argues that restoring macroeconomic stability is the essential first step, while another school argues that the process can be made faster and less costly by beginning with the pegging of exchange rates. Conceptually, a good case can be made for a simultaneous approach, but, as our previous analysis suggests, this assumes that some reasonable degree of credibility is associated with governments' announced policies and with the exchange rate to which intervention is geared. The danger in beginning with the pegging of rates—whether explicitly or through the setting of target zones—is that pegging will end up being a substitute for, instead of a complement to, the adoption of prudent domestic policies. Given the poor track record of many governments over the recent past, it seems reasonable that if governments propose to take on much heavier responsibilities for exchange rate management through the use of capital controls and the like, they should first demonstrate their ability to perform well in this area by creating a stable domestic macroeconomic policy environment. We suspect that if they did this, there would be much less advocacy of the need for capital controls and for heavy direct exchange rate management.

Exchange Rate and Macroeconomic Policy Coordination. Under conditions of international economic interdependence, economic and policy developments in one country can have important effects on developments in other countries. This linkage creates a case in principle for international policy coordination.[75] Again, however, one must approach such issues from a broad political-economy perspective and not just from a narrow point of view of defining optimal economic policy. Domestic political considerations are often the source not only of impediments to achieving active macroeconomic coordination but also of economic policies that are the cause of major disturbances in the world economy.

The two instances of the strongest U.S. advocacy of international macroeconomic policy coordination in recent years—the locomotive strategy proposals of the Carter administration in the late 1970s and the surprisingly similar proposals by the Reagan administration in 1986 and 1987—both followed episodes in which the respective administration's macroeconomic policies had created major international monetary instability. A cynic might be excused for arguing that such advocacy of policy coordination was motivated more by the underlying desire to deflect attention or to help offset the effects of the administrations' own policies than by any genuine concern with the possible benefits of international cooperation.

Sound national macroeconomic policies are not a guarantee of international monetary stability; other shocks, such as the world oil price increases, do occur. Sound domestic policies, however, are certainly a necessary condition. Thus, the question becomes: How can the adoption and maintenance of sound policies best be effected? Scope certainly exists for learning from past mistakes, to bring about improvements naturally. We fear, however, that the instabilities in past macroeconomic policies have resulted as much or more from the underlying political incentive structure itself as from bad luck, inferior officials, and the use of poor economic analysis.[76]

In this regard, U.S. policy makers need to evaluate carefully the costs and benefits of certain proposed institutional reforms designed to limit the scope for variability in our own domestic monetary and fiscal policies. In recent years, considerable attention has been given to the possible use of various forms of exchange rate rules as the basis for such stabilizing reforms. This option, however, is not necessarily well advised for the United States.

The theory of optimum currency areas suggests that two basic types of criteria exist for considering whether a country's macroeconomic policy objectives should be more domestically or more internationally oriented.[77] These are (1) the institutional and structural characteristics of economies, such as their size and openness, and (2) the patterns of disturbances.

Ceteris paribus, in structural terms the smaller the economy, the stronger is the case for a primarily international orientation, and the larger the economy, the greater the case for a largely domestic orientation. When the choice of policy rules or constraints is at issue, the same types of considerations apply. Thus, for some smaller countries, the adoption of exchange rate or balance of payments rules may make considerable sense if the countries actually follow domestic policies consistent with the self-imposed external constraints. The recent experience with the European Monetary System is open to widely varying interpretations, but it is clear that ensuring the workability of its adjustably pegged exchange rate system has required the substantial use of capital controls until now; nevertheless, we would not want to argue that for all countries all reforms focused on the exchange rate should be dismissed out of hand.[78] For the United States, however, a domestically focused approach should be superior.

In terms of disturbance patterns, an exception to the foregoing structurally based criterion would occur if destabilizing shifts in asset preferences and currency substitution were the dominant disturbances faced by the U.S. economy. In this case, a monetary and fiscal policy rule based on fixed exchange rates would make considerable sense. The available evidence suggests, however, that these have not been the dominant types of disturbance faced by the U.S. economy.

Based on the considerations emphasized in the theory of optimum currency areas, then, the United States is a very poor candidate for a fixed exchange rate. Optimum currency area theory was developed within the context of Keynesian macroeconomic models, but this conclusion also holds within monetarist and new classical models as well, given the patterns of disturbances observed.[79]

Admittedly, exchange rate movements can, in conjunction with the analysis of other developments, often give useful signals for discretionary short-term macroeconomic policy making. It would be quite another matter, however, to use the exchange rate and balance of payments as the basis for long-term constraints on the behavior of U.S. monetary and fiscal policy, as would be necessary in a system of genuinely fixed exchange rates and in some proposals for target zones for exchange rates.[80]

Rules based on the exchange rate are in fact particularly unsatisfactory from the standpoint of such constraint-based approaches.[81] Consider, for example, the proposals by Ronald McKinnon that the United States should use changes in the exchange rate as guides to monetary policy.[82] Suppose that the exchange rate is falling but is still at a very high level. Should monetary policy be tightened or eased? The development of McKinnon's approach is based on the assumption that equilibrium real exchange rates are constant and that deviations from them are self reversing; the empirical evidence suggests, however, that these conditions are not closely approximated in the real world.

Furthermore, even under his own assumptions, McKinnon recognizes the need for agreement on limitations on the growth of monetary aggregates to complement the exchange rate rule. If exchange rate target zones and constraints are not expected to rein in monetary growth, then one wonders how they will succeed in inducing fiscal policy authorities to conduct policies consistent with the constraints.

In short, for the large industrial countries, constraints on monetary and fiscal policies need to be domestically focused. Recognition that economies are subject to a wide variety of shocks reduces the desirability of using any simple, one-faceted rule as a guide for policy.[83] A simple provision for wide bands for the permissible rates of growth of monetary aggregates is also unlikely to prove satisfactory, for the same types of reasons as were discussed in the case of exchange rate zones. What seems to be needed is some type of multifaceted feedback rules that would constrain monetary policy from allowing large cumulative deviations from a target range for the price level, inflation rate, or nominal income growth. These rules would need to be carefully designed to allow for variability in fiscal policy conditions and to avoid both circumvention and possible problems of dynamic instability.[84]

Concluding Remarks. International economic cooperation is clearly important, but at this point we see only a limited basis for actual active discretionary macroeconomic policy coordination. As illustrated by the wide range of views surveyed in the second and third sections, there still does not exist the kind of consensus on technical knowledge that would be necessary for the use of monetary and fiscal policy to control precisely the short-run behavior of real exchange rates.

Nor do countries' economic policies actually take shape in the politics-free atmosphere assumed in the technical literature on the theory of optimal economic policy. The pursuit of domestic political advantage from limiting short-run exchange rate variability can sometimes contribute to the development of greater disequilibrium and exchange rate movements over the longer term. Therefore, considerable scope exists for the political misuse of international policy coordination designed to limit variations in exchange rates. Very real gains would result, however, if we could at the same time limit the extent to which countries adopt monetary and fiscal policies that export instability to others.

Although the primary costs and benefits from the adoption of national policy constraint systems would occur domestically, the international dimension involved would still be important. The adoption of such constraints by the United States, for example, would limit the disturbances to which U.S. macroeconomic policies have subjected both the U.S. economy and the rest of the world. Likewise, the United States stands to gain from the reduction of policy instabilities in other countries.

Furthermore, given the technical difficulty involved, the more experts whose attention is focused on such issues, the better. Thus, efforts to design mutually beneficial sets of constraints over the variability of national monetary and fiscal policies should be a major item on the agendas of the institutions and groups concerned with international economic policy coordination.

The Path of the Dollar

A Commentary by William H. Branson

The foregoing analysis by Thomas Willett and Clas Wihlborg is characteristic of their output in that it covers the ground well and hits the important points. It is also judicious and, of course, well documented, with an entire second study in the notes. Since one author is a former colleague and coauthor of mine and the other was my student, I am pleased to be able to report that I have no deep criticism to present. The few differences that I have with the study will be noted as the discussion proceeds.

Let us focus on three important issues emphasized by Willett and Wihlborg. The first is the path of the dollar since 1980 and whether or not this path represented a persistent misalignment. The second is whether the short-term fluctuations around that path exhibited exceess volatility. The third is policy implications, especially for international policy coordination.

The path of the dollar. Our analysis here complements that by Willett and Wihlborg and follows their lead in minimizing the particular theoretical input; it summarizes the complete model discussed by William Branson and Grazia Marchese.[1]

Suppose that the current account of the United States with the rest of the world *(X)*, at approximately constant levels of employment in the United States and abroad, depends positively on the U.S. real exchange rate *(e)* through the trade component and negatively on the U.S. international debt position *(B)* through the debt service. (Here the real exchange rate is an effective average of the dollar price of foreign currencies, multiplied by the ratio of foreign to U.S. price levels.) Symbolically, $X = X(e,B)$. Then the positively sloped line marked $X = 0$ in figure 2–2 of this commentary shows the combinations of the real exchange rate and debt position that yield current account balance. In 1980 the United States was at a point such as *A* in the figure, with net investment abroad (a negative debt position) and approximate balance on current account.

Now let us assume that the United States decides to move to the

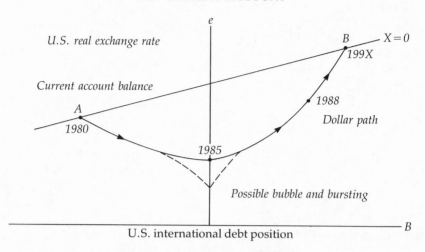

FIGURE 2–2
U.S. CURRENT ACCOUNT

e

U.S. real exchange rate

B *X = 0*

199X

Current account balance

1988

A

Dollar path

1980

1985

Possible bubble and bursting

U.S. international debt position

B

right in the figure, to a net debt position. This would happen if total investment plus the government deficit exceeded private saving, as it has since 1980, and for a period long enough to accumulate a net debt. To accumulate the debt, the United States has to run a current account deficit over that period. Let us also assume that the United States wants to stabilize the foreign debt at some point, by bringing the current account back into balance. Then the eventual equilibrium will be a point such as *B* in the figure, which is labeled 199X. At point *B*, we have a stable debt position, current account balance, and a real exchange rate that is above the level at point *A* (the dollar depreciated relative to *A*) in order to generate the trade surplus needed to finance the debt service.

How do we get from *A* to *B* in the figure? In order to generate the current account deficit that is the foreign borrowing, the dollar must appreciate from point *A* and then eventually reverse its direction to end up at point *B*. So we must follow a trajectory such as the solid path in the figure, going far enough below the *X* = 0 line for long enough to have accumulated the desired debt position when we arrive at point *B*. This is the underlying path of the dollar since 1980, shown (upside down) in figure 2–1 of the Willett and Wihlborg study. The United States passed from net creditor to net debtor position in 1985 and in 1988 had a real exchange rate that was slightly above the 1980 level, by Organization of Economic Cooperation and Development (OECD) competitiveness measures. The dashed additional path around 1985 represents a possible speculative bubble and its bursting, as described by Paul Krugman.[2] The United States may have experienced a positive bubble around the underlying path in 1988.

The magnitude of the dollar appreciation from 1980 to 1985 is consistent with the increase in the trade deficit from $25 billion in 1980 to $160 billion in 1987. This was an increase of about 3 percent of gross national product (GNP). The appreciation shown in Willett and Wihlborg's figure 2–1 is about 55 percent at the peak, including the Krugman bubble. Rudiger Dornbusch and Jeffrey Frankel estimate that a real appreciation of 13.5 percent will reduce the trade balance by 1 percent of GNP.[3] Thus, a real appreciation of some 40 percent was needed to obtain a swing in the trade balance of 3 percent of GNP, leaving 15 percent for the bubble.

The trajectory of the dollar in figure 2–2 of this commentary is what Willett and Wihlborg refer to as a large swing in the dollar that may have very substantial economic effects. It has been widely labeled as a misalignment of the dollar—by Richard Marston, for example.[4] But this needs careful interpretation. The swing in the dollar from 1980 to 199X is an inherent part of the process whereby the amount by which investment plus the budget deficit exceeds private saving is financed abroad. In this sense, it is part of the equilibrium adjustment to whatever events caused that excess. If it had not occurred, real interest rates would have had to rise enough in the United States to reduce investment sufficiently to eliminate the excess. So the cure for the dollar misalignment was elimination of the factors that caused the domestic imbalance, including the fiscal shift that came in the early 1980s. Here I agree completely with Willett and Wihlborg's call for more stable macroeconomic policy.

Excess exchange rate volatility? The second issue we shall discuss here is excess volatility of the exchange rate around its underlying path, as well as the role of capital mobility in determining this. In the case of exchange rates, I do not have a precise definition of excess volatility. Nevertheless, Willett and Wihlborg's definition is not quite satisfactory; they define excess volatility as actual volatility greater than the volatility of equilibrium prices.

The problem with this definition is suggested by the reason that exchange rates overshoot in Dornbusch's original model.[5] Because goods prices adjust slowly to monetary disturbances in that model, exchange rates have to overadjust in the short run. In a sense, they have to do some of the work that flexible prices would have done. This seems to be a particular application of the Le Chatelier principle cited by Paul Samuelson.[6] If, in response to an external disturbance to a stable system, some variables are constrained to underadjust in the short run, then others must overadjust. This view seems implicit in Willett and Wihlborg's discussion of insufficient stabilizing speculation. In this case, the excess volatility of the flexible prices, usually in financial markets, would be the result of the insufficient volatility of the sticky prices in goods and labor markets. Research in the "new Keynesian" line of macroeconomics suggests that good reasons exist for this price stickiness—for example, those presented in the survey paper by Julio Rotemberg.[7] If good reasons do exist, some excess volatility, in terms of Willett and Wihlborg's definition of it, may actually be a good thing.

The role of capital mobility in determining financial price volatility may not come through clearly in the Willett and Wihlborg analysis. An increase in capital mobility, in their definition of it (see their note 2), should make asset demands more elastic to changes in rates of return, inclusive of expected changes in exchange rates. This increased elasticity should reduce the size of fluctuations in financial prices as supplies are changed by new issues or by open-market operations or as demands fluctuate with news about relevant variables. In this sense, one would expect an increase in capital mobility to stabilize price fluctuations. It would, of course, make it harder for the monetary authorities to prevent price fluctuations, by increasing the necessary size of interventions.

In any event, recent research on exchange rate fluctuations does point to higher volatility than seems reasonable by any definition. John Campbell and Richard Clarida, for example, note that real exchange rates have been much more volatile than real interest differentials.[8] They decomposed the variance in real exchange rate innovations for the United States vis-à-vis Canada, Germany, Japan, the United Kingdom, and a trade-weighted average into variance resulting from innovations in the real interest differential and variance resulting from the implicit innovations in the fundamentals moving the long-run equilibrium real exchange rate. Across these five cases, the largest fraction of the variance in real exchange rate innovations resulting from variance in innovations in the real interest differential was 9 percent, in the case of Canada. The smallest weight that had to be assigned to the variance in the fundamentals in order to explain the exchange rate variance was 79 percent, for the United Kingdom. This is an extremely high estimate of the underlying variance of fundamentals such as fiscal policy, productivity, or demand shifts among national products. The results strongly suggest excessive variance around the underlying path given by the fundamentals, and they perhaps cast a bit of doubt on Willett and Wihlborg's belief in the reasonableness of the foreign exchange market. The results also suggest a useful role for intervention to keep the market on the track of the underlying fundamentals, if the policy authorities could figure out what these fundamentals are.

Policy implications. On policy issues, I do not differ substantially from Willett and Wihlborg. I have just presented the argument for volatility-reducing intervention. The transactions tax seems to me to be a nonstarter, because it would have to be nearly universal. And even if the major countries all imposed such a tax, if it were large enough to have a significant effect on transactions then it would also provide that large an incentive for a smaller country or other entity to provide a tax haven. I also agree with Willett and Wihlborg that the effect could be perverse, if the tax did have an effect. Along the lines of the earlier analysis of the effects of capital mobility, the tax could reduce the elasticity of asset demands with respect to changes in before-tax returns, making them more volatile rather than less. However, I see no reason in principle not to tax financial transactions as well as goods and labor transactions; it is only the practical problems that argue against it.

Willett and Wihlborg argue that macroeconomic policy should be constrained to be more stable. They do not specify how this constraint is to be applied or by whom. They also ignore the point that credible present announcements of future policy changes can have large announcement effects by moving financial market prices. The run-up in real interest rates and the dollar in 1981 following the announcement of the new budget package is an illustration. A constraint on actual discretionary variability in policy would provide an incentive for the constrained policy activist to move markets by announcing paths of gradual policy adjustment into the future. News about gradual future policy can generate large current changes via the financial markets. So Willett and Wihlborg are right to believe that the fiscal shift in 1981 was a serious error; unfortunately, no mechanism exists for ruling out its repetition other than electing more sensible people.

Let me end with a point on the controversy about policy coordination. Willett and Wihlborg make the important distinction between cooperation and coordination. I think the terms were best defined by Lamberto Dini of the Bank of Italy:

> I find it useful in this regard to distinguish between cooperation and coordination. Cooperation basically involves information exchange, consultation among authorities, and possibly common assessments of the international repercus-

sions of national policies. Coordination means that policy makers in a number of countries agree on common objectives and together take joint policy decisions that differ from those that they would have taken on their own. . . . Clearly, in this framework cooperation is the general condition, while coordination may occur sporadically, usually as the response to potential or actual conflict.[9]

There is no point in arguing about whether coordination is a good thing; it will happen when it is needed. Otherwise, cooperation is the normal state of affairs.

3
Exchange Rates, the Current Account, and Monetary Policy

Alan C. Stockman

The dramatic surge in the dollar's value relative to major European currencies was probably the most important economic event of the period between 1980 and 1984.
—Martin S. Feldstein, "The Budget Deficit and the Dollar"

As for foreign exchange, it is almost as romantic as young love, and quite as resistant to formulae.
—H. L. Mencken, *Prejudices*

Mencken's prescient comment foreshadowed considerable controversy among economists on the meaning of exchange rate changes, and it anticipated the failure thus far of all the theoretical models of exchange rates that are amenable to straightforward empirical tests. Because of the widespread perception that exchange rates and the current account are important to the U.S. and world economies—and the proper objects of wise public policy—this poses a challenge to the formulation of such a policy.

This chapter discusses the connections among exchange rates, the current account of the balance of payments, and the formulation of monetary policy. It summarizes theoretical models and related evidence and concludes that in the current state of knowledge, monetary policy should be conducted on the basis of domestic objectives

I want to thank Hali Edison, Peter Garber, Herschel Grossman, Ben McCallum, Michael Melvin, Tom Sargent, Carl Walsh, Steve Weisbrod, and particularly Phil Cagan, William Haraf, and Tom Willett, for helpful comments on an earlier draft.

and that exchange rates and the current account should play little role in its formation.

The following section summarizes the major issues regarding the role of exchange rates and the current account in the formulation of monetary policy. The next sections discusses alternative models (simple monetary models, equilibrium models, and models with sluggish price adjustment) and describes the evidence regarding each. The chapter concludes with a discussion of monetary-policy formation under uncertainty.

The Issues to Be Addressed

There are six reasons why exchange rates and the current account might appropriately play important roles in the formation of monetary policy. First, the exchange rate or the current account might properly be a target of monetary policy because of their key roles in the determination of aggregate output and employment. (The nominal exchange rate might be a good proxy for the real exchange rate because real and nominal exchange rate changes are highly correlated.)

Second, the exchange rate might be an ultimate target of monetary policy because its stability per se is desirable, for the same reasons that stability of the general nominal price level is desirable (whatever those reasons are). According to this argument, the nominal exchange rate is itself a very important price and consequently should be an ultimate target of monetary policy (along with other nominal prices).

Third, the exchange rate and current account might be useful indicators of economic conditions that affect the appropriate monetary policy. The argument here is not that the exchange rate or current account is an ultimate target, but that they provide useful information to policy makers. A currency depreciation might, for example, indicate a fall in the demand for money or a change in the supply of inside money. It might increase the probability that higher inflation will follow and may warrant a monetary policy response. Alternatively, because real disturbances to aggregate supply or demand can change real and nominal exchange rates and the current account, these changes may provide policy makers with important information about those real supply and demand disturbances. Finally, if monetary policy affects real aggregate demand or supply, the response of exchange rates and the current account may provide indirect information about these effects and aid the formulation of future policy.

Fourth, fluctuations, unpredictability, or so-called misalignments in exchange rates might cause resource misallocations (including un-employment, lower economic growth, or protectionist pressures). Appropriate monetary policy might be able to reduce the size of these exchange-rate fluctuations, make them more predictable, or reduce the size of misalignments, thereby reducing the degree of resource misallocation. The appropriate monetary policy in this case might involve a formal rule such as pegged exchange rates or target zones for exchange rates or a formal rule for official operations in the foreign exchange market such as sterilized intervention.

Fifth, monetary policy that reduces fluctuations, unpredictability, or misalignments of the exchange rate might increase the prospects for international coordination of policies in ways that would facilitate the pursuit of some policy goal (such as unobstructed international trade, full employment, greater economic growth, or lower or more predictable inflation rates).

Sixth, rules such as pegged exchange rates or target zones for exchange rates might provide desirable and enforceable constraints on monetary policy. These constraints might reduce uncertainty and facilitate efficient resource allocation and the achievement of other policy goals.

This chapter discusses these suggestions for monetary policy in light of alternative theories and evidence on the behavior of exchange rates and the current account.

Models of Exchange Rates and the Current Account

This section begins with a discussion of the simple monetary model of exchange rates with flexible prices, turns to the equilibrium model of exchange rates and the current account, and then to sluggish-price (disequilibrium) models. I discuss the implications of each type of model for monetary policy and argue that, in the current state of knowledge, exchange rates and the current account should play little role in the formation of monetary policy.

The Simple Monetary Model. Many models of exchange rates are variations on the simple monetary model, with either flexible prices or sluggish nominal prices. The simple monetary model assumes pur-chasing power parity to express the exchange rate as a ratio of price levels in two countries; it then replaces the price levels with equi-librium solutions obtained from equating money supply and demand in each country. Because money demand is affected by expected inflation and because expected inflation is connected to expected currency depreciation through the purchasing power parity assumption, this substitution implies that the current exchange rate depends on the expected future exchange rate as well as current nominal money supplies and variables, such as real income, that affect money demands. The resulting stochastic difference equation can be solved forward to obtain a solution for the exchange rate in terms of current and expected future values of nominal money and variables such as real income. With the assumption of rational expectations, statistical predictions of these future values can be substituted for the expectations, and the result is a solution for the exchange rate in terms of currently observable variables. The model is reasonably simple to work with, and it has been applied to a variety of issues such as balance-of-payments crises and devaluations as well as exchange rate determination.[1]

The main problem with the flexible-price versions of the simple monetary model is their reliance on purchasing power parity. As a result, they are unable to explain either the observed high correlation between real and nominal exchange rates (in levels or rates of change)[2] or the high variability of nominal exchange rates relative to ratios of nominal price indexes.[3] The inability of the simple monetary model with flexible prices to explain these basic and important observations suggests that it is a poor model with which to formulate policy.[4]

Equilibrium Models. These problems vanish if multiple traded (and perhaps nontraded) goods are added to the basic flexible-price monetary model. This modification, with multiple goods and real disturbances to tastes or technologies, results in so-called equilibrium models of exchange rates and the current account. The equilibrium models are dynamic stochastic general equilibrium models usually based on individual optimization. One feature of these models that makes them attractive for policy analysis is that they can overcome Lucas's critique of econometric policy evaluation. Not all of the alternative models to be discussed in the next section share this feature. This is an important consideration in determining the fitness of various economic models for evaluating monetary policy. I now summarize the equilibrium approach.

Economic theory predicts that real disturbances to supplies of goods or demands for goods (because of changes in technology, tastes, or changes in other exogenous variables such as fiscal or trade policies) change equilibrium relative prices, including the real exchange rate. In a wide variety of circumstances, these changes in the real exchange rate are accomplished at least in part through changes in the nominal exchange rate. The real disturbances also change real quantities such as production, consumption, investment, saving, and the current account.[5] Repeated real disturbances create a correlation between changes in real and nominal exchange rates. This correlation is consistent with flexible-price equilibrium in the economy, in the sense that markets clear through adjustments in price as well as in quantity. This is the basis for the equilibrium approach to exchange rate changes.[6]

To illustrate the effects of real disturbances on the exchange rate, consider a simple example. Two countries with a flexible exchange rate, the home and foreign countries, produce wheat and rice. The government of the home country operates its monetary policy to hold constant a price index that includes the nominal prices of both goods. The foreign government does the same thing with a foreign price index that differs from the home country's price index because foreigners consume more rice and less wheat.

Suppose now that the *supply of wheat increases,* so wheat's relative price falls. Because nominal price indexes are held fixed by monetary policies in each country, the exchange rate must change to depreciate the home country's money. (In an extreme case, the home country's price index includes only wheat and not rice, and the foreign country's index includes only rice and not wheat. Then the home nominal price of wheat and the foreign nominal price of rice would be unaffected. The entire change in the relative price would occur through a change in the exchange rate.) As another example, suppose a taste change reduces the demand for wheat and raises the demand for rice. The relative price of wheat must fall as before, and this must occur through a depreciation of the home country's currency.

The main points are that real disturbances can change the exchange rate, induce comovements in real and nominal exchange rates, and cause changes in exchange rates that are large relative to changes in nominal price indexes. These conclusions generalize easily to richer and more complex models (and do not require monetary policies resembling those in this simple example). The equilibrium model of exchange rates can explain, in principle, a number of observed features of exchange rate behavior. These features include a high correlation between real and nominal exchange rates and high variability of nominal exchange rates relative to nominal price levels.[7]

The equilibrium approach also has implications for the current account of the balance of payments. The current account reflects intertemporal trade. It therefore reflects the results of disturbances that affect savings or investment, that is, many of the same real disturbances that change exchange rates. These disturbances include current and expected future changes in productivity, investment opportunities, factors affecting consumption (such as wealth and interest rates), government purchases, and tax rates. Large swings in the current account and the exchange rate can occur in competitive equilibrium without any distortions or externalities that might warrant corrective government policies. These swings may be required for an optimal response of the economy to exogenous disturbances, including changes in government policies. Whether the observed behavior of the current account and exchange rate in fact represents optimal responses to these changes is, of course, another question. And, if not, whether monetary policy can be helpful, and in what way, is still another question. But the observation, by itself, of large swings in the current account and exchange rate does not imply the existence of distortions that might be rectified by government policies.

Most of the existing equilibrium models involve Pareto-optimal equilibria. As a result, there is little role for government policy in the models. That is not a necessary characteristic of those models: the equilibrium in Stockman (1980), for example, is not Pareto-efficient because asset markets are incomplete.[8] Activist government policies could in principle be designed to improve welfare in that economy. The typical absence of distortions in the equilibrium models is not meant to imply that there are no market failures or roles for government policies, including monetary policies, in the real world. Market failures clearly exist, and some of them may in fact warrant a number of activist policies. The remarkable result of the existing equilibrium models, however, is that no such market failures must be introduced into the models in order to account for key qualitative features of the behavior of exchange rates and the current account. Moreover, as I argue, certain evidence suggests that these models account for the behavior of exchange rates better than alternative models that explicitly involve distortions.

The equilibrium model without market failures has several important implications. First, the correlation between nominal and real exchange rates is not exploitable by monetary policy; attempts to affect the real exchange rate by directly changing the nominal exchange rate, whether through foreign exchange market intervention, managed floating, pegging the exchange rate, or devaluation under a system of pegged rates, will fail. The correlation is a result of real disturbances to the economy. Purely nominal disturbances would, without market failures, have purely nominal effects. Only when a nominal policy such as managed floating or devaluation is accompanied by other, real, policy changes (such as changes in capital controls) will the real exchange rate move with the nominal exchange rate. Of course, purely nominal changes could affect real output and other real variables if there were some market failure such as price sluggishness, and may do so in the real world. Equilibrium models of exchange rates are good models to the extent that these real effects of money do not explain a large fraction of exchange rate variations, and to the extent that the real disturbances emphasized by these models do.

Second, there is no simple relation between the exchange rate and the balance of trade or the current account of the balance of payments. Trade deficits do not "cause" currency depreciation, nor does currency depreciation help reduce a trade deficit. The direction of comovement of the exchange rate, the current account, and other variables depends on the source of the disturbance. A temporary increase in the demand for domestic goods, for example, accompanied by a fall in the demand for foreign goods and all goods in the future (a fall in savings) causes currency *appreciation* associated with a current account deficit. On the other hand, a temporary increase in the demand for foreign goods accompanied by a fall in the demand for domestic goods and all future goods (also a fall in savings) causes currency *depreciation* along with a current account deficit.

It is frequently claimed that the elimination of a current account deficit requires a currency depreciation. This claim is incorrect, according to the equilibrium models. Whether eliminating a current account deficit requires currency depreciation or appreciation depends on the source of disturbance that caused the deficit. Suppose that the domestic savings rate is temporarily low, perhaps because of demographic factors. This will cause a current account deficit. Suppose also that the higher domestic expenditure falls primarily on U.S. goods, leading to dollar appreciation. Then when the savings rate later returns to its original level, the fall in spending would indeed be accompanied by domestic currency depreciation. On the other hand, suppose that the current account deficit were the result of a temporary increase in the demand for foreign goods, accompanied by a fall in the demand for domestic goods and all future goods. Then the eventual elimination of the deficit would be accompanied by currency appreciation.

Suppose, for example, that the demand for U.S. goods initially rises, accompanied by a reduction in the demand for foreign goods and a reduction in savings. This would cause a U.S. current account deficit and dollar appreciation. Suppose that, subsequently, demand shifts from U.S. goods to foreign goods. Then the dollar will depreciate without eliminating the current account deficit. Suppose, finally, that domestic savings rises again to eliminate the current account deficit. Then the exchange rate could either rise or fall. The domestic currency would depreciate if the greater spending falls mainly on domestic goods, but it could appreciate if the rise in spending is accompanied by a reversal of the previous demand shift from U.S. goods to foreign goods. The usual claim that a current account deficit must necessarily be followed by depreciation results from the implicit assumptions that changes in overall spending are biased toward home goods—which is true on average though not necessarily in all cases— and that these changes in overall spending are not accompanied by relative shifts in demand for home goods versus foreign goods that would offset this average tendency. As noted, these implicit assumptions rule out certain possible exogenous disturbances a priori, such as a temporary increase in the demand for foreign goods accompanied by a fall in savings.

Third, government spending affects real and nominal exchange rates through its effects on relative demands and supplies of goods. Changes in government spending, financed by lump-sum taxes, change the real exchange rate to the extent that marginal spending propensities (on home and foreign goods) of the government and private sector differ.

Similarly, changes in tax rates change relative demands and supplies of goods. A reduction in the tax rate on investment, for example, raises the demand for investment goods, and this may fall disproportionately on domestic rather than foreign goods. Changes in tax revenue must be accompanied either by changes in government spending currently or in the future, or by offsetting future changes in taxes. Consequently, the effects of a tax change depend on what other changes accompany it. In addition, the effects of tax changes depend on both the wealth effects of changes in average tax rates and the substitution effects of changes in marginal tax rates. Under the conditions for Ricardian equivalence, a fall in the average tax rate today accompanied by an offsetting rise in the future average tax rate has no effect on resource allocation or prices.[9] A reduction in the marginal tax rate today, however, even if the average tax rate is unaffected, affects resource allocation. A reduction in the average tax rate accompanied by a reduction in the present value of government spending affects resource allocation and prices regardless of whether Ricardian equivalence characterizes the economy.

Consider a reduction in the average tax rate accompanied by either a reduction in the present value of government spending or higher future taxes in the absence of Ricardian equivalence. Suppose that consumers in each country have a higher income elasticity of demand for their own country's goods than for those of the other country. Finally, suppose that (if government spending changes) consumers in each country have a higher income elasticity for their own country's goods than does their government. Then a tax cut in the United States raises the demand for U.S. goods relative to foreign goods. This causes dollar appreciation to raise the relative price of U.S. goods.

Similarly, a reduction in the marginal tax rate on investment (given the average tax rate) raises investment. Suppose that changes in investment expenditure in each country fall relatively more on that country's goods than on those of the other country. Then a reduction in the marginal tax rate on investment in the United States raises the demand for investment goods, and particularly that for U.S. goods. This causes dollar appreciation and raises the relative price of U.S. goods.

Fourth, government budget deficits (given the present value of government spending) can affect the current account and real and nominal exchange rates if Ricardian equivalence does not characterize the economy.[10] The reduction in savings associated with the tax cut shows up as a current account deficit. A budget deficit does not necessarily cause currency appreciation even if it causes a current account deficit. The domestic currency appreciates if the increased spending by domestic households falls, at the margin, mostly on domestic goods. In the opposite case it depreciates.[11]

Fifth, the dynamics of real and nominal exchange rates are related and can take a variety of forms.[12] The real and nominal exchange rates will be highly autocorrelated—and look very much like random walks—if the underlying disturbances tend to be permanent in nature. Observed real exchange rates have this characteristic, as discussed later. Edward Prescott and others who have studied the productivity shocks required to replicate features of the real world in real business cycle models have typically found that underlying productivity shocks are highly persistent and closely approximated by random walks.[13] So the assumption of permanent, or highly persistent, exogenous disturbances may not be a bad one.

Sixth, arbitrage ensures that the expected percentage of change in the real exchange rate between two countries is equal to the difference between expected real interest rates in those countries. Expected real interest rates may differ even if nominal interest rates are related to each other by interest rate parity (another arbitrage condition), because price deflators differ across countries. In other words, the word *real* refers to a different bundle of "goods" in each country. Any difference between the expected "own returns" on these two bundles of goods is reflected in an expected change in their relative price, that is, the real exchange rate. If disturbances affecting the real exchange rate have large transitory components, then a large fraction of changes in the real exchange rate would be associated with these differentials in real interest rates. If the disturbances are mainly permanent, then only a small fraction of changes in real exchange rates would be associated with international differentials in real interest rates.

The evidence on equilibrium exchange rate models suggests that they should be taken seriously even though there are gaps in the evidence at present, associated primarily with the absence of a fully convincing identification of the fundamental exogenous disturbances. The models can nevertheless account for a number of important features of the data, such as the high correlation between real and nominal exchange rates and the greater variability in exchange rates than in purchasing power parity price ratios.

A satisfactory model should also be able to explain certain other features of exchange rate data. Expected changes in exchange rates in the real world tend to be small relative to unexpected changes. Changes in real exchange rates tend to be nearly permanent (on average) or to persist for a very long time. This is consistent with the view that most changes in real exchange rates are the result of real shocks with a large permanent component. Because changes in real and nominal exchange rates are very highly correlated and have similar variances, it is also consistent with the view that most changes in nominal exchange rates are the result of largely permanent real disturbances. These features of actual exchange rate behavior place restrictions on the nature of disturbances in equilibrium models.

The question of whether most changes in exchange rates are due to changes in long-run equilibrium real exchange rates, as the equilibrium models with permanent disturbances imply, or to short-run expected real interest differentials, as the equilibrium model with transitory disturbances (and some other models discussed later) imply, has been addressed econometrically by John Campbell and Richard Clarida.[14] Their results are summarized in table 3–1. They found that most of the variation in the U.S. exchange rates with Canada, the United Kingdom, Germany, and Japan is the result of changes in the long-run equilibrium real exchange rate. The first column of the table shows the fraction of real exchange rate innovations attributable to expected real interest rate differentials. The second column shows the fraction attributable to changes in the long-run equilibrium real exchange rate. The third column shows the fraction that could be attributed to either of the first two columns, because of their covariance. Even if the explanatory power of the covariance is apportioned so as to maximize the fraction of innovations in the real exchange rate attributable to expected differentials in real interest rates, the table shows that those numbers range from 2 percent to 27 percent, except for the trade-weighted dollar, where that fraction for the second model reaches 42 percent.[15] The fraction attributable to changes in the long-run equilibrium real exchange rate is, on the other hand, *at least* 73 percent to 98 percent, except in the last row where it may be as low as 58 percent.

The issue of permanent and transitory components in real-exchange rate changes has also been investigated by Huizinga[16] and

TABLE 3–1

FRACTION OF VARIANCE OF REAL EXCHANGE RATE CHANGES, 1979:10–1986:3

Exchange Rate[a]	Changes in Ex-ante Real Interest Differential (percent)	Changes in Long-run Equilibrium Exchange Rate (percent)	Their Covariance (percent)	C^{*b}
U.S.–Canada				
Model 1	9	85	6	.95
Model 2	16	75	9	.92
U.S.–UK				
Model 1	8	79	13	.96
Model 2	21	198	−119	.98
U.S.–West Germany				
Model 1	4	98	−2	.98
Model 2	27	126	−52	.89
U.S.–Japan				
Model 1	4	81	15	.98
Model 2	2	91	7	.99
U.S. trade-weighted dollar				
Model 1	6	84	10	.97
Model 2	42	188	−130	.90

a. Campbell and Clarida used two different models of the risk premium on foreign exchange.
b. C^{*} is the estimated correlation between innovations in the actual real exchange rate and the long-run equilibrium real exchange rate.
SOURCE: John Y. Campbell and Richard H. Clarida, "The Dollar and Real Interest Rates," in K. Brunner and A. H. Meltzer, eds., *Empirical Studies of Velocity, Real Exchange Rates, Unemployment, and Productivity,* Carnegie-Rochester Conference Series, vol. 27 (1987), pp. 149–215.

by Kaminsky.[17] Both studies found that real exchange rates are non-stationary with both permanent and transitory components. Huizinga found that the variance of the permanent component accounts for about one-half to three-fourths (the average estimate was .58) of the variance of changes in the real exchange rate for the U.S. dollar over the period since 1973, assuming that covariances are taken from as far back as eleven years.[18] Monte Carlo evidence by Galan[19] and by Kaminsky suggests that the kind of procedure Huizinga used results in systematic understatement of these numbers in small samples, so there is reason to believe that the number 58 percent substantially understates the true fraction of the variance of changes in real exchange rates accounted for by the permanent component.[20] For bilateral British pound exchange rates against other currencies, Huizinga's results are similar to those for the United States, but for bilateral Japanese yen exchange rates the permanent component explains 100 percent of the variance of changes in the real exchange rate (except against the U.S. dollar, in which case 77 percent is explained by the permanent component).

Kaminsky obtained similar results for other currency pairs. In addition, she found that real U.S. exchange rates with Germany, Britain, and Japan, and with the non-U.S. cross-rates, are cointegrated with a set of possible market fundamentals, including real outputs, accumulated trade balance surpluses as a fraction of output, accumulated government budget deficits as a fraction of output, the price of oil, and Britain's oil output. One implication that Kaminsky draws from her econometric study is that the disturbances affecting exchange rates have been predominately real rather than monetary.[21] A second implication of this evidence is that it is inconsistent with the view that exchange rate changes result from a class of so-called rational bubbles.[22]

The finding that most of the variation in real exchange rates can be attributed to a permanent, long-run equilibrium component should not be taken to imply that transitory disturbances are unimportant. As noted earlier, current account deficits and surpluses reflect intertemporal trade. The existence of large current account deficits is itself prima facie evidence that there are either important transitory disturbances or permanent disturbances that are partly anticipated. In either case, one can expect that these would be associated with some transitory components in real exchange rates.[23] Whether or not these transitory components represent efficient equilibrium dynamics is more difficult to ascertain.

The equilibrium models have, as noted earlier, implications regarding the effects of fiscal policies. The models imply that changes in tax rates affect exchange rates through their effects on demands for goods (and supplies of goods). One possible explanation for the appreciation of the U.S. dollar from 1980 to 1985 is the reduction in tax rates in 1981 (which was partially anticipated with the 1980 election results). The increase in corporate investment taxes with the 1986 tax legislation (which was partially anticipated from the end of 1984) may play a major role in the explanation of the depreciation of the U.S. dollar since 1985.

Longer-term evidence supports this suggestion. Vittorio Grilli examined the exchange rate between the U.S. dollar and the British pound from 1870 to 1984.[24] He found that a reduction in U.S. taxes relative to gross national product leads to dollar appreciation over this period and that a reduction in British taxes relative to gross national product leads to dollar depreciation. In contrast, the ratio of the budget deficit to gross national product had no effect on the exchange rate.[25]

A more commonly asserted reason for dollar appreciation from 1980 to 1985 was the U.S. government budget deficit per se.[26] By now, that explanation seems strained because of the fall in the value of the dollar from 1985 to 1988 in the face of very little change in the current or prospective budget deficit situation. There is also some other evidence against this hypothesis. First, there is the (mixed) evidence supporting the Ricardian equivalence hypothesis.[27] Second, there is little evidence that budget deficits are connected with changes in exchange rates.[28] Those empirical studies that find effects of budget deficits on exchange rates typically fail to distinguish between the effects of deficits and the effects of current and expected future government spending. (One must hold fixed both current and expected future spending to have a Ricardian experiment.) In fact, there is some evidence that changes in real government spending affect the real and nominal exchange rates.[29] Third, as Campbell and Clarida point out, most models imply that the effects of a temporary government budget deficit on today's real exchange rate and on the long-run equilibrium real exchange rate are in opposite directions.[30] The budget deficit raises the domestic interest rate and induces currency appreciation today. But the long-run effect of the deficit is to reduce domestic wealth and therefore to cause long-run depreciation. This occurs because the long-run stock of accumulated foreign debt must be serviced through a trade surplus, which requires a lower price (real depreciation) to achieve, because the fall in long-run domestic wealth reduces domestic expenditure, and this reduction falls disproportionately on domestic goods. So if temporary government budget deficits were responsible for the dollar's appreciation in the 1980s, the correlation between innovations in the real exchange rate and the long-run equilibrium rate should be negative. This correlation is reported as C^* in table 3–1. It is not negative; instead, it is strongly positive for all of the exchange rates examined. This evidence casts doubt on the hypothesis that government budget deficits play a major role in explaining changes in real exchange rates.[31]

The main implication of the equilibrium models for monetary policy is that, if those models are good approximations of the actual economy, we have little basis for conducting monetary policy in ways that depend heavily on exchange rates or the current account. While changes in exchange rates and the current account may be related to changes in aggregate output, no correlation among them is exploitable by monetary policy. While the exchange rate and current account could in principle provide information to policy makers about disturbances to tastes or technology that might bear on the optimal monetary policy actions, in the present state of knowledge little information can actually be obtained from these changes.

This leaves two other possible roles for monetary policy in the equilibrium models. First, the exchange rate might be an ultimate target of monetary policy because stability in the exchange rate might be desirable per se. The usual reasons for concern about nominal prices, however, do not justify concern over the prices of particular items but, rather, over stability of nominal prices in general. Although the exchange rate (multiplied by foreign nominal prices) is one component of this general price level, the proper focus would be on the general price level itself. Moreover, if the underlying disturbances to the economy are real, then stability in the nominal exchange rate may be inconsistent with stability in the overall level of prices. If stability of the latter is the goal, then optimal policy involves allowing the exchange rate to adjust endogenously.

Second, rules such as pegged exchange rates or target zones might provide useful constraints on monetary policy. There may indeed be important reasons to constrain monetary policy makers. It is not clear, however, that a particular system of exchange rates is a better method of constraint than many alternatives, such as a constitutional rule on money growth rates or a rule specifying a target value for a more general index of prices. In the presence of large real shocks (which, I have argued, characterize the data), a rule of this form could constrain monetary policy makers to choose (implicitly) inflation rates that are nonzero on average and highly variable. Surely there are better ways to constrain policy makers.

Models with Sluggish Nominal Price Adjustment. An alternative model of exchange rates, the so-called disequilibrium model, results from the assumption of sluggish nominal price adjustment. The problems with the simple monetary model of exchange rates can be "solved" by assuming nominal price sluggishness, though new problems replace the old. With sluggish nominal prices in the model, even purely nominal disturbances can change the real exchange rate because the nominal exchange rate changes rapidly while price levels do not. The model predicts that real and nominal exchange rates are highly correlated and that nominal exchange rates vary more than do nominal price levels. The model can result in "overshooting" of the exchange rate, as in Dornbusch's study, in which the short-term response of the exchange rate to an exogenous disturbance exceeds its long-term response.[32] Whether the particular version of the disequilibrium model results in overshooting, these models generally imply that the nominal and the real exchange rates exhibit predictable (intrinsic) short-term variations. The change in the real exchange rate will have a large predictable component associated with price adjustment. If the exogenous shocks are monetary rather than real, then this predictable component will be temporary. The short-term response of the real exchange rate will be reversed in the longer run and possibly eliminated as nominal price levels adjust to their equilibrium levels.

The sluggish-price version of the monetary model has other implications for the real exchange rate. First, the anticipated percentage change in the real exchange rate equals the ex ante differential in real interest rates as in the equilibrium models. As noted earlier, however, most of the changes in real exchange rates seem to be associated with changes in the long-run equilibrium rate rather than with short-term expected differentials in real interest rates.[33] This casts doubt on the empirical importance of the predictable component of real exchange rates associated with sluggish nominal price adjustments.[34]

Huizinga found that differences between the real exchange rate and its implied long-run equilibrium level are autocorrelated.[35] He examined the dollar-pound exchange rate and found that it undershoots rather than overshoots—in other words, that changes in the long-run equilibrium real exchange rate are accompanied on average by smaller changes (in the same direction) in the actual rate. Huizinga then imposed overshooting on the data. Even after doing this, he found substantial depreciation of the long-run real exchange rate of the dollar before 1980, substantial appreciation of the long-run real exchange rate from 1980 to 1985, and substantial depreciation after that. His estimates are consistent with the notion that most of the

dollar's appreciation from 1980 to 1985 and its subsequent depreciation reflect changes in the long-run component. In fact, before imposing parameter values to force overshooting on the data, he found that
the long-run exchange rate actually appreciated more from 1980 to
1985 than did the actual exchange rate.

Second, disequilibrium models suggest that changes in the exchange rate should be useful predictors of future changes in the
nominal price level, because the former adjusts rapidly to disturbances while the latter adjusts with a lag. Changes in the money
supply should also help explain changes in real exchange rates.
Nevertheless, neither of these implications is borne out strongly by
the data.[36]

Third, according to these models, differences between the real
exchange rate and its implied long-run equilibrium level should be
eliminated slowly as the nominal price level adjusts toward its new
equilibrium after a disturbance. Huizinga's estimates (when overshooting is imposed on the data) show, however, that differences
between the actual and long-run real exchange rates are eliminated
suddenly rather than gradually. As he points out in his study, this is
"inconsistent with the view of real exchange-rate overshooting that
comes from the 'sticky-price' models of exchange rate determination."

Fourth, disequilibrium models suggest that the real exchange rate
should vary more under a system of floating nominal exchange rates
than under a system of fixed nominal exchange rates, because the
short-term variations in the real exchange rate, due to changes in the
nominal exchange rate, would vanish. This particular prediction is
clearly borne out by the data. In "Real Exchange Rate Variability under
Pegged and Floating Nominal Exchange Rate Systems: An Equilibrium Theory" (in Karl Brunner and A. H. Meltzer, editors, Carnegie-Rochester Conference Series [Amsterdam: North-Holland,
forthcoming]) I present an equilibrium model of exchange rates that
also has this feature. The troublesome aspect of the evidence that real
exchange rates vary more under floating than under pegged exchange
rate systems is that equilibrium and disequilibrium models both predict that other macroeconomic and international-trade aggregates
should be affected by the exchange rate system.[37] There is little or no
evidence, however, to support this.[38]

If the disequilibrium exchange-rate model is appended to a standard macroeconomic model in which sluggish adjustment of nominal
prices leads to real-output effects of monetary policy, then it has
further implications. Disturbances to the money supply or money
demand should lead to temporary real and nominal depreciation
associated with temporary increases in real output above trend.

Fifth, the real and nominal value of the currency should show countercyclical responses from monetary disturbances. There is little statistical evidence of this, although it could reflect the preponderance of real disturbances. (The U.S. dollar, for example, appreciated rapidly in real terms during the recovery from the 1982 recession until 1985.)

The model also predicts that, in response to monetary shocks, the half-life of the temporary changes in real exchange rates and in output relative to trend should be similar, because both result from the same sluggish nominal-price behavior. The apparent permanent component in real exchange rates could be a highly persistent temporary component, but its half-life would be much too long relative to deviations of real output from trend. The statistical evidence that most of the variation in real exchange rates is explained by this permanent component is inconsistent with the disequilibrium view that nominal shocks, or even temporary real shocks, cause most of the important changes in exchange rates. The evidence instead supports the view that most changes in real exchange rates are the result of real shocks with a large permanent component. Models with sluggish nominal price adjustment necessarily imply some intrinsic dynamics for real exchange rates as prices adjust toward equilibrium. The transitory component in real exchange rates may be a result of sluggish price adjustment following real disturbances.[39]

Some versions of the disequilibrium model also imply that currency depreciations should be accompanied by current account deficits, and appreciations by current account surpluses. This occurs in part because current account deficits are viewed as reducing domestic (and raising foreign) wealth, which reduces the demand for domestic money and leads to nominal and real depreciation. It also occurs in part because the reallocation of wealth reduces the demand for domestic goods and raises the demand for foreign goods; this raises the relative price of foreign goods, which entails nominal and real depreciation. There is little evidence, however, that currency depreciations are accompanied by current account deficits, and vice versa, as these models predict. Nor is there much evidence that changes in the money supply are associated with the current account.

Some versions of the disequilibrium model invoke the assumption of irrational expectations. Jeffrey Frankel and Kenneth Froot, for example, present a model that explains the behavior of the dollar in the 1980s in this way.[40] Survey evidence of dealers in foreign exchange markets, and subsequent exchange rate behavior, supports their claim that expectations were biased. The Frankel-Froot model is subject to many of the same criticisms made here of other disequilibrium models. The survey evidence is disconcerting, but it does not accord with evidence about expected exchange rates from the forward market. This raises the question of why these dealers, if they accurately reported their beliefs, did not take larger positions in the forward market and cause a change in the forward rate. The forward exchange rate is itself not an unbiased predictor of future spot exchange rates. The forward rate contains a risk premium. Given rational expectations, this risk premium must be large and variable. As with the so-called equity premium on stocks relative to bonds, the risk premium on forward foreign exchange is larger than can be rationalized with commonly assumed degrees of risk aversion and existing equilibrium models. The presence of a similar problem with equities, however, suggests a common explanation. Econometric estimates of the variability of the risk premium are also subject to the problem that the statistical behavior of exchange rates is extremely complex. Some progress has been made recently with nonparametric methods.[41]

Fiscal deficits affect the real exchange rate through two new channels in the disequilibrium model. Typically, the models assume that the conditions for Ricardian equivalence are violated in the usual direction (that is, a cut in current taxes and offsetting rise in future taxes raises perceived current wealth). The models also assume that households in each country have a greater income elasticity of demand for their own country's goods than for the other country's goods. Then an increase in the deficit resulting from a tax cut (with no change in the path of government spending) tends to induce currency appreciation as in the equilibrium model. The two new effects on the real exchange rate in the disequilibrium model work in opposite directions. First, a government budget deficit raises perceived wealth and therefore raises the demand for money, which leads to nominal and real (because of sluggish nominal prices) currency appreciation. Second, a government budget deficit raises the real interest rate, and therefore the nominal interest rate, and so reduces the demand for money; this causes nominal and real depreciation. These two forces affect the nominal exchange rate in the equilibrium model. In the disequilibrium models they also affect the real exchange rate. Devaluation, domestic credit expansion under pegged exchange rates, and official operations in the foreign exchange market under flexible rates all have real effects in the disequilibrium model through these channels. Each affects real wealth by changing the stock of official reserves held by the government, which is not included in private wealth when Ricardian equivalence does not hold.

The disequilibrium model of exchange rate changes implicitly underlies many media reports and policy discussions. It implies that the correlation between real and nominal exchange rate changes is exploitable by monetary policy. In contrast, the equilibrium models imply that exchange rate changes are not "causes" of changes in relative prices, but part of the process through which the changes occur in equilibrium. The disequilibrium model implies that currencies may become overvalued or undervalued relative to their equilibrium levels, that these are associated with changes in international "competitiveness" that are not justified by real comparative advantage, and that they cause welfare losses. The equilibrium model, in contrast, implies that it is incorrect to blame decreased competitiveness on the exchange rate or to expect an alternative exchange rate system, by itself, to affect competitiveness.[42] The equilibrium model implies that the question of whether a change in the exchange rate— or more general exchange rate volatility—is "good" or "bad" for the economy is not correctly posed, because the exchange rate is an endogenous variable. The right question, according to that model, is whether the underlying disturbances to the economy are "good" or "bad," so (of course) the answer varies with the disturbance.

The implications of the disequilibrium model for monetary policy involve several trade-offs. Each trade-off involves parameters that would be difficult to estimate in the current state of knowledge. The model suggests that it is feasible and desirable for monetary policy to take as one of its goals the exchange rate and the current account, on the grounds that monetary policy can affect real output and employment (as well as its distribution across sectors) through its influence on these variables. Monetary expansion, by causing real depreciation, raises international competitiveness and (consequently) output and employment in the export sector, though it may reduce output in sectors using imported inputs. The disequilibrium model also implies that it is feasible and desirable for monetary policy to help prevent large fluctuations, unpredictability, or misalignments in the level of the exchange rate in order to prevent resource misallocations. Monetary policy, however, can create as well as alleviate resource misallocations in the disequilibrium model. This makes the policy problem difficult. Maurice Obstfeld, for example, argues that "only when it is known that a particular goods-market shock will be reversed within several years is there a case for resisting its real exchange rate effect through monetary policy so that excessive relocation costs are avoided," through various government policies.[43] Even then, he notes, attempts to prevent misalignments through monetary policy alone may "encounter serious pitfalls." The disequilibrium model also implies that the exchange rate and the current account contain information about the sources of other exogenous disturbances to the economy that might impinge on monetary policy. Acquiring this information, however, is not easy.

The model does not have unambiguous implications about the optimal exchange rate system, except in special cases. Arguments can be made with this model for pegged exchange rates or target zones. The slope of the short-run Phillips curve may be steeper under floating exchange rates rather than under fixed,[44] so if monetary policy is used to try to stabilize output, a case can be made for pegged exchange rates. Pegged rates would also entail less real exchange rate variability or misalignment resulting from monetary disturbances and would eliminate undesirable current account behavior resulting from inappropriate exchange rates.[45] On the other hand, pegged exchange rates would entail periodic finite adjustment unless other policies were changed. These adjustments might create uncertainty about the credibility of the pegged rates, leading to speculative attacks, interest rate variability, and the possible imposition of controls, restrictions, and taxes on international trade and payments. Arguments based on the variability or misalignments of exchange rates are not necessarily arguments for pegged exchange rates but rather for appropriate monetary (and other) policies that can be followed under a system of flexible rates. Finally, if the economy is subject to real disturbances that require changes in the equilibrium real exchange rate, then a system of floating exchange rates could be better than a system of pegged rates because (with sluggish nominal price adjustment) floating permits relative prices such as the real exchange rate to adjust more quickly to the equilibrium level. That is, flexibility of exchange rates can substitute for flexibility of nominal prices of goods.

Whether these policy arguments should be taken seriously depends largely on whether the model on which they are based is to be taken seriously for purposes of evaluating alternative policies. Also relevant is the robustness of the policy arguments to alternative assumptions and models. Here arises an objection to disequilibrium models. They are not "structural" in Lucas's sense, and so they cannot be relied on for evaluations of alternative policies.[46] One part of the problem is the treatment of market failures. Rather than modeling market failures (such as price sluggishness) from microeconomic foundations, disequilibrium models postulate market failures at a macroeconomic level. By now there are many examples showing that this methodology leads to incorrect inferences. The models do not adequately explain the reasons for nominal price sluggishness or why that sluggishness—if it exists—affects real resource allocation.[47]

In the face of this evidence, it is difficult to take disequilibrium models seriously as a basis for policy formulation.[48] Nevertheless, policy makers should not entirely dismiss the implications of these models until the alternatives are better developed and empirically checked.[49] But policies should be based on this class of models only if they are robust to those alternative models that are more consistent with the data.[50]

Conclusions for Monetary Policy Formation

Monetary policy must be formulated in a situation of uncertainty about which of the models discussed above gives a better approximation of the world for this purpose. I have argued that the equilibrium model is the best model for this purpose, but, as Mencken said, foreign exchange is resistant to formulae. Formally, one could set up a decision problem for monetary policy makers, assign probabilities to each of the competing theories (as well as their intersections), and derive the policy that would maximize expected utility. I do not attempt that formal exercise here. Instead, I argue that if one places some positive probability on both the equilibrium model and the model with sluggish nominal prices, while also taking into account the existing evidence, then one will find that a reasonable monetary policy places little weight on exchange rates and the current account, and most weight on domestic inflation or output stabilization and growth.

If the equilibrium model were true, then there would be nothing to be gained from a monetary policy geared to exchange rates or the current account, and the losses would all occur in the resulting behavior of inflation. If the model with sluggish nominal-price adjustment were true, then gains *could* result from monetary policies directed at changing the exchange rate and the current account. If we could be sure that one model or the other is a good description of the world, then the relevant trade-offs would involve inflation against the potential gains from monetary policy through reductions in resource misallocations resulting from real exchange rate misalignments and variability or from inappropriate levels of the current account.

Unfortunately, all of the important effects of monetary policy are unlikely to be captured adequately and accurately by either of these models alone, or even in combination. If monetary policy can affect the real exchange rate, but most changes in real exchange rates are the result of real disturbances altering the long-run equilibrium level, then monetary policy aimed at offsetting any particular change in the real exchange rate, or attempting to change its level, is at least as likely to be harmful as beneficial. If policy makers had detailed and accurate knowledge of the market failures in the economy as well as all of the parameters and relevant disturbances in a timely fashion, then they could calculate the value of the real exchange rate that would maximize some social welfare function. If the market failures had certain characteristics (such as involvement of nominal variables in some fundamental way), then perhaps policy makers could use monetary policy to move toward the level of the real exchange rate that maximizes welfare. But without all this information in the minds of policy makers, attempts to improve welfare by conducting monetary policy to manipulate the real exchange rate or current account are likely to *reduce* welfare.

This does not suggest that all attempts at activist monetary policy would be likely to reduce welfare. In particular, the argument of this chapter is not that scientific uncertainty always translates into no recommendation for policy makers. Countercyclical rules such as those proposed by McCallum may increase welfare on average, even though a similar argument applies to these rules.[51] But if monetary policy affects real output, then (for example) monetary expansion following a decline in the growth rate of total output is likely to reduce rather than raise welfare if that decline in output growth was an optimal market response to external disturbances (as, say, in real business cycle models). The difference between the two cases is that it may be much easier to isolate changes in aggregate output that are inefficient responses to external circumstances than it is to isolate inefficient responses of the current account and exchange rates and then to identify accurately the effects of these inefficient responses on output. If output is a major concern for monetary policy, it is more efficient to concentrate policy directly on it than to go through the slippery, roundabout channels related to exchange rates and the current account.[52]

Zen and the Art of
Modern Macroeconomics

A Commentary by Jeffrey A. Frankel

Alan Stockman addresses one of the most difficult and interesting questions that international economists have to consider: what to say of use to monetary policy makers rather than to fellow economists only. He first evaluates two competing theories, namely, the equilibrium model—short for "dynamic stochastic general equilibrium models based on individual optimization"—and the sluggish-price or disequilibrium models.

Stockman's discussion sounds reasonable enough. It admits to some "gaps in the evidence" for the equilibrium models. It does not insist that the transitory component to the real exchange rate is zero, only that it is much smaller than the permanent component. Stockman is even willing to put some probability on the possibility that he is wrong and that the sluggish-price model is right. Furthermore, the main conclusion is one with which I agree, for reasons to be discussed at the end of my comments: "A reasonable monetary policy places little weight on exchange rates and the current account and most weight on domestic inflation or output stabilization and growth."

All this is reasonable and modest. But it can also be a bit misleading. Stockman does not bang on the table and say, "I know the right answer." He does the opposite. His answer to the question "What does the theory have to say about what policy makers should do?" is, in essence, "Nothing." The misleading part lies in the danger that the answer, "I have nothing to recommend to policy makers" becomes "I recommend that policy makers do nothing." The word "nothing" will play a key role in my comments. The word does not often appear explicitly in the writings of equilibrium theorists. The popular phrase in the econometric writings is "random walk." (The usual conclusion is stated as "I have found that such and such a variable follows a random walk" or, at best, "I cannot reject the hypothesis that this variable follows a random walk." You seldom hear someone say,

"After studying this variable for six months, I have absolutely nothing to say that would help to predict its movements." But the statements mean the same thing.) In Stockman's discussion, the telling phrase is "in the current state of knowledge," as in "In the current state of knowledge . . . exchange rates and the current account should play little role [in the conduct of monetary policy]."

I should make clear that my remarks do apply not just to Stockman but equally to other "equilibrium" writings, and indeed to much of modern macroeconomics. I shall refer to the disease as the "Zen" of modern macroeconometrics, that is, the search for perfect nothingness.[1] Let me explain.

The goal in econometric work was once to get results that were statistically significant, to reject the null hypothesis. In order to stand in front of a conference proudly or to expect to publish a paper in a journal, the author first sought significant results.[2] Significant results are difficult to obtain in macroeconomics. The world is a complicated place; it is unlikely that the few key variables that emerge from the particular theory that one has developed will actually go far toward explaining a real-world time series. So what we have done—quite cleverly—is to redefine the rules. Now the goal is to fail to reject the null hypothesis—that is, we now try to get results that are statistically insignificant, or, in essence, to find *nothing*. It is far easier to find nothing than to find something. Typically one fails to reject many hypotheses every day, even in the shower or on the way to work.

Examples abound of the goal of finding nothing, from tests of Euler conditions to Ricardian equivalence.[3] But I shall pick an example that is central to Stockman's evaluation of the two competing theories of exchange rates: the question of whether the real exchange rate follows a random walk.[4]

Not long ago, it was argued that (1) purchasing power parity held fairly well, even in the short run—that is, that there was a near-infinite speed of adjustment of the real exchange rate toward a long-run equilibrium constant (or slow-moving trend)—and that (2) this was evidence in favor of the equilibrium view of goods markets. Subsequently, clear statistical rejections established the fact that purchasing power parity does not hold in the short run, and the question became whether it holds in the long run. Many of the equilibrium theorists now claim that (1) the speed of adjustment of the real exchange rate toward purchasing power parity is zero, or close to it, and (2) this is evidence in favor of the equilibrium view of goods markets.

It is true that it is difficult to reject the hypothesis that the real exchange rate follows a random walk, or comes close to it. A typical estimate is that the speed of adjustment of the real exchange rate to long-run equilibrium is 3 percent a month (an autoregressive coefficient of .97), or 30 percent a year (an autoregression coefficient of .70) and that this speed is not significantly greater than zero. But (even waiving the change in position) one might wonder why anyone would consider the finding of a zero speed of adjustment as evidence in favor of the equilibrium view.

The logic goes as follows. When one has finished running through some mathematics of dynamically optimizing equilibrium, one comes out with nothing to say about movements in the real exchange rate. The rate can move up as easily as down. (The problem is that the equilibrium theorists have not identified the "fundamental disturbances"; this is the "gap in the evidence" to which Stockman refers. As Stockman says, in his 1987 study, the theory is still in its infancy.)[5] In other words, as far as the theorist knows, the real exchange rate follows a random walk.

The sticky-price model of Rudiger Dornbusch, on the other hand, *does* have something to say of use in predicting movements in the real exchange rate. It says that when the real exchange rate has overshot its long-run equilibrium (in response, for example, to a shift in the monetary-fiscal policy mix), as the dollar clearly had by 1984, the best expectation is for it to return gradually toward that equilibrium.[6] So a failure to reject the hypothesis that the real exchange rate follows a random walk is (understandably) interpreted as evidence against the sticky-price theory. But it is also interpreted as evidence in favor of the equilibrium theory, even though the latter has no more testable implications for the real exchange rate than does the proposition that nine is a prime number.

Stockman has offered a second kind of evidence. In addition to arguing that some of the things predicted by the sticky-price model seem not to be true (the adjustment of the real exchange rate toward a long-run equilibrium), he argues that some of the things that the model does successfully predict can also be explained by varieties of the equilibrium theory.[7] Two examples stand out.

One piece of evidence that is traditionally considered to support the sticky-price model is the observation that fluctuations in the real exchange rate are very highly correlated with fluctuations in the nominal exchange rate. But Stockman has an explanation of how such behavior can also come out of an equilibrium model. To begin with, there are always real shocks to productivity, technology, tastes, trade policy, and taxes that would move the real exchange rate no matter what the regime. Why do these movements in the real exchange rate happen to show up almost entirely as movements in the nominal exchange rate instead of the price level? He says that it is because the monetary authority tries to stabilize the price level.

The second piece of evidence that is traditionally considered the exclusive preserve of the sticky-price model is the observation that the fluctuations in the real exchange rate are much greater for countries and time periods in which there is a floating exchange rate than when there is a fixed exchange rate. Surely this clinches the case? No. Stockman has recently shown how to coax out of the equilibrium theory an explanation for this fact, too.[8] This story begins with the proposition that under fixed exchange rates, governments are likely to put on (and take off) trade controls more often, in order to protect their foreign exchange reserves. Then Stockman turns loose his dynamically optimizing agents, who manage to adjust to this behavior on the part of the government in such a way as to smooth out fluctuations in the real exchange rate. Voilà! An equilibrium model that is "consistent" with the facts. Such explanations are clever and make for good journal articles that are popular among academic economists. But that does not make them true.

Speaking of agents, spy novels are a good analogy for stories that are clever and make entertaining reading but that may not necessarily represent the truth. Datum: At the conference at which Alan Stockman's discussion and the present commentary were originally presented, I got up from my chair next to Alan Stockman on the stage and walked over to take my place at the lectern. At the least, the following three hypotheses could have emerged:

- I was a spy for a foreign power, Alan was a CIA counterspy who was about to assassinate me, and so I had gotten up to move out of range. This hypothesis is "consistent with the facts" in the sense that, if true, it would explain them. But it is convoluted and not very plausible.
- John Le Carré was in British intelligence before he began his second career as a novelist. This hypothesis is an interesting subject for speculation. I have no idea whether it is true or not. It is also "consistent with the facts" in the weak sense that it does not contradict the datum. But it seems no more relevant than the statement that nine is a prime number, the proposition that economic agents dynamically optimize, or the hundreds of other hypotheses that I "fail to reject" every morning in the shower.
- I went to the lectern for the simple reason that the American Enterprise Institute invited me to comment on Alan's study. While not as clever as the other propositions, this hypothesis is simple, plausible, and consistent with the facts in the strong sense that it would explain them while most other hypotheses would not.

I will leave it to the reader to decide which hypothesis is the correct one.

Thus far I have addressed two kinds of empirical claims in favor of the equilibrium theory—namely, that it is "consistent" with the statistical failure to reject a random walk on the real exchange rate (an empty statement) and that it can be made consistent with the observed variability of the real exchange rate in a regime of floating exchange rates (too convoluted). But what about the claim that if the alternative sticky-price model were correct, one should be able statistically to reject the random walk hypothesis? What about the disturbing reality that most studies have in fact failed to reject it? My answer is that one should not even *expect* to be able to reject a random walk on the basis of the mere fifteen years of post-1973 data that almost all of the tests use. Imagine that the truth is that the speed of adjustment to purchasing power parity is .03 per month or approximately .30 per year. A simple calculation suggests that one should then not expect to be able to reject statistically the hypothesis that the coefficient is zero unless one has at least forty-nine years of data.[9]

A long time series for the real exchange rate is available for the dollar-pound sterling rate (see figure 3–1). Tests of the speed of adjustment toward purchasing power parity give the following results (see table 3–2). On post-1973 data, the speed is not statistically greater

FIGURE 3–1
DOLLAR-POUND REAL EXCHANGE RATE, 1869–1987

Dollars per pound at 1929 prices

TABLE 3–2

PURCHASING POWER PARITY BETWEEN THE UNITED STATES AND THE UNITED KINGDOM, 1869–1987

	1973–1987	1945–1972	1945–1987	1869–1987
Statistics on Percentage of Deviation from Mean				
Mean absolute deviation	.120	.074	.110	.093
Standard deviation	.156	.091	.156	.121
Time trend	.001	−.001	.006[b]	−.001[b]
	(.010)	(.002)	(.002)	(.000)
Autoregression of Real Exchange Rate				
Deviation from mean	.687[b]	.722[b]	.830[b]	.844[b]
	(.208)	(.130)	(.092)	(.050)
Deviation from trend	.688[b]	.730[b]	.741[b]	.838[b]
	(.208)	(.131)	(.101)	(.052)
Regression against Nominal Exchange Rate				
Coefficient[a]	2.516[b]	1.220[b]	1.687[b]	.916[b]
	(.417)	(.103)	(.186)	(.093)
Autocorrelation coefficient	.959[b]	.989[b]	.992	.988[b]
	(.054)	(.015)	(.011)	(.014)

NOTE: Standard errors are reported in parentheses.
a. With constant term and correction for autocorrelation.
b. Significant at the 95 percent level.

than zero. On post-1945 data, it still does not quite appear statistically greater than zero;[10] as I have noted, however, this is precisely what one would expect from forty-three years of data if the true speed were .30 per year or less. On the complete data set of 1869–1987, the speed of adjustment *is* clearly statistically greater than zero.[11] In my view this not only tends to vindicate the sticky-price view but also provides a neat illustration of the irrelevance of tests that "find nothing" or "fail to reject the null hypothesis" merely because they have not looked in the right places.

Where does all this leave monetary policy? Stockman's list of six proposed reasons why monetary policy might want to pay attention to the exchange rate and the current account is very good. As should be clear by now, I reject the notion that the state of our ignorance (great as it is) is in itself a reason for policy makers to pay no attention to these two important economic variables. I do agree with the conclusion that the monetary authorities should focus primarily on the price level and real output as goals rather than the international variables. But this is because I see many advantages to targeting nominal gross national product for monetary policy.

I do not subscribe to the view that the $135 billion U.S. current account deficits of recent years should not be a subject of concern. It is important, of course, for economists to keep explaining to the general public, as Stockman does, that not all deficits are bad deficits and that a country may choose to go into current account deficit and to borrow from abroad to finance a high level of investment arising from productive opportunities or to finance a high level of consumption arising from the knowledge that income will be higher in the future. Korea's current account deficits of the 1970s are a good example. Nevertheless, the U.S. deficits of the 1980s are not of the Korean type. Their origin lies instead in our $150 billion federal budget deficits, which in turn originated in faulty economic reasoning and political gridlock, not in intertemporal optimization. I would add something to Stockman's list of proposed reasons to pay attention to the international variables—namely, that the current account deficit implies that we are going further and further into debt to the rest of the world. The only reason that I agree that monetary policy should not focus primarily on the current account deficits is that the job belongs to fiscal policy.

To say that one can construct models in which a current account deficit is "nothing" to worry about because it is the outcome of dynamic optimization is not the same thing as to say that the U.S. deficit of the 1980s is in fact nothing to worry about in the real world. It is true that we remain largely in ignorance of precisely how the economy works. But at some stage, economists have to come down from their towers of fantasy and decide what they really think. The alternative is to leave the decision making to those who may be still more ignorant.

4
Exporting the Inflation Tax

Guido Tabellini

As a result of its large current account deficits throughout most of the 1980s, the U.S. net international investment position is now negative, for the first time since World War I. As shown in figure 4–1, the U.S. net international investment position was approximately +5 percent of GNP in 1981; it is projected to be approximately −15 percent of GNP in 1990. The data concerning the U.S. net external position contain several errors in measurement and reflect arbitrary accounting conventions. But there is no doubt that during the 1980s the U.S. net external assets have been falling at a rate unprecedented in its modern history. This chapter analyzes the implications of this reduction in the U.S. net external asset position for the issue of macroeconomic policy coordination. The existing literature, surveyed briefly in the section "Monetary Policy Coordination and the Transfer Problem," has investigated some aspects of this question. Particular attention has been paid to the role of exchange rate management in helping to effect a real transfer between the United States and the rest of the world. Such a transfer eventually has to take place, if the United States restores its current account equilibrium.

This chapter focuses on a different aspect of this same issue that has been neglected so far in the literature. A large part of the capital that flowed into the United States during the 1980s has been invested in nominal dollar denominated assets. The real market value of these assets can be changed by U.S. monetary policy. In particular, an unexpected dollar devaluation would reduce the purchasing power of the U.S. external obligations, and hence would redistribute wealth from foreign to U.S. citizens. This fact may influence the incentives of

Prepared for the American Enterprise Institute Conference on Monetary Policy, held in Washington, D.C., November 14 and 15, 1988. Parts of this chapter were written while I was visiting the Board of Governors of the Federal Reserve System (International Finance Division) and the Institute for International Economic Studies (University of Stockholm). I thank both institutions for their support and hospitality. I am also grateful to Giovanna Mossetti and Thomas Willett for helpful comments. I am the only one responsible for the views contained herein.

the U.S. monetary authorities as well as the market expectations about future policy. Consider for instance the following scenario. In response to an exogenous event, the U.S. monetary authorities have to choose between raising the interest rate or accepting a devaluation of the dollar. By choosing the first option, they would raise the burden of servicing the U.S. external debt. By choosing the second option, they would instead reduce the real value of foreign claims on domestic resources. Clearly, these new consequences raise the cost of a tighter policy and increase the attractiveness of a dollar devaluation. This is the sense in which the accumulation of large dollar denominated external liabilities may have changed the incentives of the U.S. monetary authorities. The section of this chapter that discusses "Who Gains and Who Loses from a Dollar Devaluation" attempts to assess the relevance of these incentives, by analyzing in detail the data on the U.S. net external position.

Internalizing the external effects of U.S. monetary policy creates a new role for international monetary coordination. The section on

FIGURE 4–1

U.S. NET EXTERNAL ASSETS AS A PERCENTAGE OF NOMINAL GNP, 1946–1990

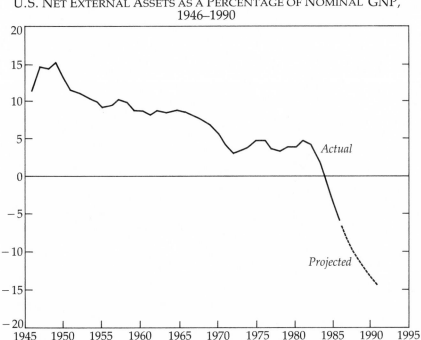

SOURCE: R. Bryant, G. Holtham, and P. Hooper, *External Deficits and the Dollar — the Pit and the Pendulum* (Washington, D.C.: Brookings Institution, 1988).

"Exporting the Inflation Tax in a Noncooperative Regime" investigates what this role is and how the gains from coordination, if any, are distributed across countries and over time. Three questions are asked. First, the subsection on the "Noncooperative Monetary Regime" investigates how monetary policy in a debtor country is affected by the incentive to extract revenue from foreign creditors in the absence of international coordination. The main finding here is that, under some conditions, the debtor country manages to collect some inflation tax from abroad, despite the fact that inflation is fully anticipated and that there is no currency substitution. Next, the subsection on "Monetary Policy Coordination" considers how the gains from coordination are distributed across countries, and how their bargaining power is affected by changes in the stock of external debt outstanding. Coordination takes the form of a fixed exchange rate agreement. The main finding here is that the distribution of these gains and the countries' bargaining power are not stable over time. Consequently, the allocation of the burden of defending the fixed exchange rate is also not stable, but depends in a predictable way on the external debt outstanding in each period. This result suggests that the incentives of the fiscal authority in the debtor country may be shaped by the nature of the internationl monetary regime. The subsection on "Fiscal Incentives and the International Monetary Regime" explores this conjecture, and argues that international monetary coordination may weaken the incentives to balance the fiscal budget in the debtor country. Finally, there are some concluding remarks in the last section.

Monetary Policy Coordination and the Transfer Problem

The U.S. current account deficit cannot keep growing forever. Eventually its growth must be arrested and the U.S. external debt must be serviced. This will involve running a trade surplus and reversing the transfer of resources that is now occurring between the United States and the rest of the world. An important question addressed in the recent literature is whether international monetary policy coordination can facilitate this process.

Exchange Rate Management. Judging from their declarations, and perhaps also from their behavior, the policy makers of the major industrial countries seem to believe that the answer to this question is positive. The Plaza Agreement of September 1985 stressed the point that "exchange rates should play a role in adjusting external imbalances" and that the Group of Five (G-5) countries (France, Japan,

United Kingdom, United States, and West Germany) would "stand ready to cooperate more closely to encourage" some further orderly depreciation of the dollar against the other main currencies—a G-5 announcement, reported by Funabashi in *Managing the Dollar: From the Plaza to the Louvre*. Similarly, at the Louvre Accord of February 1987, after the large dollar devaluation, the policy makers of the G-6 countries "agreed that the substantial exchange rate changes since the Plaza Agreement will increasingly contribute to reducing external imbalances" and that they had "now brought their currencies within ranges broadly consistent with underlying economic fundamentals." As a result, "they agreed to cooperate closely to foster stability of exchange rates around current levels"—G-6 communiqué, reported in Funabashi. This call was reaffirmed at the June 1987 Venice Summit, at the September 1987 IMF–World Bank meeting, and in other more recent communiqués.

Originally, exchange rate management was conceived as part of a more grandiose program of international policy coordination. An important aspect of this program was fiscal contraction in the United States and fiscal expansion in the rest of the world. In the implementation of the program, however, the fiscal component was not carried out. As a result, since 1985 policy coordination in practice has meant almost exclusively nominal exchange rate management.

The original program, of accompanying fiscal policy coordination with nominal exchange rate management, was in accord with current economic thinking. A fiscal contraction in the United States, accompanied by fiscal expansion abroad, would have shifted aggregate demand away from U.S. goods (because of the magnitude of the import propensities in the United States and in the rest of the world). Hence, a depreciation of the dollar real exchange rate would have been required to avoid excess supply in the United States. Because of price "stickiness" and "desynchronization" in the commodities markets, such a real exchange rate reduction would have been most easily achieved by a nominal dollar devaluation, rather than through a process of generalized deflation in the United States. This point of view has been forcefully argued in Krugman's paper, "Adjusting to the World Economy," and is shared by many economists.

Nominal exchange rate management without any fiscal adjustment on the real side is, however, much more problematic. On the one hand, if the fiscal adjustment never occurs, in the long run managing the nominal exchange rate can result in inflation, with no effect on the real exchange rate. Branson, in "The Limits of Monetary Coordination as Exchange Rate Policy," raises a similar point when he argues that the real dollar appreciation in the first half of the 1980s was an equilibrium reaction to a real shock, and hence that a monetary policy that stabilized the nominal exchange rate would have been counterproductive.

This point can be stated more generally as follows. The U.S. trade and current account deficits are real phenomena that result from an excess of investment over aggregate savings in the United States relative to the rest of the world. Reversing these deficits requires changes in real variables. Monetary policy coordination, by contrast, concerns nominal variables (such as nominal exchange rates or inflation rates). Consequently, monetary policy alone cannot correct the underlying real imbalances, although it can facilitate the adjustment process if these real variables are changed.

On the other hand, whether or not the real fiscal imbalances are corrected is not an exogenous event. Presumably, it is primarily determined by the domestic political incentives of U.S. policy makers. These incentives are not invariant across different monetary regimes. Suppose, for instance, that nominal exchange rate management succeeds, at least temporarily, in maintaining the dollar real exchange rate at just the "right" level. This might effect further improvements in the trade balance, but also might weaken the pressure on the U.S. fiscal authority to do something about its budget deficit. If fiscal policy in the United States were directed optimally by a benevolent social planner, then this consideration would not be a concern. If, however, as is more likely in the current circumstances, the U.S. budget deficit reflects a political market failure, then international monetary coordination may be counterproductive, since it may enhance the effects of the political distortion on the U.S. deficit. In other words, the economy would move from a second to a third best. This line of thought, neglected in much of the literature so far, is further elaborated in the subsection on "Fiscal Incentives and the International Monetary Regime."[1]

Monetary Policy as a Fiscal Instrument. In the recent literature, both the advocates and the critics of exchange rate management have focused extensively on the transfer problem summarized in the previous pages. But in a world with real fiscal imbalances, there is also a second important reason for monetary policy coordination to matter. Monetary policy can also be regarded as a fiscal instrument, in many ways similar to a capital levy. An unexpected monetary expansion in the United States, by devaluing the dollar, acts like a capital tax on foreign holdings of U.S. nominal external debt. The opposite is true for a monetary contraction in the United States. As such, U.S. monetary policy has external effects abroad. This creates a potential role for international monetary cooperation and exchange rate agreements, in addition to that discussed in the previous pages.[2]

Note that the base corresponding to this tax (the outstanding stock of U.S. external dollar liabilities) is partly determined by U.S. fiscal policy: the base is increased by U.S. budget deficits (to the extent that they are reflected in current account deficits); and vice versa for budget surpluses. This confirms the relevance of the issue raised at the end of the previous subsection. The incentives of the fiscal authority to balance the budget are likely to be affected by the nature of the international monetary regime—although here it seems harder to tell a priori in which direction.

The rest of the chapter looks at international monetary coordination from this point of view. Monetary policy is considered also as a fiscal instrument for redistributing wealth to or from foreigners. Budget deficits (or surpluses) are viewed also as a means to enlarge (or shrink) the tax base on which the monetary instrument can be applied in the future. Before turning to a more abstract analysis, in the next section we show that the relevance of this approach to international monetary coordination has been enhanced by the stream of large U.S. current account deficits that have accumulated during the 1980s.

Who Gains and Who Loses from a Dollar Devaluation

This section investigates how the U.S. incentives to reduce the market value of its net external liabilities by means of monetary policy changed throughout the 1980s. This requires a detailed analysis of the composition of the trend in the U.S. net international investment position depicted in figure 4–1.

Table 4–1 provides some information about the currency in which various categories of U.S. external assets and liabilities are denominated. The data are broken down by type of holder and by major type of asset. For some external assets and liabilities (essentially those held or issued by the U.S. government and its financial sector) the currency of denomination is reported in official publications. For other categories of issuer or holder (mainly the private sector other than financial intermediaries), the currency of denomination can only be estimated. The estimates are based on Hooper and Stekler's "Financing the U.S. Current Account Deficit: Who Bears the Exchange Rate Risk?"; these estimates were originally formulated for the years 1984 and 1985. In constructing table 4–1, it was assumed that the same (percentage) estimates can be applied to earlier and later periods. The way in which the general picture depends on these estimates will be discussed.

TABLE 4–1
Currency Exposure, 1980–1987
(billions of U.S. dollars)

U.S. External Assets and Liabilities	1980	1983	1984	1985	1986	1987
I. Foreign currency exposure of U.S. residents						
1. U.S. assets abroad in foreign currency						
1a. Reported	38.7	48.5	53.8	65.8	82.2	102.7
Nonbanks	2.9	3.1	2.6	2.3	2.5	3.2
Banks	5.1	8.2	12.5	16.8	28.7	51.3
Government						
Official reserve assets	26.8	33.7	34.9	43.2	48.5	45.8
Long-term	2.2	1.8	1.8	1.7	1.6	1.6
Short-term	1.7	1.7	2.0	1.8	0.9	0.8
1b. Estimated[a]	233.6	245.0	253.0	289.0	330.0	384.5
1c. Total (1a + 1b)	272.3	293.5	306.8	354.8	412.2	487.2
2. U.S. external liabilities in foreign currency						
2a. Reported	7.4	8.3	11.6	18.9	33.5	60.1
Nonbanks	3.7	3.1	3.0	3.6	3.8	5.1
Banks	3.7	5.2	8.6	15.3	29.7	55.0
2b. Estimated[b]	0.9	1.7	3.3	8.3	14.2	17.1
2c. Total (2a + 2b)	8.3	10.0	14.9	27.2	47.7	77.2
3. Net exposure of U.S. residents in foreign currency						
3a. Overall (1c − 2c)	264.0	283.5	291.9	327.6	364.5	400.0
3b. Partial (1a − 2c)	30.4	38.5	38.9	38.6	34.5	25.5
II. Dollar exposure of foreigners with respect to U.S. residents						
4. U.S. external liabilities in dollars						
4a. Reported	326.5	533.2	600.6	660.3	787.2	877.2
Nonbanks	17.9	22.2	26.4	24.3	22.0	22.1
Banks[c]	116.4	282.7	316.8	349.9	431.9	493.6
U.S. Treasury securities						
(held by private sector)	16.1	33.8	58.2	83.6	91.5	78.4
Foreign official assets	176.1	194.5	199.2	202.5	241.8	283.1
4b1. Estimated,[d] of which	157.1	250.8	291.9	391.2	515.0	589.2
4b2. Bonds	9.5	17.3	32.8	82.5	127.9	153.9
4c. Total (4a + 4b1)	483.6	784.0	892.5	1,051.5	1,302.2	1,466.4
4d. Partial (4a + 4b2)	336.0	550.5	630.4	742.8	915.1	1,031.1
5. U.S. claims on foreigners in dollars						
5a. Reported	290.0	534.0	541.2	541.2	597.5	609.1
Nonbanks	31.5	31.8	27.3	26.6	31.0	26.7
Banks	198.7	426.2	433.1	430.5	478.7	496.4
Government						
Long-term assets	59.8	76.0	80.8	84.1	87.1	86.0
5b. Estimated[e]	44.5	46.0	47.6	53.5	62.8	71.1
5c. Total (5a + 5b)	334.5	580.0	588.8	594.7	660.3	680.2

TABLE 4-1 *(Continued)*

U.S. External Assets and Liabilities	1980	1983	1984	1985	1986	1987
6. Net dollar exposure of foreigners with respect to U.S. residents[f]						
6a. Overall (4c − 5c)	149.1	204.0	303.8	456.8	641.9	786.2
6b. Partial (4d − 5c)		1.5	−29.0	44.6	148.1	254.8	350.9
7. Net gain from 10 percent dollar devaluation (percent of GNP)						
7a. (from 6a)	0.5	0.6	0.8	1.1	1.5	1.8
7b. (from 6b)	0.0	−0.1	0.1	0.3	0.6	0.8

a. 84.4 percent of direct investments, corporate bonds, and corporate stocks, computed as in B. Hooper and L. Stekler, "Financing the U.S. Current Account Deficit: Who Bears the Exchange Rate Risk?" (Board of Governors of the Federal Reserve System, Washington, D.C., 1986, mimeo).
b. 10 percent of bonds issued by U.S. corporations in foreign markets.
c. Except for liabilities to official institutions and nonmonetary organizations.
d. 100 percent of direct investment and corporate stock and 90 percent of corporate bonds (cf. B. Hooper and L. Stekler, "Financing the U.S. Current Account Deficit").
e. Direct investment, corporate bonds, and corporate stocks, less amount in line 1b.
f. U.S. is a net creditor if negative, net debtor if positive.
SOURCES: *Federal Reserve Bulletin, Survey of Current Business, Economic Report of the President,* various years.

Consider first the U.S. net position in foreign currency (lines 1–3 of table 4–1). The United States is a net creditor in foreign currency. Despite the deterioration of the aggregate U.S. net international position, the U.S. net position in foreign currency has actually improved throughout the 1980s (see line 3a). This is true even if one neglects the estimated component and only considers the assets and liabilities whose currency of denomination is reported in the official statistics (see line 3b). Note that the U.S. liabilities in foreign currency are relatively small, and that the bulk of U.S. assets abroad corresponds to line 1b of table 4–1. This line includes direct investment abroad, corporate stocks, and corporate bonds. Of these, only corporate bonds might contain large margins of error in the estimation of the currency of denomination. Since corporate bonds account for only about 20 percent of the total in line 1b, the margin of error in the estimation cannot be too large.

The counterpart of this finding is that the U.S. net debt position in dollars is much larger than its aggregate net international investment position, and has been rising even more rapidly than would be apparent from figure 4–1. As shown in line 6a, the U.S. net debt position in dollars in 1987 is more than five times as large as that in 1980. Its average rate of growth between 1983 and 1987 has been more than 40 percent per year. An even more rapidly ascending trend emerges if one neglects the estimated U.S. liabilities in dollars and only considers the assets and liabilities for which the currency of denomination is officially reported. Moreover, as indicated in line 4d, much of the increase in the U.S. external debt between 1984 and 1987 has been in nominal U.S. liabilities (reported liabilities and corporate bonds).

Line 7a of table 4–1 reports one measure of the net gain accruing to U.S. residents from an unexpected 10 percent devaluation of the dollar (accompanied by unexpected inflation), expressed as a percentage of U.S. GNP. This measure is computed by multiplying the U.S. net external debt denominated in dollars (line 6a) by 0.1, and then dividing it by nominal GNP. In 1983 this net gain was about ½ percent of GNP. At the end of 1987 it was 1.8 percent, or about 50 percent of the U.S. trade deficit for that year. These are still relatively small numbers, but they are rapidly increasing.

It might be argued that the relevant net aggregate on which to measure the net gains from a dollar devaluation is smaller than the total net international investment position. In particular, corporate stocks and direct investments might be considered as real assets, whose market value would rise in the event of a dollar devaluation. Excluding these two items from the estimated U.S. liabilities denominated in dollars leaves us with the adjusted net aggregate reported in line 6b.[3] The net gain from a 10 percent dollar devaluation computed from this aggregate is much smaller. At the end of 1987 it was still below 1 percent of GNP. But here, too, the trend is increasing very rapidly.

This trend is also shown in figures 4–2 and 4–3. Figure 4–2 depicts net private capital flows between the United States and the rest of the world. Two things are apparent. First, financial assets and not direct investment are responsible for most of the foreign capital inflows since 1982. Second, private capital inflows began to slow down during 1987; in that year, private capital flows were replaced by accumulation of dollar reserves by the foreign authorities. Figure 4–3 decomposes net private capital flows of financial assets in its two components: net purchases of U.S. financial assets by foreigners, and net purchases of foreign assets by U.S. residents. Whereas the latter have not changed significantly, foreign investors have sharply increased their net acquisition of U.S. financial assets since 1982. Also shown in figure 4–3 is the increase, up to 1987, of net purchases of U.S. Treasury liabilities by foreigners.

FIGURE 4–2
PRIVATE CAPITAL FLOWS, 1960–1987
(billions of dollars)

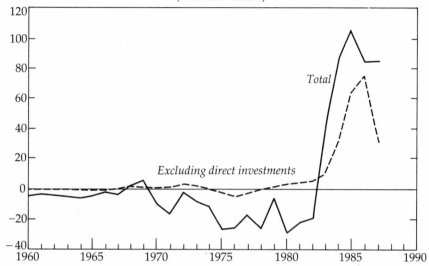

Total

Excluding direct investments

SOURCE: V. Grilli and G.Tabellini,"Il Debito Pubblico ed Estero Degli Stati Uniti Durante l'Amministrazione Reagan," ISPI Working Paper (Milan, 1988).

FIGURE 4–3
INTERNATIONAL TRANSACTIONS OF FINANCIAL ASSETS, 1960–1987
(billions of dollars)

Net foreign purchases of U.S. financial assets

Net foreign purchases of U.S. Treasury bonds

Net U.S. purchases of foreign financial assets

SOURCE: Same as source for figure 4–2

The data reported in table 4–1 are subject to several important limitations and qualifications. Taking these qualifications into account can either raise or reduce the ultimate numbers shown in line 7 of the table. But these qualifications are unlikely to change the main conclusion, namely, that the net U.S. external position denominated in dollars deteriorated substantially between 1983 and 1987. The remainder of this section discusses these data limitations in more detail.

Perhaps one of the most important issues concerns the maturity of the nominal liabilities of table 4–1. If all liabilities were of very short term, then the scope for an unexpected dollar devaluation might be reduced, unless the devaluation was very swift and sudden. Conversely, if the maturity of U.S. liabilities was long, then even a gradual and long-sustained dollar devaluation could be unexpected. Hence, the maturity of U.S. net liabilities can determine the ease with which the U.S. monetary authorities can generate a policy surprise. Perhaps more important, the maturity of U.S. net liabilities can determine the effectiveness of reputational incentives. If some reputation mechanism is in effect, then an unexpected inflationary surprise would induce the private sector to revise upward its estimate of future inflation (or devaluation). This would tend to impose costs on U.S. borrowers if their liabilities were of short maturity (or if they had variable interest rates). But these costs would be much smaller if they had borrowed long; for then, U.S. borrowers would not need to refinance their obligations at higher interest rates. Hence, in the presence of some reputation mechanism, the net gain from an inflationary surprise is higher the longer is the maturity of outstanding obligations.

Table 4–2 provides some information about recent trends in the maturity composition of some categories of U.S. external liabilities. It is apparent from the last two lines of table 4–2 that after 1983 foreign net purchases of U.S. long-term liabilities have been a large percentage of the total capital inflows in the United States, and that they have been significantly larger than in the earlier part of this decade. With respect to the U.S. Treasury alone, the average maturity of the federal government debt held by private investors has also increased during the period under consideration: it was three years and nine months in 1980; it was five years and nine months in 1987.

According to the classification scheme used for the data in tables 4–1 and 4–2, a foreigner is defined to be a foreign resident. This implies that U.S. branches of foreign companies are not considered to be foreign investors, whereas foreign offices of U.S. companies are. From the point of view of the incentives of U.S. policy makers, however, a more appropriate definition of foreigner is based on citizenship. Participation in the U.S. political process (through elections or otherwise) is more likely to be related to citizenship than to residence. Hence, it can be argued that the U.S. policy maker cares about the interests of its citizens, more than about those of its residents. Unfortunately, data on the net consolidated position of U.S. and foreign companies in general are not available. The U.S. Treasury does, however, provide some data on the consolidated foreign currency position of U.S. banks. According to Hooper and Stekler, these data suggest that U.S. banks in the aggregate did not have substantial foreign currency positions in 1985. This is consistent with the data reported in parts 1a and 2a of table 4–1. If, as it would seem likely, U.S. branches of foreign banks have a net creditor position in dollars, then the data of table 4–1 might underestimate the net debt position of the United States in dollars. Too little is known about the consolidated position of the nonbanking sector to attempt an estimate.

The foreign currency exposure of both foreigners and U.S. citizens can be altered by a variety of "off-balance-sheet" transactions. These transactions (such as forward contracts, options, futures, and swaps) would not show up in the balance-sheet data of table 4–1. Complete data on these transactions are not available. Based on estimates by market analysts and on Treasury surveys of U.S. corporations, however, something is known about the direction of these

TABLE 4–2

FOREIGN NET PURCHASES OF LONG-TERM NOMINAL ASSETS, 1980–1987
(in billions of U.S. dollars and percent)

Assets	1980	1981	1982	1983	1984	1985	1986	1987
U.S. Treasury bonds and notes								
Official institutions	3.9	11.7	14.5	0.8	0.5	8.1	14.2	31.1
Others	1.0	3.2	2.7	4.6	21.0	21.0	5.0	−5.2
Long-term securities of U.S. government corporations	2.5	1.5	−0.3	0.0	1.2	4.3	7.0	5.0
Corporate bonds	2.9	3.5	1.8	0.9	11.7	39.8	43.7	22.7
Total	10.3	19.9	18.7	6.3	34.4	73.2	69.9	53.6
% of net increase of total foreign asset in the United States	17.7	24.0	20.0	7.4	33.6	56.4	32.8	25.3

SOURCES: *Survey of Current Business, Treasury Bulletin,* various years.

transactions. Specifically, Hooper and Stekler conclude in their study that the sizable U.S. net long position in foreign currencies seems to extend to off-balance-sheet transactions as well, and that the increase in foreign dollar exposure that is apparent from table 4–1 is probably even larger if "off-balance-sheet" items are included.

Finally, the data of table 4–1 are likely to include margins of error from other sources as well. An indication of these measurement problems is provided by the large statistical discrepancy in the U.S. balance of payments accounts. Between 1975 and 1985 this discrepancy cumulated to $190 billion. According once again to Hooper and Stekler, much of this discrepancy is presumed to reflect unrecorded increases in foreign holdings of claims on the United States, including U.S. currency. If this were the case, it would provide an additional argument for believing that the U.S. net debt position in dollars is even larger than reported in table 4–1.[4]

In summary, the general picture that emerges from these data is unequivocable. First, the U.S. net external debt position denominated in dollars is very much larger (in absolute value) than the overall U.S. net position. Second, the U.S. net dollar position deteriorated very rapidly after 1983. There is great uncertainty about the exact level of this position in any given year, but not about its direction or rate of change.

What are the implications of this general picture for the incentives of the U.S. monetary authorities with respect to exchange rate policy? Presumably, as argued above, the U.S. authorities do not care much about foreign interests in the United States (except possibly indirectly, through reputational considerations). In this case, and all other things being equal, the accumulation of external dollar liabilities that took place since 1983 raised the incentives for the U.S. authorities to generate an unexpected dollar devaluation (or, equivalently, it raised the cost of an unexpected appreciation of the dollar).

Naturally, the condition that other things have remained equal is very restrictive. An unexpected change in the dollar exchange rate is associated with a web of redistributions much more complicated than that corresponding to the aggregate framework of table 4–1. Thus it is entirely possible that the position of single individuals or corporations within the United States has changed in a way that would discourage the authorities from undertaking any unexpected dollar devaluation, rather than encourage them to do so. Moreover, U.S. exchange rate and monetary policy is determined by many other considerations, generally more important than the purely redistributional aspects discussed in the previous pages; in particular, the threat of loosing the reputation earned at a high price with the Volcker disinflation is probably a severe constraint on U.S. policy makers.

For these reasons, it is impossible to extrapolate any predictions about the future course of U.S. exchange rate policy from the previous discussion alone. All that can be said is that now there is an additional factor, which will undoubtedly become increasingly important, that must be considered by the U.S. monetary authorities.

It is then interesting to inquire about the implications of these new incentives for the equilibrium exchange rate and for U.S. monetary policy in general. Specifically, how is the market going to react to the perception of these new incentives? Is anything to be gained by coordinating monetary policy internationally, beyond any advantages that might already exist in the absence of these recent trends? How are these gains distributed among the United States and other countries? How is the U.S. bargaining position in any cooperative international agreement likely to be affected? These and other questions are addressed in the remainder of this paper. For reasons of space, here we only summarize the answers to these questions. The detailed analysis is found in a previous version of this chapter.

Exporting the Inflation Tax in a Noncooperative Regime

The Noncooperative Monetary Regime. We begin with the question of whether and how a debtor country that borrowed in its own currency can collect some inflation tax from foreign holders of its external debt. Throughout this subsection it is assumed that the monetary authorities in the debtor and creditor countries behave noncooperatively. The purpose of the analysis is to understand the incentives faced by the monetary authorities in the United States and in the other major industrial countries in the absence of international policy coordination, given the economic trends described in the previous section.

It is easy to show that, in the absence of international cooperation, the equilibrium rate of inflation in the debtor country increases with the size of the net nominal external claims to be repaid in the current period. Intuitively, the larger the net claims that are being repaid, the greater the redistribution associated with unexpected inflation, and hence the greater the incentive to inflate. If private lenders are fully informed and have rational expectations, they realize that issuing external debt alters the incentives of the monetary authorities in the debtor country; thus, they anticipate any forthcoming inflation. This implies that the equilibrium inflation rate is fully incorporated in the nominal interest rate when the debt is issued. Hence, the debtor country cannot directly collect any inflation tax from foreign debt holders.

Yet, despite this fact, without policy commitments a monetary policy of zero inflation is not credible, and hence would not be expected by foreign lenders. This result is well known in the existing literature on rules versus discretion in monetary policy (see for example Calvo's article "On the Time Consistency of Optimal Policy in a Monetary Economy" and Kydland and Prescott's "Rules Rather Than Discretion: The Inconsistency of Optimal Plans"). It is due to the fact that the rate of inflation in the debtor country is chosen only afterward that foreign investors have made an irrevocable decision to buy domestic nominal debt. Given this timing, it is optimal for the monetary authorities to try to devalue the outstanding debt obligations by creating inflation. But this ex post optimality is fully perceived by foreign investors, ex ante, before making their investment decision. As a result expected inflation drives up the nominal interest rate, and the debtor country is trapped in the equilibrium with high inflation.[5]

In this setup, however, unlike in a closed economy, the monetary authorities in the debtor country are not the only ones trapped in a time-consistent suboptimal equilibrium. If the outstanding debt is sufficiently large, the government of the creditor country also has a credibility problem: it cannot refrain from intervening in defense of the debtor currency. The reason is the same: to redistribute wealth in favor of its own citizens who hold nominal external claims. It can be shown that the creditor's intervention in defense of the debtor's currency tends to be larger in proportion to the amount of the stock of external debt outstanding. This intervention too is fully anticipated by the market; hence, it does not achieve any redistribution of income in favor of the debt holders. On the contrary, by intervening the creditor government pays seigniorage to the foreign authorities. This seigniorage is totally wasted from the point of view of the creditor government: more intervention by the creditor simply encourages the debtor country to print even more currency. Yet, despite this fact, the foreign authorities cannot refrain from intervening. They are not being irrational. Like the government of the debtor country, the foreign authorities are simply subject to an incentive compatibility condition. They cannot credibly precommit not to buy domestic currency. Anticipating their purchases, the domestic (debtor) central bank then keeps printing money, up to the point where the foreign authorities are fully satiated and domestic prices and the exchange rate are at the equilibrium level. This equilibrium level is fully anticipated by the market, which receives the required real rate of return on its lending.

This finding illustrates an important asymmetry concerning who gains and who loses in this attempt to export the inflation tax. For low levels of external debt the creditor government does not intervene in defense of the debtor currency. Hence, in this case the domestic country is the only loser, since it bears the full costs of inflation and yet extracts no seigniorage from abroad. If the level of debt is sufficiently large, however, the creditor country does intervene. Hence, in this second case, the losses are shifted to the foreign (creditor) country, and take the form of seigniorage revenue paid through the official intervention in the exchange rate market.

This discussion suggests that the authorities in the creditor country ought to discourage their own citizens from acquiring large quantities of external nominal assets. The foreign individual investor is atomistic and hence does not perceive that his investment decision alters the incentives of the policy maker in its own country: it is perfectly rational, from his point of view, to invest, taking as given the behavior of his own authorities. But his purchase decision has a negative externality: it increases the incentives of the authorities to bail him (and the other investors) out, by intervening in the foreign exchange market. Hence, by restricting the private acquisition of external assets, the foreign authorities can reduce the seigniorage that they pay abroad.

Since 1987, foreign central banks have substantially increased their purchases of dollar denominated assets (see the section "Who Gains and Who Loses from a Dollar Devaluation" and Hale's article, in the *Wall Street Journal*, "Accounting for the Dollar Glut"). This behavior on their part may be interpreted as evidence of policy coordination. However, the results of this subsection suggest another possible interpretation. According to the theoretical results presented above, an increase in foreign official intervention in defense of the dollar might be expected even in the absence of cooperation, given the remarkable increase in the U.S. external dollar obligations that took place since 1983.

Monetary Policy Coordination. Attempts of the debtor country to export the inflation tax abroad result in a net inefficiency for the world economy. This suggests that there are gains to be had from international policy coordination. This subsection investigates how these gains are distributed between the two countries if a coordinated monetary policy can be implemented.

By policy coordination we mean that the policy instruments at home and abroad are arranged to maximize social welfare in both countries, with weights on each country that depend on their relative

139

bargaining power. Thus, we can think of monetary policy coordination as a binding agreement whereby the two countries delegate the choice of their policies to a (fictitious) international agency. The goal of this agency reflects the preferences of the countries involved in the agreement, with weights that depend on their bargaining position. I neglect here the question of how the binding agreement can be enforced.[6] I focus instead on the questions of how the gains from coordination are distributed between the debtor and the creditor, and the forms that they take.

In a world where inflation is costly, any cooperative equilibrium must satisfy an obvious requirement—to have zero inflation at home and abroad. Inflation only causes a loss of real resources. Any international transfer of resources dictated by the cooperative agreement can be effected without inflation, simply by means of official intervention in the market for foreign exchange. Thus, for instance, if under the agreement the domestic country has to transfer income abroad, it would simply buy reserves of foreign currency (sterilizing the impact of that purchase on its price level). The reverse would hold if the transfer is to be effected in the opposite direction. The question addressed in this subsection concerns the direction and size of transfers that occur in the cooperative equilibrium.

Consider first what happens if the international agreement is signed ex post, once foreign investors have bought nominal external debt. In this case, the debtor can be shown to have more bargaining power than the creditor. Moreover, the bargaining position of the debtor country improves as its nominal debt increases. Hence, in equilibrium the debtor receives a larger amount of transfers as its debt rises. The key to this result is that the agreement here is signed ex post, after nominal debt has been purchased by the foreign investors. In such a situation, an increase in debt improves the bargaining position of the debtor country, since it increases the loss of income that can be inflicted abroad through inflation in the event of a disagreement. Conversely, and for the same reason, a higher level of debt weakens the position of the creditor country.

Next, consider the case in which the cooperative agreement is signed ex ante, before any external debt is issued by the domestic country. Suppose further that the real amount borrowed and the currency of denomination of the debt are determined independently of the nature of the monetary regime, and are taken as given when the monetary policy agreement is entered into. In other words, think of this ex ante monetary cooperation as a contingent contract signed by the domestic and foreign monetary authorities in anticipation of the debt policies pursued by the government, accepting these policies as given. In this case, inflation does not involve any redistribution between debtor and creditor. If the two countries fail to reach the ex ante agreement, the foreign lenders fully anticipate the forthcoming inflation. Thus, failure to reach an agreement does not involve any loss for the foreign lenders: the flow of real interest payments on the external borrowing of the domestic country is the same irrespective of whether there is monetary cooperation.

This implies that here the creditor is in the stronger bargaining position: he receives most of the gains from cooperation, the more so the larger is the debt outstanding. It is almost as though the debtor has to pay the creditor to induce him to cooperate. In a sense, by entering into the cooperative agreement, the debtor "buys" from the creditor the capacity to precommit to a zero inflation rate. In a different context, in their article in the *European Economic Review* Giavazzi and Pagano interpret the cooperative agreement that gave rise to the European Monetary System (EMS) along these same lines.

This finding, that for the creditor country it is preferable for monetary cooperation to occur ex ante rather than ex post, and that the opposite is true for the debtor, is very intuitive. The evaluation of the players' welfare at the noncooperative disagreement point is different ex ante from ex post. Ex post bygones are bygones; hence, the inflation that would arise if the parties fail to reach an agreement redistributes real resources between the debtor and the creditor country. If, however, the disagreement is evaluated ex ante and it is fully anticipated when the debt is purchased, then inflation causes no real redistribution but only brings about a loss for the domestic country. Thus, the debtor is in a stronger bargaining position if it negotiates the agreement ex post, after the foreign private sector is locked into a nominal investment position, rather than ex ante.

An important implication follows from this result. Any change in the nominal net debt position of a country creates incentives to renegotiate preexisting monetary agreements. If the debt position increases, then the debtor has an incentive to renegotiate, since its bargaining power has increased. If on the other hand the external debt decreases, then it is the creditor that has the incentive to recontract. In the real world there is no institutional device that would prevent foreign governments from renegotiating their previous contracts. This suggests that only ex post cooperation is likely to be implemented: the two countries would not enter into a contract being both aware that the terms of the contract would be changed in the future.

Fiscal Incentives and the International Monetary Regime. The results of the previous two subsections suggest that the fiscal authorities in the debtor country may have an incentive to use debt policy to gain a strategic advantage over its creditors. In particular, because of the strategic effects of external debt, the debtor may borrow more or less than he otherwise would. This subsection briefly investigates how the incentives to borrow for the debtor government are shaped by the nature of the international monetary regime.

For simplicity, I assume that the borrower can only issue debt denominated in domestic currency.[7] The question is whether the real marginal cost of borrowing (inclusive of interest payments, the domestic costs of inflation, and the eventual transfers across countries) is higher with or without monetary cooperation. Note that there is no reason that the motives that induce the government to borrow (such as tax smoothing or intertemporal revenue redistribution) should be affected by the nature of the international monetary regime. Hence, a finding that the marginal cost of borrowing is lower under one regime than in the other implies that in equilibrium the government borrows more in that regime.

To answer this question, note first of all that the real interest payments must be the same under both regimes: since investors have rational expectations, they correctly anticipate the equilibrium inflation rate in either regime, and obtain the same real rate of return from their lending. Hence, the cost of borrowing can differ across the two regimes only because of the other two effects of issuing debt: the effect on domestic inflation (in the noncooperative equilibrium) and the effect on the international transfers associated with the exchange rate intervention.

In the absence of cooperation, the debtor country has to bear the costs of inflation. Hence the marginal cost of issuing external debt, besides the payment of interest, consists of the marginal output loss due to the forthcoming higher inflation. If on the other hand the countries cooperate, then inflation is zero. It can be shown that the marginal cost of borrowing is always lower with than without monetary cooperation. It can also be shown that the marginal cost of issuing debt is lowest if cooperation occurs ex post. This is because of the results described in the previous subsection: with ex post cooperation, the bargaining power of the debtor country increases with the size of its external debt obligations; hence, by issuing more debt, the borrowing country can reduce the transfers that it pays (increase the transfers received) under cooperation. As such, the marginal cost of issuing debt is lowest.

This finding may have important implications. The government of the borrowing country, anticipating that monetary policies will be set cooperatively, should borrow more under a cooperative monetary regime than if monetary cooperation is ruled out. If government borrowing is optimal from the point of view of society as a whole, then cooperation is bound to be welfare improving for the debtor country. But if the fiscal deficit reflects some political distortion, then monetary cooperation would enhance the effect of this distortion. In this case, it is conceivable that monetary cooperation would be counterproductive, in the sense that economic welfare in the borrowing country would be higher in a monetary regime without cooperation than in the cooperative regime. This would happen if the beneficial effect of cooperation on the rate of inflation is more than offset by its adverse effect of enhancing the domestic political distortion. Investigating these issues more in detail, in a model where the political distortion is explicit, would be an interesting task for future research (see note 1).

Finally, note that the findings summarized above provide a counterexample to the widespread opinion that fixed exchange rate agreements may act as a discipline device on the fiscal authorities of a country. This idea probably makes a lot of sense for a small open economy that unilaterally pegs its nominal exchange rate to that of some other country. For in this case, a fixed exchange rate regime constrains the rate of domestic credit expansion, and hence may raise the cost of running a fiscal deficit.[8] In the case of a large open economy like the United States, however, the burden of defending an exchange rate target is likely to fall on all countries participating in the exchange rate agreement, and not just on the weak currency country. The point of this subsection is to argue that the distribution of the burden of defending a fixed dollar exchange rate is not exogenous, but is likely to depend also on the amount of external debt outstanding: the larger the debt, the greater the U.S. ex post bargaining power, and hence the more the United States will benefit from the agreement. It is this factor that may weaken (rather than reinforce) the incentives to balance the budget for the U.S. authority in a fixed compared to a flexible exchange rate regime.

Conclusion

Since 1983, the United States has accumulated large external liabilities denominated in dollars. This has increased the attractiveness of an unexpected dollar devaluation for the U.S. authorities. The results of this chapter suggest that in the absence of international monetary cooperation these new incentives can lead to either of two outcomes or to a combination of both. They can lead to a high equilibrium

143

inflation rate in the United States and to a dollar devaluation. Alternatively, they can force the foreign monetary authorities to intervene in defense of the dollar by acquiring dollar denominated assets, thereby also placing a ceiling on the equilibrium rate of inflation in the United States. In this second case, the United States would be able to extract some seigniorage revenue from the creditor countries, even if its incentives are fully understood by foreign investors and inflation is perfectly anticipated.

Because inflation is costly, there are gains from international monetary policy coordination, but the distribution of these gains among countries can vary, depending on when coordination occurs. If it occurs ex ante, before the debt is issued, then monetary coordination would involve a transfer from the debtor to the creditor. Here cooperation essentially provides a commitment technology for the debtor country; hence, the debtor would be willing to pay a price to lend credence to a noninflationary policy.

If on the other hand cooperation occurs ex post, after the debt has been issued, then the direction of the transfer is reversed, with the creditor paying the debtor to induce him not to inflate. The reason is that once investors are locked into a nominal debt contract, inflation redistributes real resources from the creditor to the debtor; thus, the debtor country is in a stronger bargaining position ex post rather than ex ante, in direct proportion to its exernal debt outstanding.

Two general implications follow from these results. First, in a world with fiscal imbalances a cooperative monetary regime might not be stable over time, since the bargaining power of the countries involved would change with their external debt position, and hence the allocation of the burden of defending the exchange rates would also change. Second, engaging in monetary cooperation in such a world might weaken the incentives for the debtor country to correct its fiscal deficit. This happens because monetary cooperation reduces the cost of borrowing, particularly if cooperation, as it is likely, occurs ex post.

Naturally, these results only suggest the way in which the behavior of policy makers and financial investors in the major industrial countries may be affected by the current U.S. external deficit. In practice, several other factors play a much more important role in shaping this behavior; among them, probably one of the most important is the concern of the U.S. monetary authorities for their reputation, which would tend to weaken the incentives analyzed in this chapter.

Internationally Negotiable Inflation Taxes

A Commentary by Jacob S. Dreyer

Before commenting on Guido Tabellini's interesting essay, I will summarize his core observations and conclusions:

1. Accumulation of net external debt makes inflationary policies in the debtor country more tempting because a large part of the inflation tax burden is borne by foreigners.

2. There exists a unique equilibrium level of reserves denominated in the debtor country currency that the central bank of the creditor country is willing to accumulate.

3. This unique equilibrium level is a function of the actual (or, alternatively, prospective) size of net indebtedness and depends on whether the inflation tax is imposed on foreigners by the debtor unilaterally or is essentially negotiated by the debtor's and creditor's central banks.

The technology underlying Tabellini's essay is a two-country two-period-game theoretical model. The setup of the model and its basic assumptions are crucial for arriving at his results. I will discuss these assumptions and the setup later.

First, let me remark on the proposition that the rising net indebtedness itself intensifies temptations to tax via inflation. In the first part of his essay Tabellini presents numbers reflecting growing U.S. external debt, which in turn form the basis for subsequent inferences about rising incentives to pursue inflationary monetary policies in the United States.

This observation about intensifying inflationary incentives, while apparently self-evident, is not, strictly speaking, an external debt problem but an external balance sheet problem. Some ten years ago, when the United States was still a creditor country and its net external assets were close to 5 percent of GNP, many economists and the international financial community were engaged in a spirited debate.

145

The debate was about the dollar overhang, the inflationary incentives it creates, and the desirability of managing the implied risk of the ensuing wealth transfers through international cooperation, which was then presented in the guise of the substitution account of the International Monetary Fund (IMF). More than twenty years ago, when the creditor position of the United States was some 10 percent of its GNP, Jean-Jacques Servan-Schreiber, speaking about the "American challenge" to Europe, observed that U.S. corporations had been borrowing large amounts in the still-young Eurodollar market and using the proceeds to acquire real assets located in Europe. He postulated that such a mismatch in the currency denomination of the balance sheet may give the U.S. authorities a strong motive to inflate and thereby boost U.S. corporations' net worth at the expense of European lenders. Suspicions of the U.S. propensity to inflate predate its recent slide into a net debtor position.

For the sake of accuracy and fairness, this distinction between the net-asset and gross-balance-sheet positions in no way affects Tabellini's results. His formal model is set up in such a manner that a problem of denomination mismatch just cannot arise.

Another of his key findings is a demonstration that the bargaining power of the debtor country increases with the size of its debt. But Brazil, say, or Mexico, can extract substantial concessions from its creditors even though the debt is denominated in currencies other than their own. One would naturally expect that an issuer of debt denominated in his own currency would have an even greater leverage. In addition to such a debtor's ability to reduce the real value of his liabilities through inflation, he can resort to debt repudiation, default, suspension of interest payments, and other actions potentially available to debtors when creditors' claims are, as a practical matter, unenforceable. The greater the ability of a particular participant in such a game to impose on others a transfer of wealth in his own favor, through an inflation tax or otherwise, the greater is his bargaining power. This point is so self-evident that one hardly needs to develop a model of the bargaining parties' behavior to establish it.

Similarly, the bargaining power of the debtor is enhanced by the ability to sneak up, so to speak, on the creditors. In other words, if the creditors are faced with the fait accompli of unenforceable claims *already* accumulated, they would be willing to grant the debtor more generous concessions than they would if they had known *in advance* that the debtor intended to incur debts with uncertain prospects for their full repayment in real terms. This point is also so obvious as to not require further elaboration.

Much more interesting is Tabellini's finding that when the debt level exceeds a certain threshold—that is, potential gains arising from imposing an ex post inflation tax on foreign holders of debt become sufficiently attractive—cooperative management of the exchange rate by the debtor and creditor countries may result in a lower rate of inflation in the debtor country than a non-cooperative exchange rate management would produce. In Tabellini's context, cooperation means in essence that the creditor country purchases a certain amount of the debtor's currency, and in exchange the debtor country keeps the inflation rate lower than it would without such purchases of its currency by the creditor's monetary authorities. Thus in Tabellini's discussion cooperation results in zero inflation. Under a cooperative arrangement of this sort, the debtor country agrees to a reduced inflation tax levy on foreigners in exchange for lower inflation at home. The creditor country transfers to the debtor less wealth than under a noncooperative regime resulting from the creditor's ability to persuade the debtor that his output gains because of lower inflation exceed the opportunity costs of a reduced wealth transfer.

Tabellini's statements are based upon a skillfully setup, economical, and transparent model that allows him to derive the equilibrium values (in terms of its relevant parameters) for the amount of debtor country currency purchased by the creditor's central bank. As mentioned, the model he employs and the assumptions he uses are, understandably, crucial for obtaining his results.

Crucial assumption one is that inflationary policy would be pursued by the debtor country for the *sole* purpose of imposing a tax on foreign holders of domestic nominal debt. Inflation in Tabellini's essay has no benefits at all; as the rate of inflation goes up, output losses rise more than proportionately. Quite logically therefore the Nash equilibrium presumes zero inflation. This assumption eliminates, however, all incentives to conduct inflationary policy even in an open economy with a neutral external balance let alone in a closed economy. If, contrary to this assumption but in unfortunate conformity with experience, some inflation is perceived by the government to be desirable (either as a demand stimulant in a Keynesian framework or as a means of taxing *domestic* holders of debt), then surely the trade-off specified by Tabellini would be affected, and consequently the bribe paid by the debtor to the creditor—that is, the equilibrium level of official reserves purchased by the latter—would be understated.

Another, and related, assumption is that nominal depreciation of the debtor's currency is uniquely related to the rate of inflation but has no other effects. The model employed does not distinguish between tradeables and nontradeables—that is, it leaves no room for reallocation of resources—and takes care of distributional effects by postulat-

147

ing a lump tax cum subsidy. The interest rate serves to translate future values into present values but is not otherwise related to the size of the debt, level of intervention, or rate of inflation. While Tabellini has to abstract from these effects of currency depreciation to make his model manageable, allowing for these effects affects the trade-off faced by the debtor and thus generally yields a different equilibrium level of the debtor's currency purchased by the creditor than the one derived in absence of such effects.

Next, support by the creditor of the debtor's currency value, that is, his foreign exchange intervention, is assumed to be always fully sterilized. If the assumption of total sterilization is relaxed and inflationary consequences of official intervention are allowed, the game becomes quite complicated. Now the creditor faces an additional cost of intervening because of inflation-induced output loss over and above the cost of the direct wealth transfer. It stands to reason that in this case his incentives to acquire the other country's currency would be diminished.

Furthermore, Tabellini postulates a peculiar difference in perceptions and behavior between private agents and monetary authorities. The wealth transfer occurs in his essay as a result of seigniorage extracted by the debtor from the creditor, which in fact means that foreign monetary authorities receive less than fully inflation-adjusted nominal interest rate on their reserve holdings. Both private and official foreign holders of the debtor's currency may misjudge future inflation when they purchase nominal debt. But curiously the same result holds when the inflation is fully anticipated. Even more curiously the seigniorage-producing transfer is present in a cooperative regime even though the creditor, through his purchases of the debtor's currency, determines the nominal exchange rate and thus, in Tabellini's setup, the debtor's rate of inflation.

Despite this litany of reservations, objections, and misgivings, I enjoyed Tabellini's essay. The model he chose to deal with the problem analyzed in the essay was cleverly conceived and skillfully executed. But by defining the problem of cooperative exchange rate management as purely a transfer problem between governments, the author sacrificed applicability of his findings to the ongoing policy debate.

It is a reasonable postulate that, ceteris paribus, the mounting external dollar liabilities of U.S. residents intensify temptations for a more inflationary monetary policy. There is little doubt that foreign governments have an interest in protecting the wealth position of their citizens against real depreciation of dollar-denominated claims they hold. This interest would, at the margin, make foreign governments more willing to support the exchange value of the dollar than they would be inclined otherwise. Everybody is in agreement with these propositions. Neither do I have a problem with Tabellini's conclusion that purchases of dollars by foreign central banks reduce pressures on the U.S. government to bring the fiscal deficit down (as do, for that matter, purchases of U.S. assets by private foreigners). This is true not only for current but also for expected purchases.

Beyond that, however, neither the equilibrium level of dollar purchases by foreign central banks nor the relationship between cooperative monetary policies and the U.S. rate of inflation depends primarily on the desire of foreign governments to shield dollar assets of their citizens from dollar depreciation. Regarding the latter, once allowance is made not only for interactions among governments but also for interactions between governments and private agents within each country, monetary cooperation is more likely to have an inflationary bias than an anti-inflationary one. Regarding the former, my reading of Funabashi and other interpreters of coordination accords is that managing the process of international wealth transfer is not at all the predominant motive of the negotiating parties. Their main motive appears to be a desire to reduce price and output fluctuations said to be caused by exchange rate movements. Whether joint exchange rate management is desirable is a separate matter. But given this objective, the paradigm chosen by Tabellini is applicable to neither a positive nor a normative analysis of international monetary cooperation.

5

Future Challenges to the International Monetary System

Richard N. Cooper

The international monetary system is a broad and complex topic, more than can be discussed satisfactorily in a brief essay. I shall therefore concentrate on just one aspect of it here, namely the prospects for eliminating the large trade imbalances that now characterize the world economy. Concretely, I shall focus on the prospect for eliminating the U.S. current account deficit over the next five years, by 1993, an objective that many would consider highly desirable and indeed if anything somewhat too leisurely. The subtitle of my remarks might be "some unpleasant arithmetic concerning the U.S. trade deficit."

I shall begin by establishing the base line and making some assumptions. The U.S. current account deficit in 1987, what I assume will be the peak in this century, amounted to $154 billion. It grew to that level over five years, starting with a small surplus of $7 billion in 1981. It seems reasonable that we should eliminate it over five years: that would not require a pace of decline greatly different from the pace of increase. To start with, elimination would require a correction of $154 billion, some combination of reduced imports and increased exports of goods and services. Of course, we must allow for the debt that will accumulate between 1987 and 1993 while the deficit is declining. Servicing that debt—I assume it will not have to be repaid for some time—would require an additional $40–50 billion, leaving a total required improvement of roughly $200 billion to eliminate the deficit.

Agricultural policies throughout the world have distorted agricultural markets, leading to large surpluses of temperate zone products. These policies are likely to be modified during the next five years, because the economic and fiscal burden of continuing them is too great. The process, however, will be slow and politically difficult, so I assume that within the next five years no consequential help to the required improvement will be coming from agricultural exports.

Service industries will continue to expand their export activities, but service imports will also continue to rise. There might be a net improvement from this source, along with a little help from agriculture, of perhaps $20 billion. That leaves by subtraction an improvement of about $180 billion per year required in net exports of manufactured goods.

This amount understates the magnitude of the required adjustment, moreover, insofar as it makes no allowance for the likelihood that in order to sell that much more, American products would have to become somewhat cheaper relative to foreign ones—and that in turn implies that at today's prices the swing in U.S. net exports and hence in foreign net imports would have to be even greater than $180 billion.

Domestic Changes

Is such an improvement possible over the next five years? Is it likely? Two aspects must be taken into account, the domestic side and the international side. Can the United States produce an additional $180 billion in manufactured goods per annum by 1993, for export or to substitute for manufactures that we are now importing from the rest of the world? At present U.S. manufacturing output is running around $950 billion a year, at capacity utilization rates of about 84 percent. If we assume that full capacity is about 90 percent, then an additional $57 billion could be produced by increasing utilization rates. For the rest, though, new capacity will be required. If we assume a capital-output ratio of 2 in manufacturing, an additional $120 billion of output will require $240 billion in new plant and equipment and working capital, or an average of $60 billion a year over the next four years. I assume that this will be an incremental requirement, above the $146 billion that was spent on plant and equipment in manufacturing in 1987, much of which was for replacement and modernization.

This additional investment requirement amounts to about 1¼ percent of gross national product (GNP). The steady improvement in the trade balance of, say, $40 billion a year amounts to about ¾ percent of GNP. Together the required investment and improvement in net exports amount to about 2 percent of GNP, nearly the current natural growth rate of the economy. That would leave very little for increases in public plus private consumption (including housing) over the next five years, a prospect that will not be welcome either to the public or to an administration running for reelection in 1992.

My conclusion from the arithmetic on the domestic side is that it would be possible to make the adjustments in output and absorption required to eliminate the current account deficit by 1993, but it will be difficult. Moreover, policies are not in place to accomplish that result. They are not even being seriously discussed.

International Changes

Let us turn now to the international side. Who will be on the other side of this large swing of $180 billion in world trade in manufactured goods? Although developing countries would like to increase their imports, they are limited by their ability to earn through exporting and to borrow more. Although the current debt situation may ease somewhat, net capital inflows to debt-ridden developing countries are not likely to increase by more than $10–20 billion a year over the next several years—that would be optimistic. Allow a further $20 billion for Taiwan, Korea, the Communist countries, and a few others; that leaves $140–150 billion for Europe and Japan.

Even within Europe, many countries now run current account deficits. The large surpluses are concentrated in the Federal Republic of Germany, the Netherlands, and Switzerland. Those countries could be on the other side of a major U.S. correction. However, Japan and West Germany especially have keyed their economies over the past decade or longer to export-led growth. The same is true of Taiwan and Korea. Will they be able to adjust, psychologically as well as economically, to a prolonged period of relative export stagnation, to a decline in net exports of manufactures on the order of $75 billion each? Will they be able to rely instead on domestic demand to fuel economic growth? Japan seems to have started the process of adjustment, and the Japanese discuss publicly the major structural changes that will have to take place in their economy, although much disagreement exists on their detailed direction. Discussion of the need for structural change along these lines is much less evident in Europe.

No doubt the first $25 billion reduction each in the surpluses of Japan and Germany (in which term I include its smaller immediate neighbors) will be welcome, as it contributes toward better world balance relieves protectionist pressures in the United States, and reduces foreign calls for market opening (in Japan) and fiscal expansion (in Germany). The second $25 billion reduction each in the surpluses of Japan and Germany is likely to generate concern, as the manufacturing industries suffer from loss of export markets or stiffer foreign competition in the domestic market, and rumblings about the need to reduce the rate of deterioration. The third $25 billion reduction each in their trade surpluses (but not the current account surpluses, because their earnings on foreign investments will be growing continually), all in a five-year period, will, in my view, create such high anxiety—*angst* in German, which has more visceral, less cerebral connotations than the English word *anxiety*—that the publics will call on their governments for strong and effective steps to halt the deterioration, and the governments will comply. Countries that have identified social virtue with export performance will find such rapid and extensive deterioration traumatic and unacceptable.

The issue can be put another way. At current levels of income, demographic structure, interest rates, and so on, Japan and West Germany generate private savings far in excess of the willingness of domestic investors to borrow and invest in plant and equipment. Although the governments absorb some of this saving through their budget deficits, large amounts of savings are invested abroad, especially in the United States. Developing countries would be happy to absorb this excess saving as a way to finance investment to improve future standards of living. Since the debt crisis of 1982, net lending to capital-importing developing countries has dropped dramatically, falling from $103 billion in 1981 (admittedly an exceptional year) to an estimated $14 billion in 1987, and the brunt of this decline has fallen on investment in those countries. Private investors in the rich countries are leery about investing in most developing countries. Although matters may improve somewhat over the next several years, barring world recession, there is no clear prospect in the medium run that the borrowing capacity of developing countries will improve by more than $10–20 billion per year.

Disposition of Excess Savings

So if the United States succeeds in correcting its imbalance between savings and investment, the counterpart of its trade deficit, where will the excess world savings go? Without careful management directing it into public or private spending, it will be dissipated through world recession. A decline in income will eliminate excess savings. To avoid this, the governments of Japan and Europe must absorb more of the excess savings through increases in expenditure or reductions in taxes that encourage private spending, that is, in higher budget deficits. This recommendation does not fit comfortably with conventional prudence in national fiscal management. We learned long ago, however, that if everyone, households and businesses as well as governments, is fiscally prudent, modern economies will not prosper. Spending is required to generate income and output.

An obvious solution in the near term would be substantial increases in aid to developing countries, many of which would be happy to spend the funds. A certain disenchantment with foreign aid has set in in most donor countries, though, due to demonstrable mismanagement of funds here and there, to investments that turned out poorly, and, it must be said, to investments that turned out successfully but produced output that competed with products from industrialized countries. There is no doubt some merit to all of these complaints. Industrialized countries, however, do not hold their own investments to the same high standard: for example, commercial office space in U.S. cities was substantially overbuilt with the help of strong tax incentives during the early 1980s, and Europe has made numerous public investments, like those in steel and civil aircraft, that do not meet reasonable standards of returns to investment. Furthermore, over the decades 1960–1980 developing countries grew at extraordinary rates, and it is hard to believe that inflows of capital from the rest of the world, including foreign aid, were not essential to this outstanding performance.

In view of the reluctance of private investors, renewed capital flows to developing countries must come from public sources or from private sources with public guarantees. Public money would increase budget deficits and conflicts with canons of conventional fiscal prudence. Although guarantees do not create this problem, they do create potential exposure to future defaults. Nevertheless, some combination of public loans and guarantees to developing countries perhaps represents the most socially useful way to correct the major imbalances in the world economy. The Japanese government has committed itself in principle to invest $30 billion in developing countries over the next three years, but it has not yet found the modalities.

The leading alternative, if world recession is to be avoided, will be continued lending to the United States. That is not desirable from the American perspective unless substantial new and productive opportunities for investment are found. Without new mechanisms to help developing countries increase their imports by $40–50 billion a year, though, that is what will ocur.

Conclusion

It is worth noting that northern Europe and Japan are entering a period of slow economic growth in the labor force, with an aging population. The United States is also experiencing a decline in the natural growth of the labor force for the next seven or eight years. But immigration will augment growth in the American labor force, to an extent that will not occur in northern Europe and Japan. America, therefore, can use investment productively for equipping and housing a growing labor force, whereas in northern Europe rich investment opportunities will be limited to those created by technological change, and even those will be discouraged by strong currencies. It is therefore likely that capital will continue to flow in large volume from Europe and Japan to the United States. For this reason, it may be a mistake to try to eliminate the U.S. current account deficit entirely within the next five years. To the extent that the United States runs a deficit in the mid-1990s, the problem of adjusting the world structure of trade will be eased.

6
The International Monetary System, the European Monetary System, and a Single European Currency in a Single European Market

Gottfried Haberler

The international monetary system is still one of widespread, loosely managed floating, although it has come under increasing criticism. The criticism has been especially severe in Europe, leading to the formation of the European Monetary System (EMS) in 1979. The EMS, a Bretton Woods–type of arrangement of stable but adjustable exchange rates, has seven members: Belgium, Denmark, France, Germany, Ireland, Italy, and the Netherlands. Britain is conspicuously absent, and Greece, Portugal, and Spain are not yet ready to join.

In 1987 and 1988 two landmark agreements were reached by the European Community (EC), which are binding for all its twelve members. The so-called Single European Act of 1987 provides that by the end of 1992 all remaining restrictions on trade between EC members must be removed. In 1988 it was agreed that by mid-1990 all restrictions on capital flows must be phased out. In other words, the currencies of the EC countries will become fully and freely convertible. (Greece, Ireland, Portugal, and Spain can delay compliance until 1992.)

It stands to reason that this has far-reaching monetary implications, especially for the members of the EMS, for stable exchange rates and free convertibility of currencies require as a minimum very tight coordination of monetary policy.

This is an abbreviated version of the essay that appeared in English in a volume of essays, *Geldwertsicherung und Wirtschaftsstabilität*, in honor of Professor Helmut Schlesinger, vice president of the German Bundesbank, edited by Norbert Bub, Dieter Duwendag, and Rudolf Richter (Frankfurt am Main, West Germany: Fritz Knapp Verlag, 1989).

No decision has yet been made on how to handle the monetary problems posed by free mobility of capital. A radical solution that has generated much attention in the media and that France supports but not Britain is to create a European central bank that would issue a single European currency. At the Hanover EC Summit in June 1988 a high-level committee of the governors of the central banks, chaired by Jacques Delors, chairman of the European Commission, was set up to make concrete proposals.

The sections in this chapter deal with the problem of fixed exchange rates versus floating, trade liberalization in the EC, the EMS, and the problem posed by free capital flows.

Fixed or Floating Exchange Rates?

In the past few years the present system of loosely managed floating has again come under sharp criticism.[1] On February 19, 1988, a blast came from an unexpected source. None less than His Holiness, Pope John Paul II in his encyclical "The Social Concerns of the Church" ("*Sollicitudo Rei Socialis*") said: "The world monetary financial system is marked by an excessive fluctuation of exchange rates and interest rates, to the detriment of the balance of payments and the debt situation of the poorer countries." Naturally, the pope did not make concrete proposals for change. The encyclical says, "The Church does not have technical solutions to offer." Still, the pope's statement has been widely interpreted as a rejection of the present system of floating exchange rates. The gold bugs in the *Wall Street Journal*, for example, were delighted. They spent several days "observing the performance of some of the world's notable economic thinkers" and awarded a silver medal to the pope. A gold medal went to Edouard Balladur, the French minister of finance.

French governments, both President Mitterrand's Socialist and Prime Minister Jacques Chirac's conservative, have urged a return to some sort of fixed exchanges.[2] Balladur has spelled out the French position on several occasions, for example, in his article "Rebuilding an International Monetary System: Three Possible Approaches."[3]

In his *Wall Street Journal* article Balladur mentions several alleged failures of floating exchange rates to achieve expected results: never have international balances been so large, nor fluctuations of these imbalances so wide, and so forth, as during the period of floating exchange rates. Although I could go through the list of alleged failures and show that what happened was not the consequence of floating, I shall not take the time to do so, because this criticism of floating falls to the ground if we consider the nature of the proposed

157

alternatives to floating and what would have happened if any one of them had been in force in the 1980s.

The suggested alternatives for floating are variants of the Bretton Woods system of "stable but adjustable exchange rates," embellished by target zones and guided—or misguided—by commodity price indexes, including the price of gold. There is no reason to assume that a Bretton Woods–type of system would have functioned better in the 1980s than it did in the 1960s and 1970s. On the contrary, it is easy to see that it would have broken down just as it did in the early 1970s.

In 1982 the U.S. economy took off on a vigorous, noninflationary expansion. Foreign capital from Europe and other countries poured into the United States, the dollar soared, and a large trade deficit developed. The expanding U.S. economy pulled the world economy out of the recession.

Now consider what would have happened if in that situation the world economy had been in a straitjacket of fixed exchange rates. Europe would have come under severe deflationary pressure, and any fixed-rate system, with or without a target zone, would have collapsed. The response would have been imposition of controls, and the world economy probably would have been plunged into a recession.

The Achilles' heel of the system of stable but adjustable exchange rates à la Bretton Woods is its vulnerability to destabilizing speculation. Very briefly, if under that system a currency weakens and the country loses reserves, the speculators (market participants) know that the currency can only go down; it cannot go up. Furthermore, they have learned from experience that a devaluation is bound to be large, because the authorities want to make sure that they will not have to go through the painful operation again soon. Therefore, if the speculators have guessed correctly and the currency is devalued, they make a large profit. If they have misguessed, they merely lose transaction costs.

Under floating, the situation is different. A currency under pressure goes down immediately. Therefore, the speculators can never be sure whether the market has not already overshot and the currency will go up again. In other words, under fixed exchange rates speculators speculate against the central banks whose hands are tied. Under floating, speculators speculate against each other, which obviously is much more risky.

Up to 1914 exchange rates of the major industrial countries were credibly fixed under the gold standard, which therefore was not so vulnerable to destabilizing speculation as a Bretton Woods–type of system. Still, it is hardly necessary to argue at length why a return to the gold standard is out of the question. Suffice it to ask the question, Who would want to entrust the course of the world price level and, therefore, the economic stability of the Western world to the mercy of Soviet Russia and South Africa, the dominant producers of gold?

Of course, this does not settle the question of floating versus fixed rates. I believe that floating should continue, but I do not want to exaggerate the case for floating. In a sense, floating is merely a second best: if any two countries of any group of countries agree to fix the exchange rates of their currencies, it would be the best solution— provided that two conditions are fulfilled. First, currencies are fully convertible in free markets; in other words, there is no exchange control, either open or disguised, as, for example, import restrictions on balance-of-payments grounds. Surely, fixed rates propped up by a battery of controls is the worst system. Second, the fixed rate must not impose heavy unemployment or inflation on any participating country.

Unfortunately, those conditions are only rarely met in the present-day world. The European Common Market and the EMS are no exceptions. Some real exceptions can be found among the many countries that peg their currency to the dollar, the yen, or the German mark, like Austria. The Austrian schilling has been pegged to the prestigious D-mark. True, Austria still has some controls on capital flows. The controls are mild, however, and if the links to the D-mark were broken, the confidence of the people in the schilling would suffer, and the controls would be tightened.

All this was different under the gold standard before 1914. For one thing, exchange control was unknown; and for another, wages were more flexible than they are now, and the tolerance for unemployment greater than now. In passing, it might be mentioned that if wages and prices were perfectly flexible, the whole problem of fixed versus flexible exchange rates would disappear.

In a few cases the failure to change the exchange rate or to float caused great damage. In the 1920s the British pound was grossly overvalued, because it had been restabilized at the prewar parity with gold and the dollar. As a consequence, the British economy was sharply depressed throughout the 1920s. John Maynard Keynes criticized the policy in his famous pamphlet *The Economic Consequences of Mr. Churchill*, Churchill being chancellor at the time. In 1931 the pound was cut loose from gold and depreciated, taking along the currencies of many countries—Australia, New Zealand, and Canada among them. The Federal Reserve reacted by tightening money—in the midst of a severe depression! Continental European countries were hit hard; they, too, tightened money and imposed all sorts of controls on trade and payments. The case of Germany deserves special mention, because sharply rising unemployment helped Hitler come to power. France, Switzerland, Belgium, Holland, and Poland, the "gold bloc," suffered a second deflationary shock when two years later (1933–1934) the dollar was devalued vis-à-vis gold.

Developments after World War II were infinitely better than in the interwar period. Bretton Woods was a great improvement over the gold standard. For about twenty years it served the Western world well by permitting realignments of exchange rates. Late in the 1960s, however, trouble arose, and the Bretton Woods agreement collapsed in the early 1970s and was replaced by widespread managed floating.

The reasons for the troubles and collapse of Bretton Woods are briefly these. In the late 1960s the U.S. dollar lost its position of unquestioned dominance because of two developments. First, inflation rose in the United States when President Johnson financed the increasing cost of the war in Vietnam and the equally costly Great Society programs at home by bank credit rather than by taxes, and, second, rivals to the dollar emerged: the German mark and the Japanese yen (not to mention the currency of tiny Switzerland, that island of democracy and prosperity that survived unscathed two world wars and the Great Depression).

A fact of crucial importance is that the interdependence of financial markets in the Western world has sharply increased and that capital flows across national boundaries have become very large. This situation has accentuated the vulnerability to destabilizing speculation of the Bretton Woods system of stable but adjustable exchange rates. Thus when the dollar came under pressure in the 1960s and gold flowed out of the country—the dollar was still convertible into gold for foreign central banks—more and more investors at home and abroad concluded that sooner or later the dollar would be devalued. Foreign central banks had to buy billions of dollars to hold the line. In August 1971 President Nixon closed the gold window, imposing a 10 percent import surcharge to induce other countries to upvalue their currencies. This was achieved in December 1971, resulting in a depreciation of the dollar of about 8 percent against the major foreign currencies.

Although calm returned to the foreign exchange markets, it did not last very long. In mid-1972 the dollar weakened again, and foreign central banks had to buy billions of dollars to hold the line. The end came with dramatic suddenness: on January 23, 1973, the Swiss National Bank stopped buying dollars and let the franc float up. A flood of dollars swept into Germany. During the period February 5–9, 1973, the Bundesbank bought $5 billion and then gave up. This was the end of stable but adjustable exchange rates, although the system of floating exchange rates was legalized only three years later by the second amendment of *The Articles of Agreement* of the International Monetary Fund.

For countries like Germany and Switzerland that did not want to inflate along with the United States, the only effective and efficient method is to let their currencies float. The Bretton Woods method, a one-shot appreciation of their currencies, would be a decidedly inferior approach. The reason is that neither economists nor ministers of finance or central bankers know what the equilibrium exchange rate is. This has been amply demonstrated in the past two years when the question arose over whether the dollar had declined enough to eliminate or sharply reduce the U.S. trade deficit. Time and again ministers of finance and governors of the central banks of the Group of Seven (G-7) declared that exchange rates were just about right, only to be contradicted a few months later by a further decline of the dollar. Economists, too, were by no means unanimous in their judgment. Policy makers, however, are becoming aware of their ignorance. Thus, Noburu Takeshita, prime minister of Japan, when asked whether the dollar-yen rate was right answered: "Only God knows."

Countries like Germany and Switzerland, on the one hand, that have to appreciate their currency have a strong incentive to appreciate too little rather than too much, because they do not want to run the risk of turning their trade surplus into a deficit. On the other hand, deficit countries have a strong incentive to depreciate their currency too much rather than too little, because they want to be sure that they will not have to go through the same painful process again soon.

It stands to reason that this state of affairs is unlikely to bring about a smooth adjustment of existing imbalances. Floating is a much better method, which amounts to saying that markets do a better job setting exchange rates than governments. Critics of floating point to what they call excessive volatility of exchange rates under floating. The answer is, first, that a large part of volatility has been caused by policy changes: the "open mouth policy"—that is, official statements that the dollar was too high or too low or just right—was not conducive to calming the market. Second, some of the changes called "excessive" were quite rational; for example, the sharp rise of the dollar after the election of Ronald Reagan was beneficial because the large U.S. trade deficit that developed pulled the world economy out of the recession. Third, it cannot be denied that the market sometimes makes mistakes; there are such things as speculative bubbles. Competitive markets, however, sooner or later correct themselves. Thus with the benefit of hindsight we can say that in 1984 the rise of the dollar went too far. Then in February 1985 the dollar turned around and started to decline. It is important to realize that market forces brought about the turnaround; more and more investors came to the conclusion that the dollar had risen too far.

Now if we compare the performance of the market with that of the government, we see that it is in the nature of the political process that governments are slow admitting mistakes and even slower correcting them. The U.S. budget policy is a perfect example. In the early 1980s the large budget deficits were highly beneficial because they pulled the U.S. economy out of the recession. There is almost general agreement, though, that deficit spending has gone much too far. With the trade balance now on the mend, with export- and import-competing industries booming, and with the economy operating close to full capacity, it is imperative to cut spending elsewhere to prevent inflation and recession. What is urgently needed is a credible program to phase out the structural budget deficit over a period of, say, four years. No solution of the budget problem can be expected before mid-1989.

The conclusion I draw from all this is that floating should continue. I repeat, however, that if two or more countries can agree to fix the exchange rate between their currencies, it would be the best solution, provided it can be done without imposing tight controls on trade and payments and without inflicting unemployment or inflation on any participating country. Unfortunately, these conditions are rarely met in the present-day world.

Liberalization of Trade in the EC

As mentioned, the Single European Act of 1987 provides that all remaining restrictions of trade between the twelve members of the EC must be removed by the end of 1992. The language used in official and unofficial statements about the task ahead—"to open up the European markets" or "to create a single European market"—clearly indicates how unfree and fragmented the Common Market still is. Customs inspection on the borders between the EC members is still in force, because indirect taxes have not been unified. This is not the whole reason, however; there exists a host of regulations on specific products and industries that differ from country to country and so restrict free trade and free competition in the EC, as well as imports and competition from the outside world. There are, for example, numerous health and safety regulations for trucks, all sorts of industrial machinery, and other products that differ greatly from country to country. These regulations have a strong anticompetitive effect because they restrain the operation of hundreds of small and medium-size companies. The big multinationals, such as IBM and Phillips, are less affected because they have branches in several countries. The European Commission in Brussels has been trying to harmonize regulation in certain areas. This is a very difficult and time-consuming process, and it is by no means certain that it will be completed in 1992. Perhaps the process of harmonization does not need to be finished completely to permit elimination or at least drastic simplification of customs inspection inside the EC.

The European Monetary System

The EMS is a Bretton Woods–type of arrangement of stable but adjustable exchange rates. On the whole it has been well received in official and financial circles in Europe and elsewhere. This is not surprising. For one thing, it has a natural constituency in the numerous officials and economists who have been involved in setting up and running the EMS and understandably take great pride in their creation. For another thing, the predictions of some early critics that the EMS would lead to high inflation and breakdown were not borne out by the facts.

The EMS, however, has been erroneously credited with certain improvements in the participating countries, for example, the decline of inflation. As Professor Fratianni[4] has pointed out, however, the relevant question is whether the EMS countries have performed better or worse than non-EMS countries since 1979. Actually, non-EMS industrial countries on the average have done as well or perhaps better than the EMS countries.

It has been argued that the EMS had an anti-inflationary effect because the more inflationary members, especially France and Italy, have been forced to curb inflation in order not to get too far out of line with low-inflation Germany. There is some truth in that. It is generally recognized that the EMS, contrary to the intentions of its founders, has become a hegemonic system; Germany, by virtue of the large size of its economy and its low inflation rate, has become the leader. This is highlighted by the open chafing of the French at the stern rule of the Bundesbank. The motive of the present center-left French government's renewed attempt to persuade Britain to join the EMS is surely to make the EMS more democratic and so to curb the power of the Bundesbank.[5]

Can the EMS, then, be credited with having had a beneficial disciplinary effect by linking the currencies to the D-mark? Not really: for in the absence of an EMS, there would still be a strong economic inducement for the EMS countries to follow the Austrian example of pegging their currencies, formally or informally, to the D-mark. It will perhaps be argued that for France, and possibly for Italy, formally pegging its currency to the D-mark would be politically unacceptable. We need not go into that, however, because the whole picture has been profoundly changed by the decision of the EC to phase out all control of capital flows by mid-1990.

The EC and the EMS without Exchange Control

For the following discussion it should be kept in mind that only seven of the twelve EC countries are in the EMS and that dismantling controls applies to all twelve EC countries, although four countries—Greece, Portugal, Spain, and Ireland—have been granted two more years (until 1992) to dismantle controls.

Because the EMS is a Bretton Woods–type of stable but adjustable exchange rates, it follows that the EMS is just as vulnerable as Bretton Woods was to destabilizing speculative capital flows. Actually, there have been several realignments of exchange rates, mostly devaluations against the D-mark. Not much has been heard of large capital flows preceding or accompanying exchange rate changes, however. The reason is that in several important EMS countries—France, Italy, and Belgium—controls are tight and comprehensive enough to prevent large capital flows. It is very important to understand, though often overlooked by policy makers, that in practice it is very difficult to distinguish capital from current transactions. Policy administrators know that the restrictions on capital flows are very difficult to enforce, because there are many ways to camouflage capital transactions as current transactions, for instance, by overinvoicing inputs or under-invoicing exports. The longer the controls last, the more adept investors (speculators) become in evading the controls. As a result, capital control always degenerates into more or less comprehensive exchange control.

This clearly is a most unsatisfactory state of affairs. It is, therefore, not surprising that the EC has decided to phase out capital controls by mid-1990. If the decision is carried out, 1990 will be a watershed, because with free capital mobility (absence of controls) any Bretton Woods–type of system of stable but adjustable exchange rates, such as the present EMS, becomes unworkable. As we have seen, such systems are very vulnerable to destabilizing capital flows. If a currency, say the French franc, comes under pressure, investors know that the currency will go down; and thus there will be a stampede out of the franc. This is the problem the EC faced up to the Hanover Summit in June 1988.

I will not try to describe how the Hanover decision was reached. Suffice it to say that the Hanover meeting seems to have been dominated by a radical solution of the problem: the creation of a European central bank that would issue a single European money. This proposal was rejected by British Prime Minister Margaret Thatcher, resulting in the creation of a high-level committee of the governors of the central banks, the general manager of the Bank for International Settlements (BIS), Alexandre Lamfalussy, and two other experts. This Committee of Seventeen under the chairmanship of Jacques Delors, president of the European Commission, will make concrete proposals in a year.[6]

Following the example of Tommaso Padoa-Schioppa who in a much-quoted paper speaks of the "inconsistent quartet," we can formulate the problem as that of an "inconsistent tercet": one cannot have at the same time (1) full mobility of capital; (2) stable exchange rates; and (3) national autonomy in the conduct of monetary policy.[7]

I now discuss some policy options that could remove the inconsistency. The first that comes to mind and is often mentioned is more frequent realignments of exchange rates. The question is, how frequent? The answer is that to overcome the basic weakness of the adjustable peg—that is, vulnerability to speculation—the realignment would have to be made in small steps at high frequency. This would be equivalent to floating exchange rates, the economically best and administratively easiest solution. In the long run, it can be replaced by the radical solution of a single European currency—if and when it comes to pass. Holding out that hope would make floating more acceptable.

Another possibility can be described as a gold standard without gold. Under the gold standard exchange rates are credibly fixed; the standard is, therefore, not vulnerable to destabilizing speculations. Deficit countries are automatically subjected to monetary contraction; surplus countries, to monetary expansion.

It would not be too hard to formulate rules for monetary policy that would replicate the gold standard mechanism under modern conditions. Would it be politically acceptable? Perhaps it would be if it sailed under the popular flag of tight policy coordination.

I now come to what I call the radical solution of the problem: the creation of a European central bank that would issue a single European currency. This idea has not only found the enthusiastic support of some influential and highly competent voices in the media but also has been put forth by some high officials.

In the first group I mention two, Samuel Brittan and *The Econo-*

mist. Brittan has developed the case for a full monetary union in Europe in several articles in the *Financial Times.* He summed up his case by saying that a single European market without a single European currency would be like a house without a foundation. He also pointed out that phasing out controls on capital flows poses a problem. His solution is radical—creation of a European central bank—and he criticizes the British government and especially the prime minister for dragging their feet and not joining the EMS.

The Economist has been a strong supporter of a European monetary union. In an article "Ecu into Monnet: Some Ideas for the Next Stage of Europe's Monetary System" (London, March 5–11, 1988), *The Economist* reports a proposal made independently by Hans-Dietrich Genscher, Germany's foreign minister, and Edouard Balladur, France's finance minister, that the EC should set up a study group on the creation of a European central bank that should issue a European currency that would circulate first alongside national currencies and would later supplant them. *The Economist* accepts the goal but finds the method of setting up a study group too slow and bureaucratic; it believes that "the EEC already has the makings of a single currency in the ecu, whose value is set by a basket of European currencies." The ecu, which at present is merely an accounting unit—no ecu bank notes exist—should be turned into real money. *The Economist* further suggests that the European currency should be called the *Monnet,* which would appeal to intellectuals because of the link to Jean Monnet (1888–1979), the eminent French statesman and founding father of the European Community.

This is, of course, rather fanciful. But the idea of a European currency is taken quite seriously. The French government is fully behind it, and so is the German government. Karl Otto Pöhl, president of the Bundesbank, said that the Bundesbank was not, as is often suggested, opposed to such a goal. He even offered a name for the European currency: it could be called the *franc-fort,* the strong franc. This would please the French and would also appeal to the Germans because it sounds like *Frankfurt,* the hometown of the Bundesbank.[8]

Pöhl spelled out his ideas in the article "A Vision of a European Central Bank."[9] Naturally he thinks that the European central bank should be as independent of political pressures as the Bundesbank is and that its policy should be to ensure price stability. Chancellor Helmut Kohl too has expressed his support for the creation of a European central bank.

What shall we make of all that? As a long-run goal, the creation of a European central bank, a single currency in a single free market, is unexceptional, from both the political and the economic point of view.

As a solution posed by phasing out exchange controls, however, the situation is different. It is inconceivable that a European central bank and European currency can be set up by 1990, even if we assume that radical rejection of such a plan by the British government can be overcome.

Suppose the big four—Britain, France, Germany, and Italy—agree in principle that a Eurobank and a Eurocurrency should be set up. There will still remain important questions where strongly held divergent views have to be reconciled. For example, the German view that the Eurobank should be as independent of political pressure as the Bundesbank and that its task should be to maintain price stability will hardly go unchallenged. The conclusion is that the problem posed by phasing out controls in 1990 must be tackled in 1990 and cannot be left to be solved by a hypothetical European central bank.

Notes

CHAPTER 1: THE DETERMINANTS AND IMPLICATIONS OF THE CHOICE
OF AN EXCHANGE RATE SYSTEM

1. Alan C. Stockman, "Real Exchange Rates under Alternative Nominal Exchange Rate Systems," *Journal of International Money and Finance*, vol. 2 (August 1983), pp. 147–66.

2. Michael Mussa, "Nominal Exchange Rate Regimes and the Behavior of Real Exchange Rates: Evidence and Implications," in Karl Brunner and Alan H. Meltzer, eds., *Real Business Cycles, Real Exchange Rates, and Actual Policies*, Carnegie-Rochester Conference Series on Public Policy, vol. 25 (1986), p. 202.

3. Alan C. Stockman, "Real Exchange Rate Variability under Pegged and Floating Nominal Exchange Rate Systems: An Equilibrium Theory" (Working Paper No. 128, University of Rochester, April 1988).

4. A useful analysis of the link between exchange rate arrangements and other policy instruments in Asian countries that has implications well beyond the Asian sample considered is that by Donald J. Mathieson, "Exchange Rate Arrangements and Monetary Policy" (Manuscript, International Monetary Fund, February 1988).

5. In general, the literature on the optimum currency area focuses on factors that make countries better or worse candidates for joining a common currency area. These factors include the size of the economy, the degree of wage and price flexibility, the openness of the economy, and factors influencing the ease of adjustment to imbalances.

6. Robert H. Heller, "Determinants of Exchange Rate Practices," *Journal of Money, Credit, and Banking*, vol. 10 (August 1978), pp. 308–21.

7. The sample consists of nine countries that float and seventy-seven countries that are pegged either to a single other currency or a basket.

8. Discriminant analysis is a statistical technique used to classify a population with groups according to certain observable characteristics.

9. These countries are not included in his original sample.

10. Jacob S. Dreyer, "Determinants of Exchange Rate Regimes for Currencies of Developing Countries: Some Preliminary Results," *World Development*, vol. 6 (April 1978), pp. 437–45.

11. Merle Holden, Paul Holden, and Esther Suss, "The Determinants of Exchange Rate Flexibility: An Empirical Investigation," *The Review of Economics and Statistics*, vol. 61 (August 1979), pp. 327–33.

12. Michael Melvin, "The Choice of an Exchange Rate System and Mac-

roeconomic Stability," *Journal of Money, Credit, and Banking*, vol. 17 (November 1985a), pp. 467–78.

13. Andreas Savvides, "Real Exchange Rate Variability and the Choice of Exchange Rate Regime by Developing Countries" (Manuscript, Oklahoma State University, 1988).

14. Jean-Claude Nascimento, "The Choice of an Optimum Exchange Currency Regime for a Small Open Economy," *Journal of Development Economics*, vol. 25 (February 1987).

15. Michael Melvin, "Currency Substitution and Western European Monetary Unification," *Economica*, vol. 52 (February 1985b), pp. 79–91.

16. Hali J. Edison and Erling Vardal, "Optimal Currency Basket in a World of Generalized Floating: An Application to the Nordic Countries," *International Journal of Forecasting*, vol. 3 (1987), pp. 81–96.

17. Many studies have provided similar evidence. See, for instance, Stockman, "Real Exchange Rates"; Mussa, "Nominal Exchange Rate Regimes"; and Janice Moulton Westerfield, "An Examination of Foreign Exchange Risk under Fixed and Floating Rate Regimes," *Journal of International Economics*, vol. 7 (May 1977), pp. 181–200.

18. Other research providing similar evidence includes that by Jeffrey H. Bergstrand, "Is Exchange Rate Volatility Excessive?" *New England Economic Review*, Federal Reserve Bank of Boston (September–October 1983), pp. 5–14; and Jacob A. Frenkel and Michael L. Mussa, "The Efficiency of Foreign Exchange Markets and Measures of Turbulence," *American Economic Review*, vol. 70 (May 1980), pp. 374–81.

19. Marie Thursby, "The Resource Reallocation Costs of Fixed and Flexible Exchange Rates," *Journal of International Economics* 10 (February 1980), pp. 79–90; and "The Resource Reallocation Costs of Fixed and Flexible Exchange Rates, a Multicountry Extension," *Journal of International Economics*, vol. 11 (November 1981), pp. 487–93.

20. Sven W. Arndt, Richard J. Sweeney, and Thomas D. Willett, eds., *Exchange Rates, Trade and the U.S. Economy* (Cambridge, Mass.: Ballinger, 1985).

21. Roger D. Huang, "The Monetary Approach to Exchange Rates in an Efficient Foreign Exchange Market: Tests Based on Volatility," *Journal of Finance*, vol. 36 (March 1981), pp. 31–41; R. H. Vander Kraats and L. D. Booth, "Empirical Tests of the Monetary Approach to Exchange Rate Determination," *Journal of International Money and Finance*, vol. 2 (December 1983), pp. 255–78; Kenneth D. West, "A Standard Monetary Model and the Variability of the Deutschemark-Dollar Exchange Rate," *Journal of International Economics*, vol. 23 (August 1987), pp. 57–76; and Sushil B. Wadhwani, "Are Exchange Rates 'Excessively' Volatile," *Journal of International Economics*, vol. 22 (May 1987), pp. 339–48.

22. Jeffrey A. Frenkel and Richard Meese, "Are Exchange Rates Excessively Variable?" in Stanley Fischer, ed., *NBER Macroeconomics Annual, 1987* (Cambridge: MIT Press, 1987), pp. 117–53.

23. Behzad T. Diba, "A Critique of Variance Bounds Tests for Monetary

Exchange Rate Models," *Journal of Money, Credit, and Banking*, vol. 19 (February 1987), pp. 104–11.

24. Paul R. Krugman, "Is the Strong Dollar Sustainable?" *The U.S. Dollar— Recent Developments, Outlook, and Policy Options* (Kansas City: Federal Reserve Bank of Kansas City, 1985), pp. 103–32.

25. George W. Evans, "A Test for Speculative Bubbles and the Sterling-Dollar Exchange Rate: 1981–84," *American Economic Review*, vol. 76 (September 1986), pp. 621–36; Richard A. Meese, "Testing for Bubbles in Exchange Markets: A Case of Sparkling Rates," *Journal of Political Economy*, vol. 94 (April 1986), pp. 345–73; and Wing Thye Woo, "Some Evidence of Speculative Bubbles in the Foreign Exchange Market," *Journal of Money, Credit, and Banking*, vol. 19 (November 1987), pp. 499–514.

26. *Economic Report of the President*, Washington, D.C., 1979, p. 154.

27. Kenneth Singleton, "Speculation and the Volatility of Foreign Currency Exchange Rates," Carnegie-Rochester Conference Series on Public Policy, vol. 26 (1987), p. 18.

28. Milton Friedman, "The Case for Flexible Exchange Rates," in *Essays in Positive Economics* (Chicago: University of Chicago Press, 1953); and George N. Halm, *Approaches to Greater Flexibility of Exchange Rates* (Princeton: Princeton University Press, 1970).

29. Ronald I. McKinnon, "Monetary and Exchange Rate Policies for International Financial Stability: A Proposal," *The Journal of Economic Perspectives*, vol. 2 (Winter 1988), p. 86.

30. Jacques R. Artus, "Toward a More Orderly Exchange Rate System," in Robert Z. Aliber, ed., *The Reconstruction of International Monetary Arrangements* (New York: St. Martins Press, 1987), p. 57.

31. Michael R. Darby and James R. Lothian, "The International Transmission of Inflation Afloat," in Michael Bordo, ed., *Money, History and International Finance: Essays in Honor of Anna J. Schwartz* (Chicago: University of Chicago Press, forthcoming), p. 24.

32. Andre Farber, Richard Roll, and Bruno Solnik, "An Empirical Study of Risk under Fixed and Flexible Exchange," *Journal of Monetary Economics*, vol. 5 (Supplement, 1977), pp. 235–65.

33. Ibid., p. 263.

34. Michael Melvin and Michael Ormiston, "Investor Preferences for Fixed or Floating Exchange Rate Regimes" (Working paper, Arizona State University, 1989).

35. International Monetary Fund, *Exchange Rate Volatility and World Trade* (Washington, D.C., July 1984), p. 36.

36. Thomas D. Willett, "The Causes and Effects of Exchange Rate Volatility," in Jacob S. Dreyer, Gottfried Haberler, and Thomas D. Willett, eds., *The International Monetary System* (Washington, D.C.: American Enterprise Institute, 1982).

37. M. A. Akhtar and R. Spence Hilton, "Effects of Exchange Rate Uncertainty on German and U.S. Trade," Federal Reserve Bank of New York *Quarterly Review*, vol. 9 (Spring 1984), pp. 7–16.

38. Padma Gotur, "Effects of Exchange Rate Volatility on Trade: Some Further Evidence," *IMF Staff Papers*, vol. 32 (September 1985), pp. 475–512.

39. Peter B. Kenen and Dani Rodrik, "Measuring and Analyzing the Effects of Short-term Volatility in Real Exchange Rates," *Review of Economics and Statistics*, vol. 68 (May 1986), pp. 311–15.

40. M. J. Bailey, G. S. Tavlas, and M. Ulan, "Exchange Rate Variability and Trade Performance: Evidence for the Big Seven Industrial Countries," *Weltwirtschaftliches Archives* 122 (1986), pp. 466–77; and "The Impact of Exchange Rate Volatility on Export Growth: Some Theoretical Considerations and Empirical Results," *Journal of Policy Modeling*, vol. 9 (Spring 1987), pp. 225–43.

41. J. G. Thursby and M. C. Thursby, "The Uncertainty Effects of Floating Exchange Rates: Empirical Evidence on International Trade Flows," in S. W. Arndt, R. J. Sweeney, and T. O. Willett, eds., *Exchange Rates, Trade and the U.S. Economy* (Cambridge, Mass.: Ballinger, 1985), p. 161.

42. David O. Cushman, "Has Exchange Risk Depressed International Trade? The Impact of Third-Country Exchange Risk," *Journal of International Money and Finance*, vol. 5 (September 1986), pp. 361–79.

43. Cushman, "Has Exchange Risk Depressed International Trade?" p. 377.

44. David O. Cushman, "The Impact of Third-Country Exchange Risk: A Correction," *Journal of International Money and Finance*, vol. 7 (September 1988), pp. 359–60. He corrects a mistake in his data set and reports results that are essentially similar to those discussed here.

45. David O. Cushman, "U.S. Bilateral Trade Flows and Exchange Risk during the Floating Period," *Journal of International Economics*, vol. 24 (May 1988), pp. 317–30.

46. Keith E. Maskus, "Exchange Rate Risk and U.S. Trade: A Sectoral Analysis," Federal Reserve Bank of Kansas City *Economic Review* (March 1986), p. 28.

47. Paul De Grauwe and Bernard de Bellefroid, "Long-Run Exchange Rate Variability and International Trade," in S. W. Arndt and J. D. Richardson, eds., *Real-Financial Linkages among Open Economies* (Cambridge: MIT Press, 1987), p. 198.

48. Tijana Z. Perl, "The Overall Effect of Exchange Rate Variability versus the Effect of Pure Exchange Rate Risk on Total and Sectoral U.S. Trade" (Manuscript, Claremont Graduate School, 1988), p. 9.

49. Josef C. Brada and Jose A. Mendez, "Exchange Rate Risk, Exchange Rate Regime and the Volume of International Trade," *Kyklos*, vol. 41, no. 2 (1988), p. 277.

50. In recent years, there have been a number of papers that report model simulations that shed light on what is the direction of transmission of monetary and fiscal shocks under floating exchange rates, such as those in Ralph C. Bryant et al., eds., *Empirical Macroeconomics for Independent Economies* (Washington, D.C.: Brookings Institute, 1988). But there are relatively few empirical papers that compare the differences in monetary and fiscal policies under different exchange rate regimes or evaluate alternative exchange rate regimes under various exogenous disturbances.

51. Robert Lucas, "Econometric Policy Evaluation: A Critique," in Karl

Brunner and Allan H. Meltzer, eds., *The Phillips Curve and Labor Markets,*
Carnegie-Rochester Conference Series in Public Policy (Amsterdam: North-
Holland, 1976), pp. 19–46.

52. Ernesto Hernandez-Cata et al., "Monetary Policy under Alternative
Exchange Rate Regimes: Simulations with a Multicountry Model" (Interna-
tional Finance Discussion Paper No. 130, Board of Governors of the Federal
Reserve System, February 1979).

53. Guy V. Stevens et al., *The U.S. Economy in an Interdependent World: A
Multicountry Model* (Board of Governors of the Federal Reserve System, 1984).
The multicountry model (MCM) is a system of linked national mac-
roeconomic models at the center of which is a medium-sized model of the
U.S. economy. Linked to it and to each other are models for Canada, West
Germany, Japan, and the United Kingdom and an abbreviated model of the
rest of the world.

54. Akihiro Amano, "Exchange Rate Modeling in the EPA World Economic
Model," in Paul De Grauwe and Theo Peeters, eds., *Exchange Rates in Multicountry Econometric Models* (London: Macmillan, 1983). The Japanese Economic Planning Agency (EPA) model is a multicountry model involving nine
individual country models and a small regional block, which are linked
together through a trade linkage submodel and other channels of direct
linkages.

55. Organization for Economic Cooperation and Development, "Macroeconomic Policy and Exchange Rates," *OECD Economic Studies,* no. 3 (Au-
tumn 1984), pp. 119–44. The large OECD interlink model has twenty-three
OECD countries plus eight regions.

56. John F. Helliwell and Tim Padmore, "Empirical Studies of Macroeconomic Interdependence," in R. W. Jones and P. B. Kenen, eds., *Handbook
of International Economics,* vol. 2 (Amsterdam: North-Holland, 1985), pp. 1107–
45.

57. Michael R. Darby, "International Transmission under Pegged and Float-
ing Exchange Rates: An Empirical Comparison," in J. S. Bhandari and B. H.
Putnam, eds., *Economic Interdependence and Flexible Exchange Rates* (Cambridge:
MIT Press, 1983).

58. James M. Boughton, Richard D. Haas, and Paul R. Masson, "The Role
of Exchange Rate Movements in Transmitting International Disturbances"
(IMF Working Paper WP-86-4, 1986).

59. John Taylor, "An Econometric Evaluation of International Monetary
Policy Rules: Fixed versus Flexible Exchange Rates" (Working paper, Stanford
University, October 1986).

60. Warwick J. McKibbin and Jeffrey D. Sachs, "Comparing the Global
Performance of Alternative Exchange Rate Arrangements," *Journal of Interna-
tional Money and Finance* (forthcoming). The model is a rational expectations,
dynamic general equilibrium macroeconometric model of the world economy.
The world economy is divided into five regions consisting of the United
States, Japan, the rest of the OECD countries, the Organization of Petroleum
Exporting Countries (OPEC), and the nonoil developing countries. Each
region is linked via flows of goods and assets.

61. Warwick J. McKibbin and Jeffrey D. Sachs, "Coordination of Monetary and Fiscal Policies in the OECD," in J. Frenkel, ed., *International Aspects of Fiscal Policy* (Chicago: University of Chicago Press, 1985).

62. Hali J. Edison, Marcus H. Miller, and John Williamson, "On Evaluating and Extending the Target Zone Proposal," *Journal of Policy Modelling*, vol. 9 (1987), pp. 199–224.

63. The five MCM countries are the United States, Canada, Germany (the Federal Republic), Japan, and the United Kingdom (there is also an abbreviated rest-of-world sector, where monetary policy is left unchanged).

64. Hali J. Edison, Jaime R. Marquez, and Ralph W. Tryon, "The Structure and Properties of the FRB Multicountry Model," *Economic Modelling* vol. 4, (April 1987), pp. 115–315.

65. David Currie and Simon Wren-Lewis, "Evaluating the Extended Target Zone Proposal for the G-3" (Manuscript, London, 1987); and "Conflict and Cooperation in International Macroeconomic Policymaking: The Past Decade and Future Prospects" (Working paper, International Monetary Fund, December 1987). GEM is a large scale disaggregated model of the main OECD countries consisting of fourteen countries or sector blocs. The G-7 countries are modeled in some detail, with each country bloc containing at least twenty-five behavioral equations and more than thirty identities. The Netherlands, Belgium, and the rest of OECD are modeled in smaller blocs while OPEC, the LDCs and centrally planned economy blocs consist mainly of trade equations.

66. John Williamson and Marcus H. Miller, *Targets and Indicators: A Blueprint for the International Coordination of Economic Policy* (Washington, D.C.: Institute for International Economics, 1987).

67. One of the main differences between the two Currie and Wren-Lewis papers is that the latter paper includes two more years of data (1985–1986).

68. Jacob A. Frenkel, Morris Goldstein, and Paul Masson, "International Coordination of Economic Policies: Scope, Methods, and Effects" (IMF Working Paper WP-88-53, 1988). Multimod contains separate submodels for the G-3 countries and one additional submodel incorporating the remaining four G-7 countries and the other smaller industrial countries. Developing countries (excluding the high-income oil exporters) are modeled as one region, but with some industrial disaggregation. The submodels are linked through trade and financial flows. For more details about the model see Paul R. Masson et al., "MULTIMOD: A Multi-regional Econometric Model," *IMF Staff Studies for World Economic Outlook* (Washington, D.C.: International Monetary Fund, 1988).

69. In implementing the monetary reaction rule the target zone bands that are considered for Multimod are larger than those prescribed by Williamson. In particular, 20 percent bands rather than 10 percent bands were used, implying a lower feedback of exchange rates misalignment on interest rates.

70. Andrew Hughes Hallett, Gerry Hotham, and G. J. Hutson, "Exchange Rate Targeting as Surrogate International Cooperation" (Manuscript, University of Newcastle, September 1988).

71. Paul Levine, David Currie, and Jessica Gaines, "Simple Rules for International Policy Agreements" (Manuscript, London Business School, September 1988).

72. Patrick Minford, "Exchange Rate Regimes and Policy Coordination" (Manuscript, Liverpool University, September 1988). Andrew Blake, David Vines, and Martin Weale, "Wealth Targets, Exchange Rate Targets and Macroeconomic Policy" (CEPR Discussion Paper 247, June 1988).

73. Jacob A. Frenkel and Morris Goldstein, "A Guide to Target Zones," *IMF Staff Papers*, vol. 33 (December 1986), pp. 633–70.

74. John Williamson, "Exchange Rate Management: The Role of Target Zones," *American Economic Review*, vol. 77 (May 1987), p. 200.

75. John Williamson, *The Exchange Rate System* (Washington, D.C.: Institute for International Economics, 1985).

76. Stockman, "Real Exchange Rate."

77. Willett, "The Causes and Effects."

78. Richard C. Marston, "Exchange Rate Policy Reconsidered," in Martin Feldstein, ed., *International Economic Cooperation* (Chicago: University of Chicago Press, 1988), pp. 79–136.

79. Marianne Baxter and Alan Stockman, "For What Does the Exchange Rate System Matter?" (Working paper, University of Rochester, June 1988), p. 79.

COMMENTARY: EFFECTS OF AN EXCHANGE RATE SYSTEM

1. These arguments are developed in Jacob A. Frenkel and Morris Goldstein, "The International Monetary System: Developments and Prospects," *CATO Journal* (Fall 1988), pp. 285–306.

2. Contrast, for example, the target zone scheme in John Williamson, *The Exchange Rate System* (Washington, D.C.: Institute for International Economics, 1985), with that in John Williamson and Marcus H. Miller, *Targets and Indicators: A Blueprint for the International Coordination of Economic Policies* (Washington, D.C.: Institute for International Economics, 1987).

3. See Jacob A. Frenkel, Morris Goldstein, and Paul Masson, "International Economic Policy Coordination: Rationale, Mechanisms, and Effects," in William Branson, Jacob A. Frenkel, and Morris Goldstein, eds., *International Policy Coordination and Exchange Rate Fluctuations* (Chicago: University of Chicago Press, forthcoming); and Frenkel, Goldstein, and Masson, "Simulating the Effects of Some Simple Coordinated versus Uncoordinated Policy Rules" (Brookings Institution Proceedings, Washington, D.C., 1988).

4. See Francesco Giovazzi and Alberto Giovannini, "Can the EMS Be Exported?" in Bronson, Frenkel, Goldstein, eds., *International Policy Coordination.*

5. Ibid.

CHAPTER 2: INTERNATIONAL CAPITAL FLOWS, THE DOLLAR, AND U.S. FINANCIAL POLICIES

1. For further analysis of the role of the growth of international capital mobility in contributing to the breakdown of the Bretton Woods system, see

Robert Solomon, *The International Monetary System* (New York: Harper & Row, 1989); John Williamson, *The Failure of World Monetary Reform* (New York: New York University Press, 1977); and Thomas D. Willett, *Floating Exchange Rates and International Monetary Reform* (Washington, D.C.: American Enterprise Institute, 1977).

2. We use the term "capital mobility" synonymously with the degree of international financial market integration as discussed, for example, in Jeffrey A. Frankel, "Monetary and Portfolio-Balance Models of Exchange Rate Determination," in Jagdeep S. Bhandari and Bluford H. Putnam, eds., *Economic Interdependence and Flexible Rates* (Cambridge: MIT Press, 1983), pp. 84–115, and Clas Wihlborg, "Flexible Exchange Rates, Currency Risks, and Integration of Capital Markets," in Assar Lindbeck, ed., *Inflation and Employment in Open Economies* (Amsterdam: North-Holland Press, 1974), pp. 169–87. In essence, capital mobility is perfect if the returns on otherwise equivalent securities denominated in different currencies and issued in different countries but otherwise identical are equalized at all times through international arbitrage. In other words perfect capital mobility implies perfectly (infinitely elastic) arbitrage schedules. Where exchange risk and risk aversion are present, then we must distinguish between covered and uncovered arbitrage schedules. In such circumstances the amount of capital that moves in response to a change in international interest rate differentials is a function of the elasticities of both the covered arbitrage and speculative schedules. Capital mobility can be perfect in the sense of the law of one price holding for international investments where exchange risk is eliminated through forward contracts; that is, the covered arbitrage schedule is perfectly elastic, yet there is little capital flow because risk aversion and uncertainty make the speculative schedule inelastic. In such a case a country may have considerable monetary independence even though international arbitrage enforces covered interest parity at all times. Imperfect capital mobility in the senses used here is not necessarily an indication of market inefficiency.

One useful way in which to think of the degree of capital mobility is in terms of the offset coefficient, which reflects the degree to which an autonomous change in domestic monetary aggregates is offset by induced international capital flows. For a small country, perfect capital mobility implies an offset coefficient of one; that is, there is no scope for independent domestic monetary policy. Zero capital mobility implies an offset coefficient of zero. For further discussion of concepts of capital mobility and empirical evidence relevant to these concepts, see Ralph C. Bryant, *International Financial Intermediation* (Washington, D.C.: Brookings Institute, 1987), and Jeffrey A. Frankel, "International Capital Mobility and Exchange Rate Volatility" (Paper delivered at Federal Reserve Bank of Boston conference on international payments imbalances, Bald Peak, N.H., October 5–7, 1988) and the references cited there.

3. On the effects of international capital mobility and the Eurodollar market on U.S. monetary conditions, see the analysis and references in Ralph C. Bryant, *Money and Monetary Policy in Interdependent Nations* (Washington, D.C.: Brookings Institution, 1980), and *International Financial Intermediation;*

Jacob Dreyer, Gottfried Haberler, and Thomas D. Willett, eds., *Exchange Rate Flexibility* (Washington, D.C.: American Enterprise Institute, 1975); Richard J. Sweeney and Thomas D. Willett, "Eurodollars, Petrodollars, and Problems of World Liquidity and Inflation," in Carnegie-Rochester Conference Series on Public Policy (1977), pp. 277–310; and John Wenninger and Thomas Klitgaard, "Exploring the Effects of Capital Movements on M1 and the Economy," *Federal Reserve Bank of New York Quarterly Review* (Summer 1987), pp. 21–31.

4. For recent analysis and references to the literature on the effects of floating exchanges on inflation, see Marion Bond, "Exchange Rates, Inflation and Vicious Circles," *IMF Staff Papers* (Washington, D.C.: International Monetary Fund, December 1980), pp. 679–711; Andrew Crockett and Morris Goldstein, "Inflation under Fixed and Flexible Exchange Rates," *IMF Staff Papers*, no. 3 (Washington, D.C.: International Monetary Fund, 1976), pp. 509–44; Thomas D. Willett and John Mullen, "The Effects of Alternative International Monetary Systems on Macroeconomic Discipline and the Political Business Cycle," in Raymond Lombra and Willard Witte, eds., *Political Economy of International and Domestic Monetary Relations* (Ames: Iowa State University Press, 1982), pp. 143–59; and Thomas D. Willett and Matthias Wolf, "The Vicious Circle Debate," *Kyklos*, fasc. 2 (1983), pp. 231–48. For analysis of the recent U.S. experience, see J. Harold McClure, Jr., "Dollar Appreciation and the Reagan Disinflation," in Sven Arndt, Richard J. Sweeney, and Thomas D. Willett, eds., *Exchange Rates, Trade and the U.S. Economy* (Cambridge, Mass.: Ballinger Publishing, 1985), pp. 267–72; and Jeffrey Sachs, "The Dollar and the Policy Mix: 1985," Brookings Papers on Economic Activity, no. 1 (Washington, D.C.: Brookings Institution, 1985), pp. 114–97.

5. For recent contributions and detailed surveys of this literature, see Arndt, Sweeney, and Willett, *Exchange Rates, Trade and the U.S. Economy;* Jagdeep S. Bhandari, ed., *Exchange Rate Management under Uncertainty* (Cambridge: MIT Press, 1987); Bhandari and Putman, *Economic Interdependence and Flexible Exchange Rates;* David Bigman and Teizo Taya, eds., *Exchange Rate and Trade Instability: Causes, Consequences, and Remedies* (Cambridge, Mass.: Ballinger Press, 1983); J. Bilson and Richard Marston, eds., *Exchange Rate Theory and Practice* (Chicago: University of Chicago Press, 1984); Bryant, *Money and Monetary Policy;* Bryant et al., eds., *Empirical Macroeconomics for Interdependent Economies* (Washington, D.C.: Brookings Institution, 1988); and Ronald W. Jones and Peter B. Kenen, eds., *Handbook of International Economics*, vol. 2 (Amsterdam: North-Holland, 1985).

6. For a recent analysis of this approach and its extensions in recent years, see Jacob A. Frenkel and Assaf Razin, "The Mundell-Fleming Model a Quarter Century Later," *IMF Staff Papers* (Washington, D.C.: International Monetary Fund, 1987), pp. 567–620.

7. See Ronald I. McKinnon, "The J-Curve, Stabilizing Speculation, and Capital Constraints on Foreign Exchange Dealers," in David Bigman and Teizo Taya, eds., *Floating Exchange Rates and the State of World Payments* (Cambridge, Mass.: Ballinger Publishing, 1984), pp. 101–25.

8. See the analysis and references in Dallas D. Batten and R. W. Hafer, "Currency Substitution: A Test of Its Importance," *Federal Reserve Bank of St.*

Louis Economic Review (August–September 1984), pp. 5–11; Ronald I. McKinnon et al., "International Influences on U.S. Inflation: Summary of an Exchange," *American Economic Review* (December 1984), pp. 1132–34; F. Spinelli, "Currency Substitution, Flexible Exchange Rates, and the Case for International Monetary Cooperation," *IMF Staff Papers* (Washington, D.C.: International Monetary Fund, December 1983), pp. 755–83; Douglas H. Joines, "International Currency Substitution and the Income Velocity of Money," *Journal of International Money and Finance* (September 1985), pp. 303–16; and Thomas D. Willett et al., "Currency Substitution, U.S. Money Demand, and International Interdependence," *Contemporary Policy Issues* (July 1987), pp. 76–82.

9. Recent rational-expectations open-economy models tend to focus on informational efficiency under different patterns of disturbances. See, for example, Jagdeep S. Bhandardi, "Informational Efficiency and the Open Economy," *Journal of Money, Credit, and Banking* (November 1982), pp. 457–78; Robert P. Flood and Robert Hodrick, "Optimal Price and Inventory Adjustment in an Open Economy Model of the Business Cycle," *Quarterly Journal of Economics* (August 1985), pp. 887–914; Reuven Glick and Clas Wihlborg, "The Role of Information Acquisition and Financial Markets in International Macroeconomic Adjustment," *Journal of International Money and Finance* (September 1986), pp. 257–83; Reuven Glick and Clas Wihlborg, "Real Exchange Rate Effects of Monetary Shocks under Fixed and Flexible Exchange Rates," Working paper (Los Angeles: University of Southern California, 1987); Kent P. Kimbrough, "Aggregate Information and the Role of Monetary Policy in an Open Economy," *Journal of Political Economy* (February 1984), pp. 268–80; Kimbrough, "The Information Content of the Exchange Rate and the Stability of Real Output under Alternative Exchange Rate Regimes," *Journal of International Money and Finance* (April 1983), pp. 27–28; and Bo Sanderman Rasmussen, "Stabilization Policies in Open Economies with Imperfect Current Information," *Journal of International Money and Finance*, vol. 7, no. 2 (June 1988), pp. 151–66.

Most of these models assume perfect capital mobility, but Glick and Wihlborg allow for limited capital mobility in the form of noise in the uncovered interest rate differential. A particularly interesting result from this literature is the argument by Kimbrough that output variability will be less under flexible than under fixed exchange rates because of the additional information about the nature of disturbances provided by exchange rate movements under flexible rates.

10. It is sometimes argued that inappropriate changes in the exchange rate also impose important economy-wide externalities. See, for example, Richard N. Cooper, "I.M.F. Surveillance over Exchange Rates," in Robert Mundell and Jacques Pollak, eds., *The New International Monetary System* (New York: Columbia University Press, 1977), pp. 69–83. For a critical analysis of this view, see Thomas D. Willett, "Alternative Approaches to International Surveillance of Exchange-Rate Policies," in *Managed Exchange Rate Flexibility* (Boston: Federal Reserve Bank of Boston, 1978), pp. 148–72.

11. For examples of some types of cases in which destabilizing speculation may be profitable to the speculators and increase rather than reduce the welfare of consumers, see David Feldman and Edward Tower, "Optimal Destabilizing Speculation," *De Economist,* vol. 134, no. 3 (1986), pp. 368–77. See also Milton Friedman, "In Defense of Destabilizing Speculation," in Milton Friedman, *The Optimum Quantity of Money and Other Essays* (Chicago: Aldine Publishing, 1969), pp. 285–91.

12. See Milton Friedman, *Essays in Positive Economics* (Chicago: University of Chicago Press, 1953).

13. See Fritz Machlup, "Equilibrium and Disequilibrium," *Economic Journal* (March 1958), pp. 1–24. In the perfect capital-mobility Keynesian rational-expectations models pioneered by Dornbusch, sluggish adjustment in the domestic economy causes the short-run equilibrium exchange rate to overshoot its long-run equilibrium level. This form of overshooting occurs with stabilizing speculation. Thus destabilizing speculation is a possible but not a necessary cause of exchange rate overshooting.

14. The importance of this possibility was emphasized in the early days of floating by Ronald I. McKinnon, "Floating Exchange Rates 1973–74: The Emperor's New Clothes," in Karl Brunner and Allen H. Meltzer, eds., *Institutional Arrangements and the Inflation Problem,* Carnegie-Rochester Conference Series on Public Policy, vol. 3 (1976), pp. 79–114. While Willett, *Floating Exchange Rates,* has argued that McKinnon's original analysis overstated the generality of this problem, we argue later that at times this can be an important consideration.

15. For recent contributions to and surveys of this literature on exchange market efficiency, see Arndt, Sweeney, and Willett, *Exchange Rates, Trade and the U.S. Economy;* Paul Boothe and David Longworth, "Foreign Exchange Market Efficiency Tests: Implications of Recent Empirical Findings," *Journal of International Money and Finance,* vol. 5 (June 1986), pp. 135–52; Jeffrey A. Frankel and Richard Meese, "Are Exchange Rates Excessively Variable?" in Stanley Fisher, ed., *National Bureau for Economic Research Macroeconomics Annual 1987* (Cambridge: MIT Press, 1987), pp. 117–53; Robert J. Hodrick, *The Empirical Evidence on the Efficiency of Forward and Future Foreign Exchange Markets* (New York: Harwood Academic Publishers, 1987); Richard M. Levich, "Empirical Studies on Exchange Rates: Price Behavior, Rate Determination and Market Efficiency," in Jones and Kenen, *Handbook of International Economics,* pp. 980–1040; Ronald MacDonald, *Floating Exchange Rates Theories and Evidence* (Winchester, Mass.: Allen & Unwin, 1988); and Richard J. Sweeney, "Beating the Foreign Exchange Markets," *Journal of Finance* (March 1986), pp. 163–82.

16. See, for example, William H. Branson, "Causes of Appreciation and Volatility of the Dollar," in *The U.S. Dollar—Recent Developments, Outlook, and Policy Options* (Federal Reserve Bank of Kansas City); William H. Branson, "The Limits of Monetary Coordination as Exchange Rate Policy," Brookings Papers on Economic Activity, no. 1 (Washington, D.C.: Brookings Institution, 1986), pp. 175–94; Jacob A. Frenkel, "Commentary on 'Causes of Appreciation

and Volatility of the Dollar,' " in *The U.S. Dollar*, pp. 53–63; and Jeffrey Sachs, "Is There a Case for Greater Exchange Rate Coordination?" in *The U.S. Dollar*, pp. 185–212.

17. This could likewise explain the substantial bias over this period in the predictions implied by forward rates. See, for example, Karen Lewis, "The Persistence of the 'Peso Problem' When Policy Is Noisy," *Journal of International Money and Finance* (March 1988), pp. 5–21.

18. See Jeffrey A. Frankel, "The Dazzling Dollar," Brookings Papers on Economic Activity, no. 1 (Washington, D.C.: Brookings Institution, 1985), pp. 199–217, and Jeffrey A. Frankel, "International Capital Flows and Domestic Economic Policies," in Martin Feldstein, ed., *The United States in the World Economy* (Chicago: University of Chicago Press, 1988), p. 625.

19. See, for example, Frankel, "The Dazzling Dollar," and Michael Gavin, "The Dollar as a Speculative Bubble: 1984–1985" (Paper delivered at conference on trade imbalances and exchange rate volatility, Clark University, Worcester, Mass., September 1987).

20. For recent surveys and discussions of the empirical literature on the degree of international capital mobility, see Bryant, *International Financial Intermediation*; Frankel, "International Capital Mobility"; Maurice Obstfeld, "Capital Mobility in the World Economy: Theory and Measurement," in Karl Brunner and Allan H. Meltzer, eds., *The National Bureau Method, International Capital Mobility and Other Essays*, Carnegie-Rochester Conference Series on Public Policy, vol. 24 (Spring 1986), pp. 55–103; and Thomas D. Willett, "Highlights of a Brookings-World Bank Workshop on the International Consequences of Budget Deficits and the Monetary-Fiscal Mix," Brookings Discussion Papers in International Economics, no. 37 (Washington, D.C.: Brookings Institution, October 1985).

21. See Paul Sarmas, "The Term Structure of Interest Differentials and the Expected Dollar Exchange Rate Paths" (Ph.D. diss., Claremont Graduate School, 1989).

22. See, for example, the analysis and references in Arndt, Sweeney, and Willett, *Exchange Rates, Trade and the U.S. Economy*; John Y. Campbell and Richard H. Clarida, "The Dollar and Real Exchange Rates," Carnegie-Rochester Conference Series on Public Policy, vol. 27 (1987), pp. 104–40; Robert J. Hodrick, *The Empirical Evidence on the Efficiency of Forward and Future Foreign Exchange Markets* (New York: Harwood Academic Publishers, 1987); Richard Marston, "Exchange Rate Policy Reconsidered," in Martin Feldstein, ed., *International Economic Cooperation* (Chicago: University of Chicago Press, 1988), pp. 79–136; and Sweeney, "Beating the Foreign Exchange Markets."

23. The evidence of risk aversion is indirect and based on systematic patterns of the forecast error of the forward rate and interest rate differentials. An alternative interpretation of these systematic errors is that they are caused by learning of structural parameters and policy rules. This interpretation is favored by the difficulty of explaining patterns of implied time-varying risk premiums.

24. In recent years economists have appropriately emphasized the limits to the effectiveness of sterilized intervention. The combination of the wide-

spread belief in close to perfect capital mobility and the low power of tests of forward rate bias led, however, to a tendency to assert that sterilized intervention could have virtually no effect apart from signaling. Recent empirical research suggests that such a view itself is too strong. On these issues see Bryant, *International Financial Intermediation;* Dale W. Henderson and Stephanie Sampson, "Intervention in Foreign Exchange Markets: A Summary of Ten Staff Studies," *Federal Reserve Bulletin,* vol. 69 (November 1983), pp. 830–36; Peter B. Kenen, "Exchange Rate Management: What Role of Monetary Policy in an Open Economy," *Journal of Political Economy* (February 1984), pp. 248–80; Marston, "Exchange Rate Policy Reconsidered"; Maurice Obstfeld, "Can We Sterilize? Theory and Evidence," *American Economic Review* 72 (May 1982), pp. 45–50; and Thomas D. Willett, "The Causes and Effects of Exchange Rate Volatility," in Jacob Dreyer, Gottfried Haberler, and Thomas D. Willett, eds., *The International Monetary System* (Washington, D.C.: American Enterprise Institute, 1982), pp. 25–64.

25. In the literature about the principal agent, there are theoretical arguments for a short-term bias in managers' decision making even when stockholders know of this bias. Essentially, agents (managers) favor projects with a high return in the short term over projects that are better in present value terms but provide a return in the longer term only. The reason is that principals cannot disentangle perfectly whether the high return in the short run results from skill or other factors. If the manager chooses the better project in present value terms, there is a positive probability that a low return in the short run is due to a lack of skills. Thus, principals expect agents to have a short-term bias, which forces them to operate with such a bias in order not to look bad. See, for example, Tim Campbell and Anthony Marino, "On the Incentive of Managers to Make Myopic Investment Decisions," Working paper (Los Angeles: University of Southern California, 1988), and Bengt Holstrom, "Agency Costs and Innovative Activity," in D. Day, G. Eliusson, and C. Wihlborg, eds., *Markets for Innovation, Ownership, and Control* (forthcoming). This reasoning seems applicable to a wide variety of economic (and academic) behavior.

26. See, for example, John Rutledge, "An Economist's View of the Foreign Exchange Market," in Dreyer, Haberler, and Willett, *Exchange-Rate Flexibility,* pp. 83–88.

27. Shafigul Islam, "Dollar and Policy-Performance-Confidence Mix," Princeton Essays in International Finance, no. 170 (Princeton: Princeton University Press, July 1988).

28. Ibid.

29. See Richard M. Levich, "Empirical Studies of Exchange Rates: Price Behavior, Rate Determination and Market Efficiency," in Jones and Kenen, *Handbook of International Economics,* pp. 980–1040.

30. For additional recent discussions along at least partially similar lines, see Paul S. Armington, "Toward Understanding Major Fluctuations in the Dollar," Brookings Discussion Papers in International Economics, no. 39 (Washington, D.C.: Brookings Institution, November 1985); Paul S. Armington and Catherine Wolford, "A Model-Based Analysis of Dollar Fluctua-

tions," Brookings Discussion Papers in International Economics (Washington, D.C.: Brookings Institution, January 1984); Jeffrey A. Frankel and Kenneth A. Froot, "The Dollar as an Irrational Speculative Bubble: A Tale of Fundamentalists and Chartists," *Marcus Wallenberg Papers on International Finance*, vol. 1 (International Law Institute, 1986), pp. 27–55; Islam, "Dollar and Policy"; and Willett, "Consequences of Budget Deficits" and "The Dollar and the Deficit."

31. On the possible role of such approaches in economics, see the discussion and references in Robin Hogarth and Melvin W. Reder, eds., *Rational Choice: The Contrast between Economics and Psychology* (Chicago: Chicago University Press, 1987). For macroeconomic applications see M. H. Pessaran, *The Limits to Rational Expectations* (Oxford: Blackwell, 1987).

32. See, for example, Bryant, *Money and Monetary Policy*, and Jeffrey A. Frankel, *Obstacles to International Macroeconomic Policy Coordination*, Princeton Studies in International Finance (Princeton: Princeton University Press, forthcoming).

33. Clas Wihlborg, "The Incentive to Acquire Information and Financial Market Instability," in Day, Eliasson, and Wihlborg, *Markets for Innovation*.

34. See Roman Frydman, "Towards an Understanding of Market Processes," *American Economic Review* (September 1982), pp. 652–68, and Margaret M. Bray and N. E. Savin, "Rational Expectations Equilibrium, Learning and Model Specifications," *Econometrica*, vol. 54 (September 1986), pp. 1129–60.

35. Some might question how we could believe in the possibility of an insufficiency of stabilizing speculation when the volume of transactions in the foreign exchange market is so high. The answer is that the vast majority of transactions are undertaken by banks and brokers who do not take on substantial unbalanced positions over extended periods. Thus the market can be thin for net speculative positions even though gross turnover is quite high.

36. See James Hamilton and Charles Whiteman, "The Observable Implications of Self-Fulfilling Expectations," *Journal of Monetary Economics* (November 1985), pp. 353–74; Lewis, "The Persistence of the 'Peso Problem,'" pp. 5–21; and Guido Tabellini, "Learning and the Volatility of Exchange Rates," *Journal of International Money and Finance*, vol. 7, no. 2 (June 1988), pp. 243–50.

37. See Richard Meese, "Testing for Bubbles in Exchange Markets: The Case of Sparkling Rates," *Journal of Political Economy* (April 1986), pp. 345–73.

38. Because of offshore offerings of dollar-denominated obligations, there need not be a one-to-one relation between net U.S. international capital flows and exchange market pressures for the dollar. See, for example, the discussions by Richard N. Cooper, "Economic Interdependence and the Coordination of Economic Policies," in Jones and Kenen, *Handbook of International Economics*, pp. 1195–234, and Rudiger Dornbusch, "Flexible Exchange Rates and Excess Capital Mobility," Brookings Papers on Economic Activity, no. 1 (Washington, D.C.: Brookings Institution, 1986), pp. 209–26.

39. See, for example, Peter Isard, "Exchange Rate Modeling: An Assessment of Alternative Approaches," in Bryant et al., *Empirical Macroeconomics*, pp. 183–201; and Richard A. Meese and Kenneth Rogoff, "Was It Real? The

Exchange Rate–Interest Differential Relation over the Modern Floating Rate Period," *Journal of Finance,* vol. 43, no. 4 (September 1988), pp. 933–48.

40. See, for example, J. Bilson, "Discussion," in Dreyer, Haberler, and Willett, *International Monetary System,* pp. 116–19.

41. See, for example, Jacob A. Frenkel, "Turbulence in the Foreign Exchange Markets and Macroeconomic Policies," in Bigman and Taya, *Exchange Rate and Trade Instability,* pp. 3–27, and Charles Goodhart, "The Foreign Exchange Market: A Random Walk with a Dragging Anchor," Financial Markets Group Discussion Paper (London: London School of Economics, 1988).

42. For further analysis of the economic developments over this period and the possibility that there may have been an insufficiency of stabilizing speculation at this time, see Steven Kohlhagen, "The Experience with Floating: The 1973–1979 Dollar," in Dreyer, Haberler, and Willett, *International Monetary System,* pp. 142–79; Herbert Stein, *Presidential Economics,* 2d ed. (Washington, D.C.: American Enterprise Institute, 1988); and Thomas D. Willett, "The Fall and Rise of the Dollar," AEI Reprint, no. 196 (Washington, D.C.: American Enterprise Institute, April 1979).

43. William H. Branson, "Sources of Misalignment in the 1980s," in Richard C. Marston, ed., *Misalignment of Exchange Rates: Effects of Trade and Industry* (Chicago: Chicago University Press, 1988), p. 9.

44. See William H. Branson, "The Limits of Monetary Coordination as Exchange Rate Policy," Brookings Papers on Economic Activity, no. 1 (Washington, D.C.: Brookings Institution, 1986), pp. 175–94.

45. See Martin Feldstein, "The Budget Deficit and the Dollar," in *National Bureau of Economic Research Macroeconomics Annual 1986* (Cambridge: MIT Press, 1986), pp. 355–92.

46. Islam, "Dollar and Policy," p. 18.

47. For a range of empirical analysis of this issue, in addition to Feldstein, see Bryant et al., *Empirical Macroeconomics;* Ralph C. Bryant, Gerald Holtham, and Peter Hooper, eds., *External Deficits and the Dollar: The Pit and the Pendulum* (Washington, D.C.: Brookings Institution, 1988); Paul Evans, "Is the Dollar High because of Large Budget Deficits?" *Journal of Monetary Economics,* vol. 18 (1986), pp. 227–49; Michael M. Hutchinson and David H. Pyle, "The Real Interest Rate/Budget Deficit Link: International Evidence, 1973–1982," *Federal Reserve Bank of San Francisco Economic Review,* vol. 4 (Fall 1984), pp. 26–35; and Michael Hutchinson and Charles Pigott, "Real and Financial Linkages in the Macroeconomic Response to Budget Deficit," in Sven W. Arndt, and J. David Richardson, ed., *Real-Financial Linkages among Open Economies* (Cambridge: MIT Press, 1987), pp. 139–66.

48. See, for example, Islam, "Dollar and Policy," p. 18; Maurice Obstfeld, "Comment," in Marston, *Misalignment of Exchange Rates,* pp. 31–38; and Frankel, "The Dazzling Dollar."

49. See, for example, Islam, "Dollar and Policy"; William Poole, "Discussion," in Federal Reserve Bank of Kansas City, *The U.S. Dollar;* and Poole, "U.S. International Capital Flows" (Paper delivered at the Western Economic Association meeting, Los Angeles, July 1, 1988).

50. For an interesting exchange of views on this issue, see Branson, "Limits of Monetary Coordination"; Richard N. Cooper, "Dealing with the Trade Deficit in a Floating Rate System," Brookings Papers on Economic Activity, no. 1 (Washington, D.C.: Brookings Institution, 1986), pp. 195–207; also in this Brookings volume, see Rudiger Dornbusch, "Flexible Exchange Rates and Excess Capital Mobility," pp. 209–26, Stanley Fischer, "Symposium on Exchange Rates, Trade and Capital Flows: Discussion," pp. 227–32, and John Williamson, "Target Zones and the Management of the Dollar," pp. 165–74.

51. Safe-haven arguments have taken a number of different forms. Originally the term was used about capital flows from Europe generated, for example, by prospects of Mitterand's socialist policies in France. The term came to be used more broadly to include capital flight from the developing countries and milder views that the U.S. had become increasingly safe economically relative to other areas. An interesting variant is the argument and evidence presented by Robert Ayanian, "Political Risk, National Defense, and the Dollar," Economic Inquiry (April 1988), pp. 345–51, that the build-up in defense spending in the United States bolstered confidence and induced capital flows.

Most of the economists who have looked at the issue have concluded that safe-haven–motivated capital flows have generally not been a major cause of the rise of the dollar in the 1980s. See, for example, Frankel, "The Dazzling Dollar"; Peter Isard and Lois Stekler, "U.S. International Capital Flows and the Dollar," Brookings Papers on Economic Activity, no. 1 (Washington, D.C.: Brookings Institution 1985), pp. 219–36; and Islam, "Dollar and Policy"; these criticize dismissals of the safe-haven argument on the grounds that economists tend to ignore factors that are nonquantifiable. While there is some truth in this general assertion, it misses the point; many of the analyses of this issue argue, for example, that where safe-haven considerations are dominant, we should be seeing a decline in interest rates in the United States relative to Europe as a result of capital inflows. Likewise it is not clear why a shift in net capital flows between the United States and the developing countries should influence the value of the dollar relative to the yen or the mark.

52. See, for example, Frankel, "The Dazzling Dollar," and Paul R. Krugman, "Is the Strong Dollar Sustainable?" in The U.S. Dollar—Recent Developments, Outlook, and Policy Options, (Kansas City, Mo.: Federal Reserve Bank of Kansas City, 1985), pp. 103–32.

53. The analysis by Jeffrey A. Frankel and Kenneth A. Froot, "Using Survey Data to Test Standard Propositions regarding Exchange Rate Expectations," American Economic Review, vol. 77 (March 1986), pp. 133–53, draws on surveys by the American Express Banking Corporation, the Economist Financial Report, and Money Market Services. American Express polled more than two hundred central bankers, private bankers, corporate treasurers, and economists. The other two surveys focus on a smaller set of international bankers.

54. See, for example, Maurice Obstfeld, "Comment," in Marston, Misalignment of Exchange Rates, pp. 31–8.

55. See Jeffrey A. Frankel, The Yen/Dollar Agreement: Liberalizing Japanese

Capital Markets, Policy Analyses in International Economics, no. 9 (Washington, D.C.: Institute for International Economics, 1984).

56. See William H. Branson, *Financial Capital Flows in the U.S. Balance of Payments* (Amsterdam: North-Holland, 1968); Ralph C. Bryant, "Empirical Research on Financial Capital Flows," in Peter Kenen, ed., *International Trade and Finance: Frontiers for Research* (Cambridge: Cambridge University Press, 1975), pp. 321–62; Richard E. Caves and Grant L. Reuber, "International Capital Markets and Economic Policy under Flexible and Fixed Exchange Rates, 1951–1970," in *Canadian-United States Financial Relationships,* Federal Reserve Bank of Boston Conference Series (Boston: Federal Reserve Bank of Boston, September 1971), pp. 9–40; and Fritz Machlup et al., eds., *International Mobility and Movement of Capital* (New York: Columbia University Press, 1972).

57. One of the few recent studies is Stephen E. Haynes, "Identification of Interest Rates and International Capital Flows," *The Review of Economics and Statistics* (February 1988), pp. 103–09.

58. See Islam, "Dollar and Policy."

59. Willem Thorbecke, "Has Deficit News Contributed to High Interest Rates in the Eighties?" (Unpublished manuscript, 1987).

60. See Frankel, "The Dazzling Dollar."

61. Recently Jeffrey A. Frankel, "Recent Estimates of Time-Variation in the Conditional Variance and in the Exchange Rate Premium," *Journal of International Money and Finance,* vol. 7 (1988), pp. 115–25, has qualified considerably his initial analysis.

62. See William H. Branson, "Sources of Misalignment in the 1980s," in Marston, *Misalignment of Exchange Rates,* pp. 9–38.

63. See William Poole, "U.S. International Capital Flows" (Paper delivered at the Western Economic Association Meetings, Los Angeles, July 1, 1988).

64. See, for example, the *1988 Annual Report* of the International Monetary Fund and the survey of projections in the September 24, 1988, issue of *The Economist.* Most of the analyses that argue that the dollar has fallen sufficiently are based on some type of calculations of purchasing power parity that do not make allowance for major changes in equilibrium real exchange rates.

65. Jeffrey A. Frankel, "International Capital Flows," p. 572.

66. Dornbusch, "Flexible Exchange Rates," p. 223.

67. On the U.S. experience with capital controls, see Richard N. Cooper, "The Interest Equalization Tax: An Experiment in the Separation of Capital Markets," *Finanz Archiv,* vol. 24 (December 1965), pp. 447–71; Gottfried Haberler and Thomas D. Willett, *U.S. Balance of Payments Policies and International Monetary Reform* (Washington, D.C.: American Enterprise Institute, 1968); and Richard Herring and Thomas D. Willett, "The Capital Control Programs and U.S. Investment Activity Abroad," *Southern Economic Journal* (July 1972), pp. 58–71.

68. Some caution is in order in interpreting results based on interest differentials since the comparative size of these differentials does not necessarily give a good indication of the comparative effectiveness of controls in restraining capital flows. For recent analysis of the costs and benefits of

capital controls and the European experience with controls, see Giorgio Basevi, "Monetary Cooperation and Liberalization of Capital Movements in the European Monetary System," *European Economic Review* (March 1988), pp. 372–81; Bryant, *International Financial Intermediation;* E. Claassen and C. Wyplosz, "Capital Controls: Some Principles and the French Experience," in J. Melitz and C. Wyplosz, eds., *The French Economy* (Boulder, Colo.: Westview Press, 1985), pp. 237–68; Brian J. Cody, "Exchange Controls, Political Risk, and the Eurocurrency Market," Research Working Papers (Philadelphia: Federal Reserve Bank of Philadelphia, May 1988); Harris Dellas and Alan C. Stockman, "Self-Fulfilling Expectations, Speculative Attacks and Capital Controls," Working Paper no. 138, (Rochester: University of Rochester, Center for Economic Growth, June 1988); Michael Dooley and Peter Isard, "Capital Controls, Political Risk, and Deviations from Interest-Rate Parity," *Journal of Political Economy,* vol. 88 (April 1980), pp. 370–84; Francesco Giavazzi and Alberto Giovannini, "The EMS and the Dollar," with comments by David Begg and Louka Katseli, *Economic Policy* (April 1986), pp. 455–85; Takatoshi Ito, "Capital Controls and Covered Interest Parity between the Yen and the Dollar," *Economic Studies Quarterly,* vol. 37 (September 1986), pp. 223–41; Richard Marston, "Exchange Rate Policy Reconsidered," in Feldstein, *International Economic Cooperation,* pp. 79–136; Robert Miller, "Exchange Controls Forever?" in Salin Pascal, ed., *Currency Competition and Monetary Union* (Boston: Martinus Nijhoff Publishers, 1984), pp. 263–70; Conrad J. Oort, "Freedom of Capital Movements in the European Community," in Eizenga Wietze, E. Frans Limburg, and Jacques J. Polak, eds., *The Quest for National and Global Economic Stability* (Boston: Kluwer Academic Publishers, 1988), pp. 143–58; Lars Oxelheim, *Financial Integration* (Stockholm: Industrial Institute for Social and Economic Research, 1988); Nasser Saidi, "Why Do Exchange Controls Exist?" in Pascal, *Currency Competition,* pp. 270–74; and A. K. Swoboda, ed., *Capital Movements and Their Control* (Leiden: A. W. Sijthoff, 1976).

69. See James Tobin, "A Proposal for International Monetary Reform," *Eastern Economic Journal,* vol. 4 (1978), reprinted in *Essays in Economics: Theory and Policy* (Cambridge, Mass.: MIT Press, 1982), pp. 488–94. An alternative approach, not analyzed here, is to create a dual-exchange market with a separate exchange rate for capital flows. This would essentially be a price-oriented form of comprehensive controls. For a recent discussion and references to the literature on dual-exchange markets, see Ronald MacDonald, *Floating Exchange Rates.*

70. Williamson, "Target Zones," p. 233, also makes this point.

71. See Bryant, *International Financial Intermediation,* and Marston, "Exchange Rate Policy Reconsidered."

72. For further analysis of the Tobin tax proposal, see Bryant, *International Financial Intermediation;* Dornbusch, "Flexible Exchange Rates"; and Marston, "Exchange Rate Policy Reconsidered."

73. Thus, while most of the formal theoretical literature on currency substitution has focused on its potential contribution to generating exchange rate instability, Friedrich Hayek, *The Denationalization of Money* (London: Institute

for International Economics, 1987), and other advocates of currency competition have stressed the potential benefits of currency switching in disciplining national monetary authorities. For recent contributions to the debate over currency competition, see the essays on this subject in James Dorn and Anna Schwartz, *The Search for Stable Money* (Chicago: University of Chicago Press, 1987); Salin, *Currency Competition;* and Thomas D. Willett, ed., *Political Business Cycles: The Political Economy of Money, Inflation, and Unemployment* (Durham, N.C.: Duke University Press, 1988).

74. On the differences in implications of adopting a political economy in place of a traditional narrow economic perspective on financial issues, see the analysis and references in Thomas D. Willett, "Functioning of the Current International Financial Systems," in George von Furstenberg, ed., *International Money and Credit: The Policy Roles* (Washington, D.C.: International Monetary Fund, 1983), pp. 5–44; and "National Macroeconomic Policy Preferences and International Coordination Issues," *Journal of Public Policy* (forthcoming).

75. For recent analysis and references to the theoretical literature on international policy coordination and on recent policy coordination issues, see William H. Buiter and Richard Marston, eds., *International Economic Policy Coordination* (Cambridge: Cambridge University Press, 1985); Richard N. Cooper, "Economic Interdependence and the Coordination of Economic Policies," in Jones and Kenen, *Handbook of International Economics,* pp. 1195–234; Stanley Fisher, "International Macroeconomic Policy Coordination," in Feldstein, *International Economic Cooperation,* pp. 11–43; Jacob A. Frenkel, Morris Goldstein, and Paul Masson, "International Coordination of Economic Policies: Scope, Methods, and Effects," Working Paper no. 2670 (National Bureau of Economic Research, July 1988); and Thomas D. Willett, "Macroeconomic Policy Coordination Issues under Flexible Exchange Rates," *Ordo,* vol. 35 (1985), pp. 137–49.

76. See the analysis and references in Willett, *Political Business Cycles.*

77. On the theory of optimum currency areas, see the analysis and references in Edward Tower and Thomas D. Willett, *The Theory of Optimum Currency Areas and Exchange Rate Flexibility,* Special Papers in International Economics (Princeton, N.J.: Princeton University, Department of Economics, 1976).

78. For recent analyses of the EMS experience, see M. J. Artis, "The European Monetary System: An Evaluation," *Journal of Policy Modeling,* vol. 9, no. 1 (1987), pp. 175–98; Michele Fratianni, "The European Monetary System: How Well Has It Worked?" *Cato Journal* (Fall 1988), pp. 477–502; Giavazzi and Giovannini, "The EMS and the Dollar," with comments by David Begg and Louka Katseli, pp. 455–85; and Manuel Guitian, Massimo Russo, and Giuseppe Tullio, *Policy Coordination in the European Monetary System,* Occasional Paper no. 61 (Washington, D.C.: International Monetary Fund, September 1988).

79. See Thomas D. Willett, "The Deficit and the Dollar," in Arndt, Sweeney, and Willett, *Exchange Rates, Trade and the U.S. Economy,* pp. 273–81.

80. On the target zone approach to this issue, see Jacob A. Frenkel and

Morris Goldstein, "A Guide to Target Zones," Staff Papers (Washington, D.C.: International Monetary Fund, December 1986), pp. 633–73; and Williamson, "Target Zones and the Management of the Dollar."

81. See Thomas D. Willett, "A Public Choice Analysis of Strategies for Restoring International Economic Stability," in New International Arrangements for the World Economy (Berlin: Springer-Verlag, 1989), pp. 9–30.

82. See Ronald I. McKinnon, An International Standard for Monetary Stabilization (Washington, D.C.: Institute for International Economics, 1984), and Ronald I. McKinnon, "The Dollar Exchange Rate as a Leading Indicator for American Monetary Policy," in Academic Conference Volume (San Francisco: San Francisco Federal Reserve Bank, Fall 1985), pp. 161–206.

83. See Thomas Mayer and Thomas D. Willett, "Evaluating Proposals for Fundamental Monetary Reform," in Willett, Political Business Cycles, pp. 398–423.

84. For examples of different possible types of multipart rules, see Allan H. Meltzer, "Monetary Reform in an Uncertain Environment," Cato Journal (Spring 1983), pp. 93–112, and Thomas D. Willett, "A New Monetary Constitution," in Dorn and Schwartz, The Search for Stable Money, pp. 145–62.

COMMENTARY: THE PATH OF THE DOLLAR

1. William H. Branson and Grazia Marchese, "International Imbalances in Japan, Germany, and the U.S.," in International Payments Imbalances in the 1980s (Boston: Federal Reserve Bank of Boston, 1988), pp. 19–50.

2. Paul R. Krugman, "Is the Strong Dollar Sustainable?" The U.S. Dollar—Recent Developments, Outlook, and Policy Options (Federal Reserve Bank of Kansas City, 1985), pp. 103–32.

3. Rudiger Dornbusch and Jeffrey Frankel, "Macroeconomics and the Dollar," in R. M. Stern, ed., U.S. Trade Policies in a Changing World Economy (Cambridge, Mass.: MIT Press, 1987), pp. 77–130.

4. Richard C. Marston, ed. Misalignment of Exchange Rates (Chicago: University of Chicago Press, 1988).

5. Rudiger Dornbusch, "Expectations and Exchange Rate Dynamics," Journal of Political Economy, vol. 84, pp. 1161–76.

6. Paul A. Samuelson, Foundations of Economic Analysis (Cambridge, Mass.: Harvard University Press, 1947).

7. Julio Rotemberg, "The New Keynesian Microfoundations," in S. Fischer, ed., National Bureau of Economic Research Macroeconomics Annual (Cambridge, Mass.: MIT Press, 1987), pp. 69–104.

8. John Y. Campbell and Richard H. Clarida, "The Dollar and Real Interest Rates," Carnegie-Rochester Conference Series on Public Policy, vol. 27 (1987), pp. 103–40.

9. Lamberto Dini, "Cooperation and Conflict in Monetary and Trade Policies," paper presented at the International Management and Development Institute (Milan, 1988).

CHAPTER 3: EXCHANGE RATES, THE CURRENT ACCOUNT, AND MONETARY POLICY

1. The solution to these models can also involve nonstationary solutions, typically referred to as bubbles or, sometimes, rational bubbles. These are self-fulfilling rational expectations equilibria, and there are infinitely many of them. They can be nonstochastic, exponential terms in the exchange rate, or they can be stochastic, even bursting with probability one (and, of course, agents with rational expectations know this). All of the bubble equilibria studied in these models, however, involve bubbles in *all nominal* variables, not just the exchange rate: nominal price levels would show the same paths. We do not observe nominal goods prices that behave in ways that suggest the existence of such bubbles. In addition, we observe changes in *real* exchange rates that are highly correlated with changes in nominal exchange rates; this is not a feature of these bubbles. No one has yet worked out a formal theory of these bubbles with sluggish nominal prices. Finally, even if these bubble solutions were to characterize exchange rate behavior, there may be nothing that monetary policy can do to prevent them. If markets are complete, as King, Wallace, and Weber, and Manuelli and Peck (in separate research) have shown, these bubbles have no consequences for resource allocation. Essentially, complete markets allow people to diversify completely away the risk associated with bubbles (and there is no aggregate risk, associated with bubbles, to be shared in their models). Pegging the nominal exchange rate could prevent bubbles in the nominal exchange rate, but the same bubbles in the price level could still occur (except that they would now be the same in each country). If markets are complete, the bubbles have no welfare consequences, so they do not suggest a role for government policy. If markets are incomplete, people may not be able to diversify away the risks associated with these bubbles. As a result, the bubbles may affect welfare, as may the exchange rate system. But the nature of these effects is extremely complicated. In principle there may be government policies that could improve welfare in this case. In practice, for policy purposes, this model does not seem particularly helpful. There is also a fundamental problem with the theory of these rational bubbles that has been largely overlooked. According to the theory, negative bubbles should be as likely as positive bubbles. But negative bubbles will eventually result in nonsensical negative prices.

2. I use the term "real exchange rate" here to mean the exchange-rate-adjusted ratio of nominal price levels in the two countries. If p and p^* are price indexes in the home and foreign countries and e is the appropriately defined exchange rate, the real exchange rate is ep^*/p.

3. That is, using the notation from note 2, e (or its rate of change) varies much more than p^*/p. A separate, but related, general observation is that the variances of e and ep^*/p, or of their rates of change, are nearly the same.

4. See also the discussion in Jeffrey A. Frankel and Richard Meese, "Are Exchange Rates Excessively Variable?" in S. Fischer, ed., *NBER Macroeconomics Annual*, vol. 2 (1987), pp. 117–53.

5. In this sense, the equilibrium models of exchange rates are related to "real business cycle" models that emphasize changes in tastes or technologies or equilibrium quantities and prices in closed economies.

6. See Alan C. Stockman, "The Equilibrium Approach to Exchange Rates," *Economic Review* (Federal Reserve Bank of Richmond), March–April 1987, pp. 12–31. See also Alan C. Stockman, "A Theory of Exchange Rate Determination," *Journal of Political Economy,* vol. 88, no. 4 (1980), pp. 673–98; Stockman, "Real Exchange Rates under Alternative Nominal Exchange Rate Systems," *Journal of International Money and Finance,* vol. 2 (August 1983), pp. 147–66; Stockman, "Real Exchange Rate Variability under Pegged and Floating Nominal Exchange Rate Systems: An Equilibrium Theory," in K. Brunner and A. H. Meltzer, eds., Carnegie-Rochester Series on Public Policy (forthcoming); Elhanan Helpman and Assaf Razin, "A Comparison of Exchange Rate Regimes in the Presence of Imperfect Capital Markets," *International Economic Review,* vol. 23 (1982), pp. 365–88; Helpman and Razin, "The Role of Savings and Investment in Exchange Rate Determination under Alternative Monetary Mechanisms," *Journal of Monetary Economics,* vol. 13 (May 1983), pp. 307–26; Maurice Obstfeld and Alan C. Stockman, "Exchange Rate Dynamics," in R. Jones and P. Kenen, eds., *Handbook of International Economics,* vol. 2 (Amsterdam: North-Holland, 1985); Robert J. Hodrick and Sanjay Srivastava, "The Covariation of Risk Premiums and Expected Future Spot Exchange Rates," *Journal of International Money and Finance,* vol. 5 (March 1986), pp. 5–21; Hodrick, "Risk, Uncertainty, and Exchange Rates," *Journal of Monetary Economics* (forthcoming); Lars E. O. Svensson, "Currency Prices, Terms of Trade, and Interest Rates: A General Equilibrium Asset-Pricing, Cash-in-Advance Approach," *Journal of International Economics,* vol. 18 (February 1985), pp. 17–41; Stockman and Svensson, "Capital Flows, Investment and Exchange Rates," *Journal of Monetary Economics,* vol. 19, no. 2 (1987), pp. 171–202; Sebastian Edwards, "A Real Equilibrium Model of Real Exchange-Rate Determination" (UCLA Working paper, 1987); Kevin D. Salyer, "Exchange Rate Volatility: The Role of Real Shocks and the Velocity of Money," *Economic Inquiry* (forthcoming); and Stockman and Harris Dellas, "International Portfolio Nondiversification and Exchange Rate Variability," *Journal of International Economics* (forthcoming). The approach is loosely based on Milton Friedman, "The Case for Flexible Exchange Rates," in *Essays in Positive Economics* (University of Chicago Press, 1951).

7. The prediction that changes in real exchange rates show up almost entirely as changes in nominal exchange rates does *not* require (as Frankel claims it does in his comments on this paper) the assumption, made in the simple example, that monetary authorities try to stabilize the price level. The conclusion holds as long as the real disturbances affecting the real exchange rate have little effect on money demands or money supplies.

8. Stockman, "A Theory of Exchange Rate Determination."

9. Robert J. Barro, "The Ricardian Approach to Budget Deficits," *Journal of Economic Perspectives,* vol. 3, no. 2 (1989), pp. 37–54.

10. The experiment here involves a change in the time path of the collection of a fixed present value of tax receipts.

11. Another argument is frequently made. Assume that assets denominated in domestic and foreign currencies are imperfect substitutes in portfolios. A tax cut in the United States, resulting in a budget deficit, would raise the real interest rate on dollar-denominated assets. Then, it is argued, the return on dollar-denominated assets exceeds the yield on assets denominated in foreign currency. To keep investors from selling dollar assets to buy foreign-currency assets, the dollar must be expected to depreciate. So the budget deficit must cause dollar appreciation in order to induce the required expected dollar depreciation.

The problem with this argument is that investors would not want to sell dollar assets to buy foreign-currency assets. The increase in the real interest rate on dollar assets is an equilibrium phenomenon: the reason the interest rate rises is that the supply of dollar assets is raised by the budget deficit, and investors must be induced to hold the greater supply. To induce them, the return on dollar assets rises above the return on foreign-currency assets. This is an equilibrium precisely because the assets are imperfect substitutes.

12. Some of these are discussed in Obstfeld and Stockman, "Exchange Rate Dynamics."

13. Edward Prescott, "Theory Ahead of Business-Cycle Measurement," in Karl Brunner and Allan Meltzer, eds., *Real Business Cycles, Real Exchange Rates, and Actual Policies*, Carnegie-Rochester Conference Series on Public Policy, vol. 25 (Amsterdam: North-Holland, 1986). pp. 11–44.

14. Campbell and Clarida estimated a state-space model that treats the expected change in the real exchange rate, the expected real-interest differential, and the long-run equilibrium real exchange rate as unobserved variables. The econometrician observes only the ex post change in the real exchange rate and the ex post real interest differential. These ex post observable variables are related to the unobserved expected variables by a forecast error that is white noise due to rational expectations. In addition, they assumed that the (unobserved) long-run equilibrium real exchange rate is a random walk. Model 1 in the table refers to results based on the assumption of no risk premium in the foreign exchange market; model 2 refers to results based on the assumption that the risk premium is linearly related to the (unobserved) ex ante real interest differential. See John Y. Campbell and Richard H. Clarida, "The Dollar and Real Interest Rates," in K. Brunner and A. H. Meltzer, eds., *Empirical Studies of Velocity, Real Exchange Rates, Unemployment and Productivity*, vol. 27, Carnegie-Rochester Conference Series (Amsterdam: North-Holland, 1987).

15. This is done by taking the maximum of column (i) and the sum of columns (i) and (iii).

16. Huizinga, "Behavior of Real Exchange Rates."

17. Graciela Kaminsky, "The Real Exchange Rate in the Short and in the Long Run" (Working paper 88–11, University of California, San Diego, 1987).

18. As Huizinga explains, his procedure does not justify the interpretation that the remaining 42 percent of the variance of real exchange rate changes is accounted for by transitory components. John Huizinga, "An Empirical Investigation of the Long-Run Behavior of Real Exchange Rates," in K. Brunner

and A. H. Meltzer, eds., *Empirical Studies of Velocity, Real Exchange Rates, Unemployment and Productivity,* Carnegie-Rochester Conference Series, vol. 27 (Amsterdam: North-Holland, 1987).

19. Manuel Galan, *Essays in Exchange Rates and Currency Options* (Rochester, N.Y.: University of Rochester, 1988).

20. Huizinga's study involves only 12 years of monthly data. The estimates obtained are not significantly different from those that would result if the real exchange rate were a random walk, nor from those that would result from white noise.

21. Kaminsky also notes that this is why the simple monetary models have performed so poorly empirically.

22. See note 1. Also see the excellent summary and critique of econometric tests for bubbles in foreign exchange markets in Frankel and Meese, "Are Exchange Rates Excessively Variable?"

23. The long-term evidence that Frankel cites in his comment on this paper indicates that *after* imposing a deterministic time trend, a low-order autoregressive process can be fit to the real exchange rate and interpreted as showing something like 30 percent per year reversion toward a mean following a shock. That evidence, however, involves the questionable imposition of a deterministic time trend to these data and ignores major differences in the stochastic process (variance, higher moments, and form of the statistical distribution) followed by real exchange rates over time. The statistical model underlying that evidence is also inconsistent with the most likely hypothesis: that there are permanent *and* transitory stochastic disturbances to real exchange rates, as indicated by the evidence reviewed in this chapter.

24. Vittorio Grilli, "Fiscal Policies and the Dollar-Pound Exchange Rate: 1870–1984," (Discussion paper No. 548, Yale University Economic Growth Center, 1987).

25. Grilli reported two sets of estimates that support this result: simple regression results and estimates from a maximum likelihood technique to correct for the fact that the probability distribution of changes in the exchange rate differs between pegged and flexible exchange rate systems. Grilli interprets the variable I have called real taxes as the permanent component of government spending; he measures it as actual real government spending minus the real deficit. Grilli's label for this variable is based on his theoretical model, which implies that the permanent component of real government spending equals the tax rate because the tax rate is adjusted to guarantee this. I prefer the more straightforward label of his variable as the level of real taxes relative to GNP. Grilli also includes separate measures of government receipts relative to GNP, but these do not correspond to the real tax rate, that is, the difference between real government spending and the real deficit. Grilli, "Fiscal Policies."

26. That is, this explanation attributes the rise in the dollar to the deficit rather than the level of government spending. This explanation implies that the dollar would depreciate in real terms if the deficit were eliminated by a tax increase, holding current and prospective future spending fixed.

27. See, for example, Paul Evans, "Interest Rates and Expected Future

Budget Deficits in the United States," *Journal of Political Economy,* vol. 95 (1987), pp. 34–58; "Do Budget Deficits Raise Nominal Interest Rates? Evidence from Six Countries," *Journal of Monetary Economics,* vol. 20 (1987), pp. 218–300.

28. See Paul Evans, "Is the Dollar High because of Large Budget Deficits?" *Journal of Monetary Economics,* vol. 18 (November 1986), pp. 227–50; Martin S. Feldstein, "The Budget Deficit and the Dollar," *NBER Macroeconomics Annual,* vol. 1 (1986), pp. 355–92; Alan C. Stockman, "Comments on 'The Budget Deficit and the Dollar' by Martin Feldstein," *NBER Macroeconomics Annual,* vol. 1 (1986), pp. 402–7; and Hodrick, "Risk, Uncertainty, and Exchange Rates."

29. See Stockman, "Comments"; Vittorio Grilli and Andrea Beltratti, "U.S. Military Expenditure and the Dollar: A Note" (Discussion paper, Yale University Economic Growth Center, 1987); and Grilli, "Fiscal Policies."

30. Campbell and Clarida, "Dollar and Real Interest Rates."

31. Direct estimation of a relationship between budget deficits and real exchange rate changes also suggests that there is no systematic relation between them. The coincidence of currency appreciation and government budget deficits, as in the United States from 1980 to 1985, is more an exception than the rule. Government spending may play a more important role than budget deficits per se; Stockman, "Comments"; Evans, "Is the Dollar High."

32. Rudiger Dornbusch, "Expectations and Exchange Rate Dynamics," *Journal of Political Economy,* vol. 84 (December 1976), pp. 1161–74.

33. Huizinga, "An Empirical Investigation," estimates that 33 to 40 percent of a change in the real value of the dollar or the British pound over any four-year interval is likely to be reversed over the following four-year interval, and that the remaining change in the real exchange rate is permanent.

34. The observed predictable, transitory component could be associated with transitory disturbances rather than slow nominal price adjustment.

35. Huizinga, "An Empirical Investigation."

36. See, for example, Behzad T. Diba, "Monetary Disturbances, Price Rigidities, and Exchange-Rate Fluctuations: An Empirical Study" (Working paper, Brown University, 1987).

37. Stockman, "Alternative Nominal Exchange Rate Systems"; Michael Mussa, "Nominal Exchange Rate Regimes and the Behavior of Real Exchange Rates," in Karl Brunner and A. H. Meltzer, eds., *Real Business Cycles, Real Exchange Rates, and Actual Policies,* Carnegie-Rochester Conference Series on Public Policy, vol. 25 (Amsterdam: North-Holland, 1986).

38. Marianne Baxter and Alan C. Stockman, "Business Cycles and the Exchange Rate Regime: Some International Evidence," *Journal of Monetary Economics* (forthcoming).

39. It is also possible that disturbances have transitory as well as permanent components, in which case the equilibrium model could explain the temporary component of real exchange rates. Alternatively, the equilibrium model might imply intrinsic dynamics due, say, to adjustment costs or differences between short-run and long-run demand elasticities.

40. Frankel and Froot, "Understanding the U.S. Dollar in the Eighties: The

Expectations of Chartists and Fundamentalists," *Economic Record* (1986), pp. 24–38.

41. A. Ronald Gallant, David Hsieh, and George Tauchen, "On Fitting a Recalcitrant Series: The Pound/Dollar Exchange Rate, 1974–83" (Working paper, University of Chicago, April 1988).

42. Studies suggesting that changes in the real or nominal exchange rate cause changes in output, employment, and so on, confuse endogenous and exogenous variables. It is sometimes argued that it is appropriate to treat exchange rate changes as exogenous when studying a particular industry. The argument is that changes in one industry will not have aggregate effects and so will not affect the exchange rate. This argument is the basis for a number of studies purporting to measure the effects of changes in exchange rates on employment, output, and so on, by industry and region. The argument is incorrect, however. For a *representative* industry, according to the equilibrium model, disturbances to supply or demand are correlated with changes in the exchange rate, so that the exchange rate is not independent of disturbances in employment or output regressions and cannot legitimately be treated as an exogenous variable. If there are a large number of industries, each with (say) supply disturbances due to technology shocks, then one of two situations occurs. Either all of the disturbances are independent, in which case there is *no aggregate disturbance* and so no change in the exchange rate as a consequence of these technology shocks (and in which case the exchange rate would be perfectly collinear with the constant term), or the disturbances are *not* independent, so that there is no aggregate disturbance and an exchange rate change as a consequence. But with dependent disturbances, the typical industry disturbance is correlated with the aggregate, and the exchange rate is not an exogenous variable.

43. Maurice Obstfeld, "Floating Exchange Rates: Experience and Prospects," *Brookings Papers on Economic Activity,* vol. 2 (1985), pp. 369–450.

44. Ibid.

45. Current account "imbalances" are sometimes thought to be bad because (i) they entail inappropriate shifts in production, for example, between traded and nontraded goods, and (ii) current account deficits reduce domestic wealth and imply less future consumption.

46. It is argued, for example, in Stockman, "A Theory of Exchange Rate Determination," that the correlation between the real and nominal exchange rate is, like the correlation between inflation and output relative to trend, not exploitable by monetary policy.

47. For an example of nominal price sluggishness that does not cause misallocations, see Robert J. Barro and Paul M. Romer, "Ski-Lift Pricing, with Applications to Labor and Other Markets," *American Economic Review,* vol. 77, no. 5 (December 1987), pp. 875–90.

The models typically assume that nominal home-currency export prices are sticky, but not import prices (which involve the product of a variable exchange rate and a sticky foreign-currency nominal export price). It seems difficult to rationalize this kind of stickiness on the basis of menu costs at the retail level.

There have been attempts to test formally disequilibrium models of exchange rates against flexible-price alternatives. Generally, these attempts involve formulating a model and either (i) estimating a parameter that determines the speed of price adjustment or (ii) performing a general specification test on the flexible-price model. See, for example, Kaminsky, "The Real Exchange Rate," who rejects the specification test and interprets this rejection as a rejection of the flexible-price assumption. The alternative interpretation is that the flexible-price model is not correctly specified in some other way. Given the numerous problems with the estimates generally obtained, this is my preferred interpretation, though others may (and do) disagree.

48. In his comments on this paper, Jeffrey Frankel argues that the fact that the equilibrium theory can be made consistent with the facts does not make it true. He is right. But surely the inconsistency of the disequilibrium model with the facts must count against it.

49. If one has sufficiently strong priors, as in the spy parable that Frankel tells in his comments, these empirical checks may be unnecessary.

50. One need not reject sluggish nominal price adjustment entirely to believe that it does not play an important role in explaining exchange rates. Aggregate business fluctuations are highly correlated across countries, so nominal price sluggishness could play an important role in business cycles without necessarily having a major effect on exchange rates.

51. Bennett McCallum, *Robustness Properties of a Rule for Monetary Policy,* Carnegie-Rochester Conference Series on Public Policy, vol. 29 (Amsterdam: North-Holland, forthcoming).

52. If there were important information in the behavior of the current account or exchange rates regarding disturbances, this conclusion would be different. All of the theories imply that there *is* such information. However, all of the evidence indicates that we do not yet know how to recover it.

COMMENTARY: ZEN AND THE ART OF MODERN MACROECONOMICS

1. This seems a more polite label than the alternative possibility, the "know nothing" school.

2. This system was not without drawbacks. Many econometricians adopted the shady practice of trying out many different functional forms, combinations of variables, and sample periods in their regressions until they found results that appeared as statistically significant.

3. If one is a believer in Ricardian equivalence, one looks for an effect of the budget deficit on interest rates or exchange rates, one typically fails to find large and significant effects, and one concludes that therefore Ricardian equivalence holds. If one does not believe in Ricardian equivalence, one looks for an effect of the budget deficit on private saving, one typically fails to find large and significant effects, and one concludes that therefore equivalence does not hold.

4. My comments here pertain, for example, to Alan Stockman, "The Equilibrium Approach to Exchange Rates," *Economic Review,* Federal Reserve Bank of Richmond (March/April 1987), pp. 12–30. In that paper, like this commentary, the author should be awarded a medal for bravery in taking on

the question what the equilibrium models have to say of use for policy makers. Many authors seek to evade the question altogether.

5. Ibid. Thus most equilibrium theorists do not wish even to hazard a guess as to what profound shifts in consumers' tastes for American products or in workers' productivity occurred in 1980–1985 (to double the dollar's value against the yen and mark) or in 1985–1987 (to halve it again).

6. Rudiger Dornbusch, "Expectations and Exchange Rate Dynamics," *Journal of Political Economy,* vol. 84 (December 1976), pp. 1161–74.

7. As far as I know, he does not offer any evidence of the third kind: things that can be explained by the equilibrium theory but *not* by the sticky-price theory.

8. Alan Stockman, "Real Exchange Rate Variability under Pegged and Floating Nominal Exchange Rate Systems: An Equilibrium Theory" (Working paper 2565, National Bureau of Economic Research, April 1988).

9. If the observations are monthly, then forty-seven years of data will do. This calculation and the test results for U.K.–U.S. data from 1869 to 1987 appear in some earlier papers of mine, as well as in Jeffrey Frankel, "Quantifying International Capital Mobility in the 1980's" (Working Paper 2856, National Bureau of Economic Research, February 1989).

10. Using the correct Dickey-Fuller test.

11. This sample period mixes different exchange rate regimes, so it would be desirable to allow for heteroskedasticity and for different speeds of adjustment during different subperiods. On the other hand, under the null hypothesis the distribution of the real exchange rate is invariant with respect to the regime. (I am indebted to Maurice Obstfeld for this point.)

Chapter 4: Exporting the Inflation Tax

1. See G. Tabellini, "Domestic Politics and the International Coordination of Fiscal Policies," *Journal of International Economics* (forthcoming), for an application of this idea to the international fiscal (rather monetary) policy coordination. See also M. Feldstein, "Distinguished Lecture on Economics in Government: Thinking about International Economic Coordination," *Journal of Economic Perspectives* (Spring 1988), for some remarks along these lines.

2. M. Canzoneri, "The Amazing Stability of U.S. Monetary Policy" (Georgetown University, 1987, mimeo), considers a model with currency substitution in which the central banks of each country may have an incentive to inflate so as to tax foreign holders of their currency. In his model there is no nominal debt, and the focus is on quite different issues. P. Wood, "Game Theory in Open Economy Macroeconomics" (Ph.D. dissertation, University of Wisconsin-Madison, 1988), also studies a model in which inflation is used to redistribute revenue from foreign to domestic residents. The mechanism in his model, however, is a pure terms-of-trade effect, and inflation is like any other tax that falls exclusively on domestic residents. A Casella and J. Feinstein, "Management of a Common Currency," in M. de Cecco and A. Giovannini, eds., *A European Central Bank—Perspectives on Monetary Unification after Ten Years of the EMS* (Cambridge: Cambridge University Press, 1989), analyze

how to collect the inflation tax from foreigners in a common currency area in which monetary policy is not fully centralized; their model is intended to apply to the current issues of European monetary integration. Finally, H. Bohn, "A Positive Theory of Foreign Currency Debt" (Wharton School, 1988, mimeo), considers optimal debt management policies for a small open economy that cannot precommit in advance to a specific monetary policy. An earlier antecedent of all this literature, including this chapter, is R. Mundell, "The Optimum Balance of Payments Deficit," in E. Claassen and P. Salin, eds., *Stabilization Policies in Interdependent Economies* (Amsterdam: North-Holland, 1972).

3. Estimated U.S. assets abroad denominated in dollars consist almost exclusively of bonds; hence, no adjustment is needed there.

4. The U.S. capital income from abroad became smaller than the capital income paid to foreigners by the U.S. during 1987. The net debt position of the United States, on the other hand, became negative two years earlier. This suggests that the market value of U.S. assets abroad is underestimated. However, these are likely to be real assets. Hence, taking account of this measurement error is unlikely to make any difference for the net dollar position of foreigners. Moreover, the trend that emerges from table 4–1 is also reflected in the data on net capital income.

5. The recent literature on rules versus discretion has explored the issue of whether reputation can reduce the ex post optimality of inflation, by creating a link between current inflation and future nominal interest rates. See the chapter by Grossman in this volume and T. Persson and G. Tabellini, "Macroeconomic Policy, Credibility and Politics" (London: Harwood, forthcoming). These reputation mechanisms could be incorporated into the present framework, without necessarily affecting the nature of the results. Clearly, the more operative the mechanism, the lower the equilibrium rate of inflation.

6. There is much literature on this issue that analyzes the role of reputation in sustaining cooperation. For instance, see M. Canzoneri and D. Henderson, "Is Sovereign Policymaking Bad?" *Carnegie and Rochester Conference Series* (Spring 1988), and the references cited therein.

7. The nature of the results should not be affected if we allowed the borrower to issue other kinds of debt, as long as we retain the assumption that debt denominated in domestic currency is the most attractive instrument from the borrower's point of view. See H. Bohn, "A Positive Theory of Foreign Currency Debt," for an analysis of optimal debt management policies for a small open economy that cannot precommit not to inflate away its outstanding nominal debt obligations.

8. This argument is also discussed in G. Tabellini, "Monetary and Fiscal Policy Coordination with a High Public Debt," in F. Giavazzi and L. Spaventa, eds., *High Public Debt: The Italian Experience* (Cambridge: Cambridge University Press, 1988), with respect to the Italian participation in the European Monetary System.

CHAPTER 6: INTERNATIONAL MONETARY SYSTEM, THE EUROPEAN
MONETARY SYSTEM, AND A SINGLE EUROPEAN CURRENCY
IN A SINGLE EUROPEAN MARKET

1. A comprehensive discussion of floating exchange rates can be found in
The Merits of Flexible Exchange Rates, Leo Melamed, ed. (Fairfax, Va.: George
Mason University Press, 1988).

2. After this was written, the conservative government of Jacques Chirac
was replaced by a center-left one. But since in the past the Socialist and
conservative governments took a similar stand, the new center-left government is not expected to bring change.

3. Edouard Balladur, "Rebuilding an International Monetary System:
Three Possible Approaches," *Wall Street Journal*, February 23, 1988. For a
detailed critical analysis of Balladur's proposals, see Robert Solomon, "Minister Balladur on International Monetary Reform," *International Economic Letter*,
vol. 8, no. 3, March 15, 1988.

4. Michele Fratianni, "The European Monetary System: How Well Has It
Worked?" (Paper presented at the Cato Institute's Sixth Annual Monetary
Conference, February 25, 1988; published in *The Cato Journal*, vol. 8, no. 2 [Fall
1988]). Fratianni presents an excellent analysis of the operation and achieve-
ments of the EMS, drawing on the extensive literature on the subject. See also
Michele Fratianni, "Europe's Non-Model for Stable World Money," *Wall Street
Journal*, April 4, 1988. Another thorough description and analysis of the
working of the EMS and a wealth of statistics can be found in Horst Ungerer,
Owen Evans, Thomas Mayer, and Philip Young, "The European Monetary
System: Recent Developments" (Occasional Paper No. 48, International Mon-
etary Fund, Washington, D.C., December 1986).

5. It is not clear, however, why Britain should be tempted to join; it has
done quite well outside the EMS. While once regarded as the sick man of
Europe, in the past five years the British economy has outperformed that of
all other members of the EC; its growth rate has been by far the highest of all
twelve members of the EMS.

6. For a detailed description of how all this came about, we shall have to
wait for the second edition of Yoichi Funabashi's best seller, *Managing the
Dollar: From the Plaza to the Louvre* (Washington, D.C.: Institute for International Economics, 1988), which surely will have a part, *Managing the European
Monetary Union*.

7. See Tommaso Padoa-Schioppa, *The EMS: A Long-Term View* (Talk given at
the "Conference on the EMS," Perugia, October 16–17, 1987, sponsored by
Banca d'Italia, Centre for Economic Policy Research and Centri Interuniver-
sitario Studi Teorici per la Political Economica, Italy). The author's quartet
contains in addition to the three items mentioned in the text above, free
trade. I leave it out, because some protection on the part of some EMS
countries, though undesirable and in violation of the spirit of the EMS, would
not prevent the functioning of the EMS.

8. See the *Financial Times* (London), July 15, 1988.

9. Karl Otto Pöhl, "A Vision of a European Central Bank," *Wall Street Journal*
(London), July 15, 1988.

A NOTE ON THE BOOK

This book was edited by
Jane Nuñez and Ann Petty of the
publications staff of the American Enterprise Institute.
The figures were drawn by Hördur Karlsson.
The text was set in Palatino, a typeface designed by Hermann Zapf.
Coghill Book Typesetting Company, of Richmond, Virginia,
set the type, and Edwards Brothers Incorporated,
of Ann Arbor, Michigan, printed and bound the book,
using permanent acid-free paper.

The AEI PRESS is the publisher for the American Enterprise Institute for Public Policy Research, 1150 17th Street, N.W., Washington, D.C. 20036: *Christopher C. DeMuth,* publisher; *Edward Styles,* director; *Dana Lane,* editor; *Ann Petty,* editor; *Andrea Posner,* editor; *Teresa Fung,* editorial assistant (rights and permissions). Books published by the AEI PRESS are distributed by arrangement with the University Press of America, 4720 Boston Way, Lanham, Md. 20706.